# Mastering Hybrid Cloud with Azure: Seamless Integration of On-Premises and Cloud Workloads

Kameron Hussain and Frahaan Hussain

Published by Sonar Publishing, 2025.

MASTERING HYBRID CLOUD WITH AZURE: SEAMLESS INTEGRATION OF ON-PREMISES AND CLOUD WORKLOADS

**First edition. April 25, 2025.**



ISBN: 979-8230461098

Written by Kameron Hussain and Frahaan Hussain.

# Azure Hybrid Cloud: Architecting the Future of Enterprise IT

**First Edition**

# Preface

In today's rapidly evolving IT landscape, organizations are no longer constrained by the binary choice of on-premises infrastructure versus public cloud. The rise of hybrid cloud computing has revolutionized how businesses architect, manage, and scale their digital environments. This book—*Azure Hybrid Cloud: Architecting the Future of Enterprise IT*—is designed to be a comprehensive guide for professionals navigating the complex and rewarding path of hybrid cloud adoption using Microsoft Azure.

Hybrid cloud models offer the flexibility to operate workloads across multiple environments, empowering enterprises to take advantage of public cloud scalability while preserving control and compliance in their own data centers. Microsoft Azure has been at the forefront of enabling these hybrid strategies, delivering a robust suite of tools, services, and integrations like Azure Arc, Azure Stack, and ExpressRoute.

Each chapter in this book builds on the core understanding of hybrid cloud principles and progresses through practical, architectural, and strategic elements to support a full-scale hybrid deployment. Whether you're an architect planning an enterprise rollout, an IT administrator managing connectivity and identity, or a business leader crafting a cloud roadmap, this book aims to provide clear, actionable insights and examples.

Chapter 1 introduces hybrid cloud computing, explores its origins, and sets the stage for understanding its relevance in modern IT. In Chapter 2, we dive into the architecture of Azure's hybrid capabilities. Subsequent chapters explore readiness planning, secure connectivity, hybrid identity, data management strategies, application modernization, and unified operations.

The later sections provide case studies and real-world use cases to ground theory in practical implementation, while the final chapter focuses on future-proofing your investment and evolving your strategies alongside emerging technologies like AI and edge computing.

Whether you're just starting your hybrid journey or refining a mature deployment, this first edition serves as a foundational resource—backed by detailed guidance and enriched with technical depth to empower you every step of the way.

# Table of Contents

C

D

E

F

G

H

I

J

K

L

M

N

O

P

Q

R

S

T

U

V

## Architecture and Best Practices

## Troubleshooting and Support

## Conclusion

# Chapter 1: Introduction to Hybrid Cloud Computing

## Defining Hybrid Cloud and Its Evolution

Hybrid cloud computing is the integration of on-premises infrastructure, private clouds, and public cloud services into a unified environment that enables consistent operations, governance, and security. Unlike a purely public or private model, hybrid cloud allows organizations to place workloads where they make the most sense—based on performance, regulatory, cost, or business continuity considerations.

The concept of hybrid cloud has been in evolution for over a decade. Early IT environments were rigid and isolated, with siloed data centers that often struggled to scale or adapt quickly. As virtualization matured, private clouds began to emerge, bringing some of the elasticity and management simplicity of public clouds into corporate data centers. Still, enterprises wanted the agility and innovation offered by public cloud vendors—without sacrificing control over sensitive data or compliance mandates. This gap gave rise to the hybrid cloud model.

Microsoft Azure's journey into hybrid cloud began with solutions like Azure Site Recovery and Azure Backup—basic services to extend disaster recovery and storage capabilities. Over time, Azure significantly expanded its portfolio to include sophisticated hybrid tooling such as Azure Arc (for multi-cloud and on-prem management), Azure Stack (for consistent hybrid infrastructure), and ExpressRoute (for high-speed private connectivity). Together, these tools allow enterprises to blur the lines between on-prem and cloud, achieving unprecedented flexibility and control.

Hybrid cloud is no longer a niche solution—it's becoming the de facto standard. Organizations are realizing that a one-size-fits-all approach to cloud simply doesn't work. With data residency requirements, latency-sensitive applications, legacy systems, and unique compliance needs, hybrid environments offer tailored solutions that adapt to diverse needs.

## Evolution Stages of Hybrid Cloud

1. **Stage 1: Basic Extension**
   Early hybrid models focused on using the cloud as an extension for backup and disaster recovery. Applications remained on-prem, while the cloud provided a low-cost redundancy layer.
2. **Stage 2: Bursting and Scaling**
   As demands grew, organizations began leveraging public clouds to handle spikes in load—an approach known as cloud bursting. These setups allowed temporary compute resources to supplement local capacity.
3. **Stage 3: Federated Identity and Networking**
   Integration of Active Directory with Azure AD and the introduction of VPN and ExpressRoute enabled secure, identity-aware communication between environments.
4. **Stage 4: Unified Management and Tooling**
   Tools like Azure Monitor, Azure Arc, and Microsoft Defender unified management and security across all assets—regardless of location.
5. **Stage 5: Strategic Hybrid Architectures**
   Now, hybrid is a design principle. Workloads are placed based on strategy, with common governance frameworks, automation, and orchestration platforms that span clouds and data centers.

## Characteristics of a Hybrid Cloud

- **Interoperability**: Systems must communicate and operate seamlessly across environments.

- **Scalability**: Ability to expand workloads into the cloud without major architectural changes.

- **Flexibility**: Businesses can decide where to host specific applications and services.

- **Consistency**: Tooling and policies apply uniformly across cloud and on-prem systems.

- **Security**: Integrated identity, access control, and encryption policies across the hybrid fabric.

## Modern Hybrid Models

Modern hybrid clouds are not limited to connecting just two environments. With the rise of edge computing, IoT devices, and multi-cloud strategies, hybrid now encompasses a spectrum:

- **Hybrid On-Prem + Azure**: The classic model, using Azure as an extension or augmentation of existing infrastructure.

- **Hybrid Cloud + Multi-Cloud**: Managing assets across Azure, AWS, GCP, and on-prem environments, often with a unified control plane via Azure Arc.

- **Hybrid Cloud + Edge**: Extending cloud capabilities to the edge—factories, retail locations, or field operations—using devices like Azure Stack Edge.

## Common Use Cases

- **Data Sovereignty Compliance**: Sensitive data remains on-prem, while compute-heavy tasks are offloaded to Azure.

- **Disaster Recovery**: Replicating VMs and data to Azure as a cold or warm standby.

- **Application Modernization**: Refactoring legacy apps gradually into microservices hosted in Azure.

- **Hybrid Dev/Test Environments**: Use Azure for scalable development and testing, while production remains on-prem.

- **Edge AI and ML**: Performing inference at the edge using Azure Stack Edge while training models in Azure.

## Key Azure Services for Hybrid Models

| Azure Service | Description |
|---|---|
| Azure Arc | Manage on-prem and multi-cloud resources with Azure Resource Manager |
| Azure Stack HCI | Run virtualized workloads on-prem with Azure integration |
| Azure ExpressRoute | High-speed, private connection to Azure from data centers |
| Azure File Sync | Extend file servers with cloud-based sync and backup |
| Azure Monitor | Centralized logging and monitoring across environments |
| Azure AD Connect | Synchronize on-prem identities with Azure Active Directory |
| Azure Site Recovery | Orchestrate disaster recovery between on-prem and Azure |

## Sample Architecture Overview (Conceptual)

While architecture diagrams are visual, here's a textual representation of a simple hybrid topology:

- **On-Prem Environment**
  - Windows Server 2022 domain controller
  - SQL Server hosting business apps
  - Local file server
  - ExpressRoute circuit connecting to Azure

- **Azure Environment**
  - Azure Virtual Network peered with ExpressRoute
  - Azure SQL Managed Instance replicating on-prem DBs
  - Azure Files connected via Azure File Sync
  - Azure Arc-enabled Kubernetes cluster managing local containers
- **Management Plane**
  - Azure Monitor and Log Analytics workspace
  - Azure Security Center monitoring hybrid endpoints
  - Azure AD with synced identities and conditional access policies

## Strategic Value of Hybrid Cloud

The business case for hybrid cloud is clear: it provides the best of both worlds. Enterprises can modernize at their own pace, adhere to strict regulations, and minimize disruption to existing systems. It enables phased migration, workload optimization, and strategic innovation.

Hybrid cloud also plays a key role in *business continuity*. During cloud outages, certain mission-critical apps can still run on-prem. Similarly, in on-prem failures, workloads can fail over to the cloud, ensuring uptime and resilience.

## Challenges of Hybrid Adoption

Despite its promise, hybrid cloud adoption is not without hurdles:

- **Complexity**: Integrating disparate systems and maintaining consistent policies requires careful planning.
- **Latency**: Applications sensitive to latency might need architecture adjustments.
- **Security Posture Management**: Ensuring consistent threat protection across the hybrid estate is critical.
- **Operational Silos**: Bridging teams that traditionally manage cloud and on-prem separately can be difficult.

### Conclusion

Hybrid cloud is more than a technological configuration—it's a strategic posture. With Azure, organizations gain access to an expansive set of tools designed specifically to ease hybrid transitions, reduce complexity, and amplify operational efficiency. As businesses seek agility without compromising on control, hybrid cloud with Azure stands as a powerful model for the present and future.

In the following sections, we will delve deeper into the components, architecture, and implementation practices to build a secure, resilient, and future-ready hybrid cloud environment.

## Business Drivers for Hybrid Architectures

Hybrid cloud architectures are not born out of technological fascination alone—they are forged in response to specific, often urgent, business needs. For many enterprises, the motivation to adopt a hybrid approach is rooted in the reality of existing investments, operational requirements, regulatory constraints, and the desire to remain competitive. This section explores in detail the major business drivers pushing organizations toward hybrid cloud strategies, with an emphasis on their practical implications in real-world environments.

## Preserving Existing Investments

One of the most immediate business drivers is the need to preserve and extend the value of existing IT investments. Enterprises often have substantial capital sunk into data centers, networking hardware, legacy applications, and skilled IT personnel. Replacing this infrastructure with a full public cloud model is not always feasible or desirable—especially for mission-critical systems that have been heavily customized over years or even decades.

Hybrid cloud allows organizations to:

- Continue leveraging legacy systems while integrating modern cloud services.
- Gradually modernize specific workloads without disrupting ongoing operations.
- Maximize ROI from already deployed infrastructure.

For example, a healthcare organization running a legacy electronic health record (EHR) system on-prem can integrate Azure services such as analytics or AI for patient insights without re-platforming the EHR entirely.

## Regulatory and Compliance Requirements

Data privacy laws and compliance frameworks (e.g., GDPR, HIPAA, PCI-DSS, ISO 27001) often restrict where and how data can be stored, processed, and accessed. In many industries—healthcare, finance, defense, and government—data residency and sovereignty requirements prevent a purely cloud-based approach.

Hybrid cloud enables compliance in such contexts by allowing:

- Sensitive data to remain on-premises or within national borders.
- Public cloud to be used for less sensitive tasks (e.g., web hosting, analytics).
- Integration with tools like Azure Policy and Azure Purview to enforce compliance.

For example, a bank in the EU may host transactional systems and personally identifiable information (PII) on-prem or in a regional Azure data center, while using cloud resources in other regions for aggregated risk analytics that do not expose PII.

## Business Continuity and Disaster Recovery

Ensuring continuous operation in the face of disruptions—natural disasters, cyberattacks, or hardware failures—is essential for business resilience. Hybrid architectures are a cornerstone of robust disaster recovery (DR) and business continuity (BC) strategies.

Using Azure Site Recovery (ASR), organizations can:

- Replicate on-prem workloads to Azure for failover in case of outages.
- Automate recovery plans and conduct DR drills without impacting production.

- Minimize downtime and data loss with near real-time replication.

Additionally, a hybrid approach ensures redundancy by having multiple execution environments. A production database may run on-prem with Azure hosting a synchronized copy for failover. Should the primary environment fail, failover is triggered automatically or manually based on the configuration.

## Latency and Performance Optimization

For workloads requiring low-latency access—such as industrial control systems, trading platforms, or real-time analytics—keeping systems close to users or devices is critical. Hybrid cloud supports edge computing strategies where data is processed closer to its source.

Azure provides solutions like:

- **Azure Stack Edge**: Run AI/ML workloads at edge locations.

- **Azure Stack HCI**: Deploy virtualized workloads in on-prem environments with cloud integration.

- **Azure Content Delivery Network (CDN)**: Cache static assets close to end-users.

This enables real-time decision-making, improved user experiences, and reduction in bandwidth usage. For instance, a logistics company could process vehicle telemetry data on edge devices and send aggregated summaries to Azure for long-term analysis.

## Flexibility and Agility

Today's enterprises operate in rapidly changing markets and require IT infrastructure that adapts just as fast. Hybrid cloud allows organizations to quickly respond to shifts in demand, regulatory changes, M&A activity, or global expansion.

With hybrid architecture, enterprises can:

- Spin up temporary cloud infrastructure for development, testing, or seasonal workloads.
- Shift workloads between environments based on business conditions or cost.
- Deploy applications closer to new market regions using Azure's global footprint.

Here's a sample scenario in code using Azure Resource Manager (ARM) templates to deploy a hybrid development environment on-demand:

```
{
"$schema": "https://schema.management.azure.com/schemas/2019-04-01/deploymentTemplate.json#",
"contentVersion": "1.0.0.0",
"resources": [
{
"type": "Microsoft.Compute/virtualMachines",
"apiVersion": "2021-07-01",
```

```
"name": "HybridDevVM",
"location": "[resourceGroup().location]",
"properties": {
"hardwareProfile": {
"vmSize": "Standard_DS2_v2"
},
"osProfile": {
"computerName": "devvm",
"adminUsername": "devadmin",
"adminPassword": "[parameters('adminPassword')]"
},
"storageProfile": {
"imageReference": {
"publisher": "MicrosoftWindowsServer",
"offer": "WindowsServer",
"sku": "2019-Datacenter",
"version": "latest"
}
},
"networkProfile": {
```

```
"networkInterfaces": [
{
"id": "[resourceId('Microsoft.Network/networkInterfaces', 'HybridDevNIC')]"
}
]
}
}
}
]
}
```

This template allows provisioning of a hybrid VM for short-term use cases, reducing the overhead of maintaining on-prem resources for temporary needs.

## Cost Optimization

Cost is always a major factor in enterprise IT strategy. While cloud promises a pay-as-you-go model, not all workloads are cost-effective in the public cloud, especially those with high network egress or sustained high resource usage.

Hybrid cloud strategies enable cost control by:

- Hosting predictable workloads (e.g., ERP systems) on-premises to avoid variable cloud billing.

- Using Azure Reserved Instances and Hybrid Benefit licensing for savings.

- Offloading backup, DR, or test environments to Azure for lower operational cost.

A cost-effective model might include on-premises hosting for databases with heavy IOPS demands, while less resource-intensive web frontends are deployed in Azure App Services. Azure Cost Management tools can track and optimize spending across both cloud and hybrid assets.

## Innovation Enablement

While operational continuity and compliance are critical, organizations also adopt hybrid cloud to unlock innovation. Azure services such as AI, machine learning, advanced analytics, and IoT are more accessible in a hybrid environment.

With hybrid integration, companies can:

- Use Azure Machine Learning to train models on cloud GPU clusters while running inference locally.

- Connect on-prem manufacturing equipment to Azure IoT Hub for predictive maintenance.

- Leverage cloud-native CI/CD pipelines with GitHub Actions and Azure DevOps to deploy hybrid applications.

These capabilities empower innovation at scale while maintaining control over critical systems. The ability to test new ideas in the cloud and extend successful ones to production on-prem makes hybrid a powerful enabler of transformation.

## Mergers, Acquisitions, and Divestitures

Corporate restructuring events often involve IT integration or separation between entities. Hybrid cloud provides the architectural flexibility needed to adapt quickly.

- Merging IT systems without fully migrating either party to the other's cloud platform.

- Isolating workloads in different environments during a divestiture while maintaining shared services like identity.

- Enabling shared access to common data layers or SaaS platforms with Azure Arc or API Gateway integrations.

## Workforce Distribution and Remote Work

In the post-pandemic era, remote work has become the norm. Hybrid cloud supports secure remote access to corporate resources through:

- Azure Virtual Desktop (AVD) for remote desktop infrastructure.

- Azure VPN Gateway and ExpressRoute for private, encrypted connectivity.

- Azure AD Conditional Access policies to enforce security regardless of access location.

This facilitates global workforce mobility without compromising on performance or compliance.

## Summary Table: Business Drivers vs Azure Services

| Business Driver | Key Azure Services |
|---|---|
| Existing Investment Protection | Azure Stack HCI, Azure Arc |
| Regulatory Compliance | Azure Policy, Azure Purview, Azure Confidential Computing |
| Business Continuity | Azure Site Recovery, Azure Backup |
| Performance Optimization | Azure Stack Edge, CDN, Azure Front Door |
| Agility and Flexibility | Azure DevOps, ARM Templates, Bicep, Azure CLI |
| Cost Optimization | Azure Hybrid Benefit, Azure Cost Management |
| Innovation and R&D | Azure ML, Azure Synapse, Azure IoT Hub |
| M&A Adaptability | Azure Arc, API Management, Private Link |
| Remote Work Enablement | Azure Virtual Desktop, Azure VPN Gateway |

## Conclusion

Hybrid cloud architecture is no longer a tactical workaround—it is a strategic necessity. It enables organizations to move at their own pace, safeguard investments, comply with evolving regulations, and serve both internal and external users with agility and intelligence. Microsoft Azure provides a mature, flexible, and secure platform that addresses all key business drivers with proven technologies, allowing organizations to modernize with confidence. In the next section, we'll explore the benefits and challenges of hybrid cloud models to further dissect how these drivers shape hybrid adoption and influence architecture decisions.

# Benefits and Challenges of Hybrid Cloud Models

Hybrid cloud models have become central to modern IT strategies, offering a balance between on-premises control and cloud agility. While the hybrid approach enables flexibility, performance, compliance, and innovation, it also introduces unique challenges that organizations must navigate with careful planning and tooling. In this section, we will explore the full range of benefits and challenges associated with hybrid cloud models, with a special emphasis on their manifestation within Azure-based architectures.

## Key Benefits of Hybrid Cloud

### Flexibility and Customization

The hallmark benefit of hybrid cloud is the ability to choose where and how workloads are deployed. Businesses can optimize infrastructure according to the sensitivity, latency, and compute intensity of each workload.

- **Sensitive customer data** can remain on-premises or in a private cloud to meet compliance needs.
- **Front-end applications** or analytics workloads can leverage public cloud scalability.
- **Temporary environments**, such as dev/test or marketing campaigns, can be spun up in Azure on demand.

This architectural freedom supports operational efficiency, financial optimization, and innovation across departments and business units.

### Incremental Cloud Adoption

Many enterprises are not prepared—or willing—to make a wholesale move to the public cloud. Hybrid cloud enables a phased migration, allowing IT teams to modernize legacy systems progressively.

For example, an organization might:

- Start with hybrid identity using Azure AD Connect.
- Move backup and disaster recovery to Azure.
- Refactor specific applications for Azure Kubernetes Service (AKS).
- Eventually transition to a more cloud-heavy posture while keeping core databases on-premises.

This approach reduces risk, avoids vendor lock-in, and builds internal capability over time.

### Regulatory Compliance and Data Sovereignty

Hybrid environments allow businesses to comply with strict regional and industry-specific regulations.

- **GDPR**: Data must remain within EU borders.
- **HIPAA**: Requires secure handling of patient data.
- **CJIS**: U.S. law enforcement data with specific residency and access rules.

Azure provides compliance-enabling services such as:

- **Azure Confidential Computing** for protecting data in use.

- **Azure Policy** and **Azure Blueprints** for enforcing governance at scale.

- **Azure Purview** for data cataloging and classification.

By hosting regulated data in an on-prem or regional facility and connecting it to Azure for compute or analytics, organizations maintain both control and capability.

**Cost Efficiency**

Hybrid cloud can reduce overall IT costs by optimizing the location and consumption model for each workload.

- **Predictable workloads** stay on-prem, avoiding variable cloud costs.

- **Bursty or seasonal workloads** run in Azure, reducing the need to over-provision on-prem hardware.

- **Backup, archiving, and cold storage** use Azure Blob Storage or Archive tiers for long-term cost savings.

Azure Hybrid Benefit allows organizations to use their on-prem Windows Server and SQL Server licenses in Azure, lowering licensing costs significantly.

Here's an example of calculating potential savings:

# Sample PowerShell command to estimate savings with Azure Hybrid Benefit

```
$vmSize = "Standard_D2s_v3"

$region = "eastus"

$osType = "Windows"

$licenseType = "AzureHybridBenefit"

Get-AzVMPriceEstimate -VMSize $vmSize -Region $region -OSType $osType -LicenseType $licenseType
```

This command (when implemented with pricing APIs or PowerShell scripts) can help forecast savings in hybrid deployments.

**Disaster Recovery and High Availability**

Hybrid cloud is ideal for creating resilient environments that continue to operate during infrastructure failures or outages.

Azure Site Recovery (ASR) and Azure Backup offer:

- Cross-location VM replication
- Automated failover/failback processes
- Application-consistent snapshots
- Backup retention policies aligned with compliance.

Critical applications can run in active-active or active-passive configurations across on-prem and Azure environments. This ensures business continuity even during major disruptions.

**Unified Management**

Tools like **Azure Arc**, **Azure Monitor**, and **Azure Security Center** provide centralized visibility and control over resources across both cloud and on-prem environments.

- Use **Azure Arc** to manage Kubernetes clusters on-prem as if they were native Azure resources.
- Use **Log Analytics** to monitor VM performance across environments with a single dashboard.
- Enforce **Azure Policy** to ensure that all VMs—regardless of location—adhere to security and tagging standards.

This leads to better operational consistency, reduced overhead, and improved auditing and governance capabilities.

**Accelerated Innovation**

Hybrid architectures empower developers and business leaders to test and implement new ideas without needing to modernize everything at once.

- Teams can run experiments or ML models in Azure using powerful GPU-based VMs.
- Web APIs can be developed in Azure Functions and connect securely to on-prem databases.
- DevOps pipelines can build, test, and deploy hybrid workloads using Azure DevOps or GitHub Actions.

This encourages agile methodologies and faster time to market for new services and features.

## Major Challenges of Hybrid Cloud

Despite its many advantages, hybrid cloud is not without difficulties. Successfully operating a hybrid environment requires advanced planning, skilled personnel, and the right set of tools and governance.

### Increased Architectural Complexity

Connecting and orchestrating disparate systems in a hybrid model introduces a new level of complexity.

- Network latency and packet loss can occur between on-prem and Azure.
- Synchronizing identity and access across environments can create mismatches.
- Configuring hybrid DNS and routing requires deep networking knowledge.

For example, setting up **ExpressRoute** involves coordination with an ISP, Azure configuration, route advertising, and failover design. A misstep in any of these areas can lead to outages or degraded performance.

### Operational Overhead

Hybrid cloud can create operational silos if not managed carefully. IT teams may have to support different toolsets, monitoring dashboards, and access control policies for on-prem versus cloud environments.

To reduce operational burden, organizations should:

- Standardize on tools that support hybrid operations (e.g., Azure Monitor, Microsoft Sentinel).
- Implement Infrastructure as Code (IaC) using Bicep or Terraform for both environments.
- Use **Azure Arc-enabled servers** to apply consistent policies.

Here's a snippet using Bicep to onboard a VM into Azure Arc:

```
resource connectedMachine 'Microsoft.HybridCompute/machines@2022-01-10-preview' = {

name: 'onprem-vm1'

location: 'eastus'

properties: {

osName: 'Windows'

osVersion: '2019'

agentVersion: '1.0.0'

}

}
```

This allows on-prem machines to be treated as first-class Azure citizens.

### Security Complexity

Security is another area that becomes more challenging in a hybrid setup. Each environment may have different vulnerabilities, access patterns, and threat models.

Key concerns include:

- Managing credentials and secrets across environments
- Securing hybrid network tunnels (VPNs, ExpressRoute)
- Ensuring consistent patch management
- Monitoring lateral movement between cloud and on-prem networks

Mitigation strategies involve:

- Using **Azure Key Vault** for centralized secret management.
- Enabling **Conditional Access** policies with **Azure AD**.
- Deploying **Microsoft Defender for Cloud** to identify misconfigurations.

### Integration and Compatibility

Legacy systems can present compatibility issues when connecting to cloud-native services. APIs, authentication methods, and data formats may require translation layers or middleware.

Example:

- A legacy mainframe system may not support modern RESTful APIs or OAuth authentication.
- Connecting it to Azure Logic Apps or Functions might require API Management or on-prem gateways.

**Data Transfer and Latency**

Transferring large datasets between on-prem and cloud can be slow and costly.

Solutions include:

- **Azure Data Box** for physical data transfer.
- **Azure File Sync** to replicate only changes.
- **Content Delivery Networks (CDN)** to cache data near users.

Organizations must also evaluate the performance impact of hybrid data flows on user experience, especially in transactional systems.

**Governance and Compliance Risk**

Inconsistent governance policies across environments can lead to:

- Shadow IT
- Incomplete auditing
- Data loss or leakage
- Regulatory fines

Azure provides tools like:

- **Azure Policy** to enforce compliance standards.
- **Azure Blueprints** to apply predefined configurations.
- **Microsoft Purview** to manage data cataloging, classification, and lifecycle.

Governance must be defined centrally and enforced uniformly, which requires cultural and technical alignment.

## Strategies for Addressing Challenges

To navigate the hybrid landscape effectively, organizations can adopt the following strategies:

1. **Design for Hybrid from the Start**
   Rather than treating hybrid as a temporary state, plan for it as a permanent architecture. Define clear patterns for connectivity, identity, and deployment.
2. **Standardize Tools Across Environments**
   Use Azure-native tools wherever possible, such as Azure Monitor, Defender for Cloud, and Arc. Avoid maintaining separate toolchains.
3. **Invest in Skills and Training**
   Hybrid requires both cloud and on-prem expertise. Provide training in DevOps, cloud networking, identity federation, and governance.
4. **Adopt IaC and Automation**
   Deploy and manage infrastructure using templates (Bicep, ARM, Terraform) to reduce drift and improve repeatability.
5. **Monitor Continuously and Secure Proactively**
   Establish unified dashboards and alerting. Use threat

detection and zero-trust principles to protect assets regardless of location.

6. **Document and Audit**
   Maintain thorough documentation of architecture, policies, and controls. Conduct regular compliance audits across the hybrid estate.

---

## Conclusion

Hybrid cloud models offer unmatched versatility and control, enabling businesses to build resilient, compliant, and high-performance environments. While challenges exist in complexity, security, and integration, they can be mitigated with thoughtful design, consistent tooling, and a culture of continuous learning.

Azure provides one of the most complete hybrid platforms available today, with tools like Azure Arc, Azure Stack, ExpressRoute, Azure AD, and more. When harnessed effectively, these capabilities empower enterprises to innovate confidently while meeting operational, financial, and regulatory goals.

The next section will dive into Azure's specific hybrid capabilities, laying the groundwork for a deeper understanding of how Microsoft's ecosystem supports hybrid workloads across infrastructure, identity, networking, and operations.

# Overview of Azure's Hybrid Capabilities

Microsoft Azure has evolved into a leader in hybrid cloud computing by delivering a comprehensive and integrated suite of services designed specifically to bridge the gap between on-premises infrastructure and the cloud. From extending identity and security across environments to managing hybrid networks, storage, applications, and compliance, Azure provides robust capabilities that enable organizations to build, deploy, and operate hybrid workloads with consistency and confidence.

This section explores Azure's core hybrid services and tools, categorized into six key capability areas: management, compute and virtualization, networking, storage and data, security and identity, and development and automation. These categories cover the full lifecycle of hybrid operations—from infrastructure provisioning and connectivity to monitoring, governance, and modernization.

## Unified Management and Governance

One of Azure's most defining hybrid strengths is its unified management layer, allowing customers to monitor, govern, and operate resources—whether they reside in Azure, on-premises, or in other public clouds.

### Azure Arc

Azure Arc is the linchpin of Azure's hybrid strategy. It allows organizations to project on-premises servers, Kubernetes clusters, SQL databases, and even third-party cloud resources into Azure, treating them as first-class Azure resources.

Benefits of Azure Arc include:

- Unified inventory and governance using Azure Resource Manager (ARM)
- Role-based access control (RBAC) and tagging across all resources

- Application of policies and compliance rules to on-premises infrastructure

- Integration with Azure Monitor, Defender for Cloud, and Azure Automation

Example of onboarding a server using Azure CLI:

az connectedmachine connect—resource-group MyResourceGroup \

—location eastus—name OnPremServer01

Once connected, the server appears in the Azure portal alongside native cloud VMs and can be managed uniformly.

**Azure Policy and Blueprints**

Azure Policy enables centralized enforcement of compliance rules across hybrid environments, including Arc-enabled resources. Azure Blueprints package policies, role assignments, ARM templates, and resource groups into reusable definitions, ensuring consistent deployments.

Example policy enforcement:

- Restricting VM sizes in specific departments

- Requiring encryption at rest for all storage accounts

- Enforcing tag naming conventions

### Azure Lighthouse

For managed service providers (MSPs) or multi-tenant organizations, Azure Lighthouse enables secure delegation of resource management across tenants without compromising control or security.

## Hybrid Compute and Virtualization

### Azure Stack Portfolio

The Azure Stack family extends Azure services and capabilities to on-premises and edge locations:

- **Azure Stack HCI**: A hyperconverged infrastructure solution that runs Windows and Linux virtual machines, containers, and Kubernetes on-premises, with full integration into Azure.

- **Azure Stack Hub**: A standalone instance of Azure services hosted in customer data centers, ideal for disconnected or regulated environments.

- **Azure Stack Edge**: A physical device enabling local compute, storage, and ML inferencing at the edge.

These technologies allow enterprises to:

- Maintain low-latency processing near users or equipment

- Run applications in remote or regulated locations

- Ensure consistent app models using ARM templates and DevOps pipelines

Here's a PowerShell snippet to create a virtual machine on Azure Stack HCI:

```
New-VM -Name "AppVM01" -MemoryStartupBytes 4GB -Generation 2 -SwitchName "vSwitch"
```

These on-prem VMs can be managed using Windows Admin Center or Azure Arc.

### Azure Kubernetes Service (AKS) Hybrid

Azure Arc also supports Kubernetes clusters. Whether you're running AKS on Azure Stack HCI or a custom Kubernetes deployment, Azure Arc can onboard and manage those clusters for consistent governance and monitoring.

---

## Hybrid Networking

Hybrid connectivity is foundational to hybrid cloud operations. Azure provides several secure and high-performance networking options.

### VPN Gateway

Azure VPN Gateway connects on-premises networks to Azure via site-to-site VPN over IPsec/IKE. It is typically used for development, testing, or smaller scale hybrid setups.

**Azure ExpressRoute**

ExpressRoute provides a private, dedicated connection between your on-premises infrastructure and Azure, bypassing the public internet.

Key benefits:

- Lower latency
- Higher throughput (up to 100 Gbps)
- SLA-backed reliability
- Compliance-ready architecture

Example: A bank with critical workloads can use ExpressRoute to maintain private, secure links to Azure while ensuring regulatory compliance and data sovereignty.

**Azure Virtual WAN**

Virtual WAN simplifies connectivity across branch offices, on-prem data centers, and Azure regions by providing a unified hub-and-spoke architecture.

- Automates connectivity with SD-WAN partners
- Integrates VPN, ExpressRoute, and Azure Firewall
- Centralizes routing, monitoring, and security policies

---

## Hybrid Storage and Data Services

Azure provides a wide range of hybrid storage solutions to support structured, unstructured, and semi-structured data across environments.

### Azure File Sync

Azure File Sync extends on-premises Windows Server file shares to Azure Files, enabling centralized cloud management while keeping frequently used data local.

Key features:

- Cloud tiering (caches only most accessed files locally)
- Multisite sync across multiple branches
- Rapid disaster recovery by spinning up a new server and resyncing

Setup involves installing the Azure File Sync agent, registering the server, and creating a sync group that includes your Azure Files share and server endpoints.

### Azure Blob Storage with AzCopy

Data backups and cold storage are often moved to Blob storage for cost efficiency.

Example command to upload on-prem data:

```
azcopy copy "C:\Backups" "https://myaccount.blob.core.windows.net/backupcontainer"—recursive
```

### Azure Data Box

For large-scale data migrations (up to petabytes), Azure Data Box provides secure, ruggedized physical appliances that are shipped to the customer, filled with data, and returned to Microsoft for upload to Azure.

### SQL Server and Azure SQL

On-prem SQL Server can be:

- Replicated to Azure SQL Database for reporting
- Migrated to Azure SQL Managed Instance for cloud-based modernization
- Managed via Azure Arc for consistent patching, backup, and policy control

---

## Hybrid Security and Identity

### Azure Active Directory (Azure AD)

Azure AD enables hybrid identity with seamless single sign-on (SSO), conditional access, and multi-factor authentication (MFA) across on-prem and cloud apps.

- **Azure AD Connect** syncs on-prem identities to Azure
- **Seamless SSO** allows users to log in without repeated prompts

- **Azure AD B2B/B2C** supports secure external collaboration

Hybrid identity example: A university can sync their local Active Directory with Azure AD, allowing students to use the same credentials to access both on-campus Wi-Fi and Azure-hosted learning portals.

**Microsoft Defender for Cloud**

Defender for Cloud delivers threat detection and security posture management across hybrid and multi-cloud environments. With Azure Arc, it can protect on-prem workloads with features like:

- Just-in-time VM access
- Vulnerability scanning
- Endpoint protection

Example configuration to enable Defender:

az security auto-provisioning-setting update \

—name default \

—auto-provision "On"

---

## Development, DevOps, and Automation

Azure supports consistent development workflows and CI/CD pipelines for hybrid environments using familiar tools.

**Azure DevOps and GitHub Actions**

CI/CD pipelines can deploy to:

- Azure App Services
- AKS clusters
- Azure Stack HCI VMs
- Arc-enabled servers and Kubernetes

Pipeline example (YAML for GitHub Actions):

```
jobs:

build-deploy:

runs-on: ubuntu-latest

steps:

- name: Checkout code

uses: actions/checkout@v2

- name: Azure Login

uses: azure/login@v1

with:

creds: ${{ secrets.AZURE_CREDENTIALS }}

- name: Deploy ARM Template

run: az deployment group create—resource-group my-rg—template-file template.json
```

**Azure Automation and Runbooks**

Runbooks can perform regular tasks such as:

- Patching Arc-enabled servers
- Restarting services
- Rotating credentials

Runbooks can be triggered on a schedule or via webhook integration with other systems.

## Summary of Azure Hybrid Capabilities

| Capability Area | Key Azure Services and Tools |
|---|---|
| Management | Azure Arc, Azure Monitor, Azure Policy, Azure Lighthouse |
| Compute & Virtualization | Azure Stack HCI, Azure Stack Hub, AKS, Arc-enabled Kubernetes |
| Networking | ExpressRoute, VPN Gateway, Virtual WAN |
| Storage & Data | Azure File Sync, Data Box, Blob Storage, SQL MI |
| Security & Identity | Azure AD, Azure AD Connect, Defender for Cloud, Key Vault |
| DevOps & Automation | Azure DevOps, GitHub Actions, Azure Automation, Bicep |

## Conclusion

Azure's hybrid capabilities provide a comprehensive and integrated foundation for building modern, resilient, and compliant enterprise environments. Whether managing virtual machines across clouds, synchronizing file systems, deploying Kubernetes clusters, or securing identity and data, Azure empowers organizations with the tools they need to operate seamlessly in a hybrid world.

By enabling consistent operations across on-premises, cloud, and edge environments, Azure not only simplifies hybrid complexity but also unlocks innovation and agility. As we move forward into deeper architectural design in the next chapter, these hybrid capabilities will serve as the building blocks for effective enterprise strategies.

# Chapter 2: Azure Hybrid Cloud Architecture

## Key Components of Azure Hybrid Infrastructure

Microsoft Azure has built one of the most robust and expansive hybrid cloud infrastructures in the market today. With increasing demands from enterprises to retain control over sensitive data, modernize legacy systems, and operate across distributed environments, Azure's hybrid solutions are designed to provide operational consistency, scalability, and compliance. In this section, we will break down the key components of Azure's hybrid infrastructure, focusing on how each one contributes to building a cohesive hybrid environment that supports both existing and new workloads.

### Azure Arc

Azure Arc is the cornerstone of Azure's hybrid and multicloud management strategy. It extends Azure's control plane to resources outside of Azure, including:

- On-premises virtual machines and physical servers
- Kubernetes clusters
- SQL Server and PostgreSQL databases
- Resources in AWS, Google Cloud, and other cloud providers

By projecting these resources into Azure Resource Manager (ARM), Arc enables administrators to apply Azure services such as:

- Azure Policy
- Azure Monitor
- Microsoft Defender for Cloud
- Role-Based Access Control (RBAC)

Arc works by installing an agent on the resource, which registers it with the Azure control plane.

Example command to onboard a Linux server:

az connectedmachine connect—resource-group HybridRG—name OnPremLinux01—location eastus

Once connected, this server behaves like a native Azure VM within the portal and CLI tools.

Benefits:

- Unified governance and compliance across environments
- Centralized logging, monitoring, and alerting
- Consistent security policies
- Inventory and asset tagging

Arc brings "cloud-native" capabilities to non-Azure resources without requiring replatforming.

## Azure Stack Portfolio

The Azure Stack family allows enterprises to run Azure services in their own data centers or edge locations. This capability is vital in environments with low connectivity, data residency requirements, or edge processing needs.

### Azure Stack HCI

Hyperconverged infrastructure (HCI) running Windows and Linux virtual machines on-premises. It's ideal for:

- Branch office deployments
- Data center modernization
- Running SQL Server, file shares, or container workloads locally

With Azure Stack HCI, you can:

- Extend clusters to Azure for cloud-based monitoring
- Enable hybrid VM backups
- Use Arc to manage workloads uniformly

PowerShell command to create a VM on HCI:

```
New-VM -Name "FinanceAppVM" -MemoryStartupBytes 4GB -Generation 2 -SwitchName "ProdSwitch"
```

**Azure Stack Hub**

A fully integrated Azure instance that runs in customer or partner data centers. It's best suited for:

- Disconnected or air-gapped environments
- Government or military use cases
- Sovereignty-sensitive workloads

With Azure Stack Hub, users can run services like App Services, Azure Functions, and Kubernetes with the same experience as in Azure Public Cloud.

**Azure Stack Edge**

A hardware-as-a-service device that offers:

- Edge computing with GPU acceleration
- ML inferencing
- Local storage with automatic Azure sync
- IoT gateway capabilities

Common use cases:

- Manufacturing floor analytics
- Video processing at retail stores
- Emergency response units

---

## Azure ExpressRoute

ExpressRoute offers dedicated, private connections between on-prem data centers and Azure, bypassing the public internet.

Key features:

- Bandwidth options up to 100 Gbps
- SLA-backed uptime and latency guarantees
- Redundant connectivity with failover options
- Compliance and security readiness

Architecture:

- Your on-premises network connects to a local ISP
- The ISP partners with Microsoft's ExpressRoute locations
- The connection terminates at Azure's edge routers, linking into your virtual network (VNet)

Configuration typically includes:

- ExpressRoute circuit
- Gateway subnet
- ExpressRoute Gateway (HighPerformance or UltraPerformance SKU)

Common use cases:

- Financial applications requiring low latency
- Healthcare systems transmitting sensitive patient data
- Real-time systems with strict performance demands

---

## Azure VPN Gateway

VPN Gateway enables encrypted communication between on-prem and Azure using IPsec/IKE tunneling.

While ExpressRoute provides a private circuit, VPN Gateway operates over the public internet and is a more cost-effective option for:

- Development environments
- SMB hybrid setups
- Initial testing and POC phases

Configuration involves:

- Creating a gateway subnet
- Deploying the VPN Gateway
- Configuring local network gateway
- Establishing site-to-site connection

Example of creating a gateway:

az network vnet-gateway create \

—name MyVPNGateway \

—resource-group HybridRG \

—vnet MyVNet \

—public-ip-address MyPublicIP \

—gateway-type Vpn \

—vpn-type RouteBased \

—sku VpnGw2 \

—location eastus

---

## Azure File Sync and Storage Solutions

For hybrid storage, Azure offers a powerful combination of local performance and cloud scalability.

### Azure File Sync

Azure File Sync allows Windows Server file shares to be extended to Azure Files, turning a traditional file server into a cloud-connected cache.

Features:

- Centralized cloud storage
- Cloud tiering (frequently accessed files cached locally)
- Multisite synchronization
- Disaster recovery through rapid resync

Deployment steps:

- Install File Sync agent on the server
- Register the server in Azure
- Create sync groups and cloud endpoints

Use case:

- Organizations with branch offices and centralized document storage needs

**Blob Storage for Backups**

Azure Blob Storage provides scalable object storage, ideal for backups, archival, and media workloads.

Combined with Azure Backup or third-party tools, it enables:

- Long-term retention
- Incremental snapshots
- Tiered storage (Hot, Cool, Archive)

---

## Azure Monitor and Log Analytics

Azure Monitor enables unified observability across hybrid and cloud resources, including:

- Performance metrics
- Log aggregation
- Alerting and notification

- Integration with external tools (ServiceNow, PagerDuty, Splunk)

Log Analytics uses Kusto Query Language (KQL) for powerful query-based insights. Example query to find CPU utilization:

```
Perf

| where ObjectName == "Processor" and CounterName == "% Processor Time"

| summarize avg(CounterValue) by Computer, bin(TimeGenerated, 5m)

| order by TimeGenerated desc
```

Azure Arc-connected servers send telemetry to Azure Monitor like native VMs, enabling consistent monitoring.

---

## Azure Active Directory Hybrid Identity

Azure AD supports hybrid identity via:

- **Azure AD Connect**: Syncs identities from on-prem to Azure AD

- **Federation**: Enables Single-Sign-On with third-party identity providers

- **Seamless SSO**: Uses Kerberos ticketing to authenticate domain-joined devices

Benefits:

- Unified identity platform

- Conditional Access policies
- MFA enforcement
- Password write-back for hybrid environments

Example deployment steps:

- Install Azure AD Connect
- Select synchronization options (Password Hash Sync, Pass-through Authentication)
- Configure OU and group filtering
- Monitor sync health via Azure AD Connect Health

---

## Microsoft Defender for Cloud

A comprehensive solution for threat detection and security posture management, supporting:

- Native Azure resources
- Arc-enabled VMs and SQL Servers
- Kubernetes clusters (AKS or Arc-enabled)

Defender for Cloud integrates with Microsoft Sentinel for SIEM capabilities, and supports custom security recommendations and remediation workflows.

---

### Summary of Key Components

| Component | Description |
| --- | --- |
| Azure Arc | Manage, monitor, and secure non-Azure resources using Azure services |
| Azure Stack HCI/ Hub/Edge | Run Azure services and VMs on-premises or at the edge |
| ExpressRoute | Dedicated private connectivity to Azure with high bandwidth |
| VPN Gateway | Secure IPsec tunnels between on-prem and Azure over public internet |
| Azure File Sync | Sync local file shares with Azure Files |
| Azure Monitor | End-to-end visibility and observability for hybrid workloads |
| Azure AD Connect | Extend on-prem Active Directory into Azure AD |
| Defender for Cloud | Threat protection and posture management for hybrid resources |

## Conclusion

The key components of Azure's hybrid infrastructure are not just disparate services—they are interconnected capabilities that collectively enable a truly hybrid enterprise architecture. From extending governance with Azure Arc to building private connectivity with ExpressRoute and enabling hybrid identity with Azure AD, these tools provide the foundation for scalable, secure, and efficient operations.

By leveraging Azure's hybrid infrastructure, organizations can embrace modernization at their own pace while maintaining control over mission-critical systems and meeting stringent compliance requirements. In the next section, we will explore how specific technologies like Azure Arc, ExpressRoute, and Azure Stack work together to support enterprise hybrid deployments.

## Role of Azure Arc, ExpressRoute, and Azure Stack

The effective implementation of hybrid cloud architecture within Microsoft Azure rests significantly on three core technologies: Azure Arc, Azure ExpressRoute, and the Azure Stack portfolio. Each serves a unique role in bridging the gap between on-premises environments and Azure's public cloud, enabling seamless operations, secure connectivity, and consistent application deployment. In this section, we will take a deep dive into how these components function individually and together to support enterprise-grade hybrid cloud strategies.

### Azure Arc: Extending Azure Anywhere

Azure Arc is a transformative technology that extends Azure's control plane to on-premises, edge, and multi-cloud environments. It allows organizations to project their resources—whether virtual machines, Kubernetes clusters, or databases—into Azure, treating them as first-class citizens within the Azure ecosystem.

#### Key Capabilities

- **Resource Projection**: Onboard non-Azure machines into Azure Resource Manager (ARM).
- **Governance**: Apply Azure Policy, role-based access control (RBAC), and tagging to Arc-connected resources.

- **Monitoring**: Collect telemetry via Azure Monitor and integrate with Log Analytics and Microsoft Sentinel.

- **Security Posture Management**: Use Defender for Cloud to assess and improve configurations.

- **Configuration Management**: Apply Desired State Configuration (DSC) and custom scripts via Azure Automation.

**Supported Resources**

- Windows and Linux servers (physical or virtual)

- Kubernetes clusters (AKS, OpenShift, Amazon EKS, etc.)

- SQL Server and PostgreSQL databases

- VMware vSphere VMs

- Third-party cloud assets (AWS, GCP, etc.)

**Use Case Example**

An enterprise with a VMware-based data center can onboard its VMs to Azure Arc, enabling centralized governance and patch management without migrating the workloads. The IT team can apply a common backup policy across all VMs, regardless of location.

**Arc Onboarding Example**

az connectedmachine connect—resource-group "HybridRG" \

—location "westeurope"—name "onprem-vm01"

Once connected, the machine appears in the Azure Portal and supports tagging, alerting, and scripting like a native VM.

**Arc for Kubernetes**

Azure Arc enables policy-driven management of Kubernetes clusters on-prem or in other clouds. With GitOps integration, teams can automate deployments and configuration management.

Example YAML snippet for GitOps configuration:

apiVersion: clusterconfig.azure.com/v1beta1

kind: GitOpsConfig

metadata:

name: arc-gitops

spec:

repositoryUrl: https://github.com/your-org/hybrid-k8s-config

operatorNamespace: arc-operator

operatorScope: cluster

---

## Azure ExpressRoute: Private Connectivity at Scale

Azure ExpressRoute is designed for enterprises that require reliable, high-speed, and secure connections between their on-premises data centers and Azure. Unlike VPNs, ExpressRoute creates a private circuit that doesn't traverse the public internet.

### Key Benefits

- **Private Connectivity**: Reduces exposure to public internet threats.
- **High Bandwidth Options**: Up to 100 Gbps for large-scale workloads.
- **Consistent Performance**: Lower latency and higher reliability.
- **SLA-Backed**: Enterprise-grade uptime commitments.

### Deployment Models

1. **Co-located**: Connect to Azure via a provider at a co-location facility.
2. **Point-to-Point**: Dedicated circuit between your data center and Azure.
3. **Any-to-Any (IPVPN)**: Leverages a provider's MPLS network.

### Common Use Cases

- Financial services requiring low-latency data feeds
- Healthcare institutions processing sensitive patient data
- Real-time analytics or high-performance computing (HPC)

**ExpressRoute Components**

- **Circuit**: Logical connection between your network and Azure.
- **Gateway Subnet**: A dedicated subnet for ExpressRoute Gateway.
- **Peering Options**: Private, Microsoft, and public peering modes.
- **Routing Domains**: BGP used for route advertisements.

Example PowerShell to create an ExpressRoute Gateway:

```
New-AzVirtualNetworkGateway -Name "MyERGateway" -ResourceGroupName "HybridRG" `
-Location "eastus" -GatewayType "ExpressRoute" -VpnType "RouteBased" `
-EnableBgp $true -Sku "Standard"
```

**Security and Compliance**

ExpressRoute is ideal for regulated environments as it helps isolate traffic, reduce attack surfaces, and facilitate compliance with standards like ISO 27001, PCI-DSS, and HIPAA.

**Redundancy and Failover**

Microsoft provisions dual circuits per ExpressRoute to support high availability. Customers can configure additional VPN Gateway connections for failover.

---

## Azure Stack: Hybrid Cloud on Your Terms

Azure Stack is a family of products that brings Azure services to your data center or edge locations. It's designed for scenarios where full cloud migration isn't feasible or desirable.

**Azure Stack Variants**

1. **Azure Stack Hub**: Full-fledged Azure instance running on-prem. Ideal for disconnected environments and sovereign cloud scenarios.
2. **Azure Stack HCI**: Hyperconverged infrastructure supporting VMs, containers, and native integration with Azure.
3. **Azure Stack Edge**: A hardware-as-a-service device with compute, storage, and GPU capabilities for edge computing.

---

## Azure Stack Hub

Azure Stack Hub allows organizations to run IaaS and PaaS services locally with a consistent Azure experience.

Key features:

- App Services, Functions, and Kubernetes support

- Integrated Marketplace
- Identity federation with Azure AD or ADFS
- Multi-tenancy for service providers or large enterprises

Common use cases:

- Government clouds with sovereignty requirements
- Maritime or aerospace deployments with poor connectivity
- Hosting regulated workloads close to data sources

---

## Azure Stack HCI

Azure Stack HCI enables organizations to run VMs and Kubernetes clusters on-prem with high availability and Azure integration.

Key integrations:

- Azure Monitor and Defender for hybrid visibility and security
- Azure Backup and Site Recovery for data protection
- Windows Admin Center for cluster management

PowerShell example to enable cluster telemetry:

```
Enable-AzStackHciTelemetry -ClusterName "HQCluster"
```

Use cases:

- Branch office virtualization

- On-prem modernization without public cloud migration
- Low-latency workloads with cloud connectivity

---

## Azure Stack Edge

Azure Stack Edge is designed for edge computing scenarios where data must be processed locally.

Key capabilities:

- AI/ML model inferencing
- Data preprocessing before sending to Azure
- IoT integration and hardware acceleration (FPGA/GPU)

Typical deployments:

- Retail stores for foot traffic analysis
- Industrial sites for predictive maintenance
- Remote medical diagnostics and imaging

---

## Interoperability and Synergy

The true power of these technologies emerges when they work together.

**Hybrid Pattern Example**

**Scenario**: A healthcare provider with an on-prem data center, rural clinics with edge devices, and a central Azure deployment.

- **Azure Stack Hub** runs clinical systems in the hospital network due to compliance needs.
- **Azure Stack Edge** deployed at rural clinics processes medical imaging locally.
- **Azure Arc** projects hospital VMs and clinic devices into Azure for monitoring.
- **ExpressRoute** links the hospital data center to Azure with high bandwidth for analytics and research.
- **Azure Monitor** and **Defender for Cloud** ensure compliance and alerting across the ecosystem.

---

## Governance Across Components

Azure Policy and Azure Blueprints can be applied consistently across Arc, Stack, and native Azure resources, providing centralized control and reducing misconfigurations.

Example policy enforcement:

- Disallowing public IP addresses on Arc-connected VMs
- Enforcing encryption on all Azure Stack Edge storage
- Requiring tag inheritance for all ExpressRoute gateways

## Developer Enablement

Developers benefit from the consistent tools across all environments:

- **Azure DevOps** pipelines deploy to Azure, Stack Hub, or Arc-enabled clusters
- **GitOps** ensures configuration compliance across hybrid Kubernetes environments
- **ARM templates** and **Bicep** streamline resource provisioning across platforms

Example Bicep file to deploy a VM (valid for both Azure and Arc-enabled HCI):

```
resource vm 'Microsoft.Compute/virtualMachines@2021-11-01' =
{

name: 'HybridAppVM'

location: resourceGroup().location

properties: {

hardwareProfile: {

vmSize: 'Standard_D2s_v3'

}

osProfile: {

computerName: 'HybridApp'

adminUsername: 'adminUser'
```

```
adminPassword: 'SecureP@ssw0rd!'
}
}
}
```

## Summary Table

| Technology | Role in Hybrid Cloud |
| --- | --- |
| Azure Arc | Extend Azure management to any infrastructure |
| Azure ExpressRoute | Provide secure, high-performance private connectivity |
| Azure Stack Hub | Run Azure services in disconnected or regulated environments |
| Azure Stack HCI | Modernize on-prem VMs and containers with cloud integration |
| Azure Stack Edge | Deliver compute and AI capabilities at the edge |

## Conclusion

Azure Arc, ExpressRoute, and Azure Stack are the foundational pillars of Microsoft's hybrid strategy. Each technology solves specific challenges—from extending governance and automating compliance to delivering high-speed, secure connectivity and running Azure services on-prem or at the edge.

Used individually, these components offer targeted solutions. Combined, they enable a fully integrated hybrid cloud architecture that is scalable, secure, compliant, and resilient. As hybrid continues to define the future of enterprise IT, these tools provide the flexibility and control needed to adapt, innovate, and grow in an increasingly complex technological landscape.

The following section will explore how Azure approaches security and compliance in hybrid environments, ensuring that the flexibility of hybrid doesn't come at the expense of trust or protection.

## Security and Compliance in Hybrid Environments

In today's digital landscape, security and compliance are not optional—they are foundational pillars for any IT infrastructure, especially when that infrastructure spans multiple environments. The hybrid cloud model, by its nature, increases complexity and attack surfaces. Managing security and compliance across both on-premises systems and cloud environments like Azure demands a cohesive, intelligent strategy backed by powerful tools and well-defined policies.

Microsoft Azure provides a rich set of features and services purpose-built to help enterprises implement robust security postures and maintain compliance across hybrid deployments. This section explores the foundational security principles for hybrid environments, the specific tools Azure offers, and the practices that help ensure consistency, reliability, and regulatory alignment.

### Principles of Hybrid Security

Securing a hybrid environment involves protecting assets in both public and private domains while ensuring seamless interoperation. The following principles should guide any hybrid security strategy:

- **Zero Trust**: Assume breach, enforce least privilege, verify explicitly.

- **Defense in Depth**: Multiple layers of protection across identity, network, data, and applications.
- **Shared Responsibility Model**: Azure secures the cloud infrastructure, but customers are responsible for securing their workloads and configurations.
- **Visibility and Control**: Unified monitoring and policy enforcement across all resources.

---

## Identity and Access Management

Identity is the new perimeter in hybrid environments. Azure Active Directory (Azure AD) acts as the centralized identity provider across cloud and on-prem systems.

### Azure AD Connect

This tool synchronizes on-premises Active Directory identities with Azure AD, allowing for single sign-on (SSO), conditional access, and multifactor authentication (MFA).

Key Features:

- Password Hash Sync and Pass-Through Authentication
- Seamless SSO with Kerberos
- Write-back support for password and group changes

Deployment involves:

- Installing Azure AD Connect on a domain-joined server

- Selecting synchronization options
- Monitoring with Azure AD Connect Health

**Conditional Access and MFA**

Azure Conditional Access policies dynamically enforce access controls based on user, location, device compliance, and application risk.

Example policy use case:

- Require MFA for access to the Azure Portal when users log in from outside the corporate network.

Policy creation via Azure CLI:

```
az ad conditionalaccess policy create—display-name "RequireMFA"
\
—conditions "@mfa-policy.json"—grant-controls "mfa"
```

**Privileged Identity Management (PIM)**

PIM provides just-in-time access to Azure resources, reducing the risk of standing administrative privileges.

## Securing Hybrid Networking

Hybrid cloud architectures often rely on complex networking models, including VPNs, ExpressRoute, and Virtual WAN. Each layer introduces risk and must be properly secured.

**Network Security Groups (NSGs)**

NSGs control inbound and outbound traffic to Azure virtual machines and subnets. Rules should enforce the principle of least privilege.

Example NSG rule creation:

az network nsg rule create \

—resource-group HybridRG \

—nsg-name AppNSG \

—name AllowWebTraffic \

—protocol Tcp \

—direction Inbound \

—priority 100 \

—source-address-prefixes Internet \

—destination-port-ranges 80 443 \

—access Allow

**Azure Firewall and Azure DDoS Protection**

Azure Firewall provides stateful packet inspection, logging, and threat intelligence integration, while DDoS Protection defends against volumetric attacks.

Combined with ExpressRoute and VPN Gateway configurations, these services harden your hybrid network perimeter.

### Private Link and Service Endpoints

These features enable secure, private access to Azure services from on-prem or VNet-connected resources, eliminating exposure to the public internet.

---

## Endpoint Security and Server Hardening

Securing virtual machines and on-prem servers is critical. Azure Defender (part of Microsoft Defender for Cloud) extends security to all Arc-enabled and Azure-native resources.

### Azure Defender for Servers

Capabilities include:

- File integrity monitoring
- Vulnerability scanning
- Just-in-time VM access
- Integration with Microsoft Defender Antivirus and EDR

Enable Defender for Arc-connected servers:

```
az security auto-provisioning-setting update \
—name default \
—auto-provision "On"
```

### Baseline Management

Microsoft provides security baselines through Group Policy templates and Azure Policy definitions, ensuring consistent hardening across environments.

Examples:

- Enforcing password complexity
- Disabling SMBv1
- Configuring TLS 1.2 for all communications

---

## Data Protection and Encryption

Protecting data at rest, in transit, and in use is vital for regulatory compliance and risk mitigation.

### Azure Disk and Storage Encryption

- All managed disks are encrypted using Storage Service Encryption (SSE) with Microsoft-managed or customer-managed keys.
- Azure Files and Blob Storage support encryption with Azure Key Vault integration.

### Azure Key Vault

Azure Key Vault allows centralized storage of secrets, certificates, and encryption keys with role-based access and audit logging.

Sample use of Key Vault to store a connection string:

az keyvault secret set—vault-name "HybridVault" \

—name "DbConnectionString" \

—value "Server=sql.local;Database=hybrid;User Id=admin;Password=pass123!"

### Confidential Computing

Azure Confidential Computing uses hardware-based trusted execution environments (TEEs) to protect data in use. Ideal for:

- Healthcare data analysis
- Financial transaction processing
- Government intelligence workloads

---

## Monitoring and Logging

Unified visibility across hybrid environments is essential for detecting and responding to threats.

### Azure Monitor and Log Analytics

Collects performance metrics, event logs, and telemetry from Azure and Arc-enabled resources.

Kusto query to identify high CPU usage:

Perf

| where CounterName == "% Processor Time"

| summarize avg(CounterValue) by Computer, bin(TimeGenerated, 5m)

| order by avg_CounterValue desc

### Microsoft Sentinel

A cloud-native security information and event management (SIEM) solution. Sentinel integrates with:

- Azure AD sign-in logs
- Defender alerts
- On-prem Windows Event Logs (via Arc)

You can create playbooks using Logic Apps to automate response actions like disabling compromised accounts.

---

## Compliance and Audit Readiness

### Azure Policy and Blueprints

Enforce security configurations and compliance requirements across hybrid resources.

Examples:

- Requiring encryption on all disks
- Enforcing naming conventions for resources
- Blocking deployment of unapproved SKUs

Azure Blueprints can package policies, RBAC roles, and templates into repeatable compliance environments.

**Microsoft Purview**

Azure Purview provides data discovery, classification, and lineage tracking across on-prem, cloud, and SaaS sources.

Capabilities:

- Automated scanning and labeling of sensitive data
- Integration with Microsoft Information Protection (MIP)
- Data access governance and lifecycle management

---

## Industry-Specific Compliance

Microsoft Azure maintains over 100 certifications and compliance offerings, supporting hybrid deployments in:

- **Healthcare** (HIPAA, HITECH)
- **Finance** (PCI-DSS, SOC 1/2/3, ISO 27001)
- **Government** (FedRAMP, CJIS, DoD IL5)

Compliance Manager in the Microsoft Purview portal helps track your compliance score, recommend improvements, and generate audit-ready reports.

---

## Challenges and Mitigations

| Challenge | Description | Mitigation |
|---|---|---|
| **Inconsistent security tooling** | On-prem and cloud systems use different platforms | Use Azure Arc and Defender for Cloud for unified coverage |
| **Latency in detecting threats** | Delays between breach and response | Use Sentinel with automated playbooks |
| **Shadow IT** | Unmonitored apps and data silos | Enforce deployment via pipelines and apply policies |
| **Configuration drift** | VMs diverge from security baselines | Use Desired State Configuration and Azure Policy |

## Summary of Key Tools

| Tool/Service | Function |
|---|---|
| Azure AD + Connect | Unified identity management |
| Conditional Access + MFA | Secure authentication and access control |
| Azure Firewall | Network protection and segmentation |
| Defender for Cloud | Threat protection and posture management |
| Key Vault | Secure secret and key storage |
| Sentinel | SIEM for real-time threat detection and response |
| Azure Policy | Governance and compliance enforcement |
| Purview | Data classification and compliance insights |

### Conclusion

Security and compliance in hybrid environments must be approached with intentionality, layered defense, and automation. Azure provides a comprehensive toolkit to help organizations secure identities, endpoints, networks, and data while maintaining continuous compliance.

With services like Azure Arc, Defender for Cloud, and Azure Policy, you can enforce consistent controls across all workloads—regardless of where they reside. This holistic approach ensures that enterprises can reap the flexibility of hybrid cloud without compromising their security posture or regulatory responsibilities.

In the next section, we will compare on-premises, cloud-native, and hybrid architectures—examining their differences, use cases, and strategic considerations to help guide architectural decision-making.

## Comparing On-Prem, Cloud, and Hybrid Architectures

Enterprises today face a diverse and evolving technology landscape, where infrastructure decisions significantly impact agility, cost, security, and scalability. The choice between on-premises, cloud-native, and hybrid architectures is not merely technical—it reflects a strategic alignment with business needs, regulatory constraints, existing investments, and future goals.

This section provides an in-depth comparison of the three dominant architectural models. It explores their strengths, weaknesses, and ideal use cases while illustrating how hybrid architectures often serve as a convergence point, blending the best features of both extremes.

## Foundational Characteristics

| Characteristic | On-Premises | Cloud-Native | Hybrid |
|---|---|---|---|
| **Location of Resources** | Local data centers or physical servers | Public cloud (Azure, AWS, GCP) | Mix of local and cloud resources |
| **Control** | Full physical control | Cloud provider controls infrastructure | Shared control between local and cloud |
| **Scalability** | Limited by physical capacity | Virtually limitless | Conditional—cloud scale + local resilience |
| **Cost Model** | CapEx heavy (hardware, licensing) | OpEx (pay-as-you-go, subscriptions) | Mix of CapEx and OpEx |
| **Latency** | Low (local) | Varies; regional data centers | Configurable based on workload placement |
| **Compliance** | Easier for strict data residency laws | Challenging for sensitive data | Customizable to regulatory needs |
| **Deployment Speed** | Slow (manual provisioning) | Fast (automation, templates) | Fast in cloud, moderate on-prem |
| **Maintenance** | In-house IT required | Cloud provider handles infrastructure | Dual responsibility |
| **Resilience** | Limited without HA setup | Built-in redundancy and DR | Configurable for business continuity |

## On-Premises Architecture

On-premises infrastructure refers to servers, storage, networking, and software hosted and operated in a private facility—whether it's a data center or server room.

### Advantages

- **Full Control**: Physical access and deep control over configuration, performance tuning, and hardware lifecycle.
- **Data Sovereignty**: Sensitive data never leaves the premises, aiding in compliance with strict regulations.
- **Latency-sensitive Applications**: Real-time applications such as manufacturing systems or trading platforms benefit from ultra-low latency.
- **Custom Hardware**: Tailored solutions for high-performance computing or specialized workloads (e.g., GPU clusters, FPGA systems).

### Challenges

- **Scalability Limits**: Hardware upgrades are capital-intensive and slow to deploy.
- **Disaster Recovery (DR)**: Requires duplicate infrastructure in geographically distinct locations.
- **Maintenance Overhead**: Patching, upgrades, hardware failures, and lifecycle management fall entirely on the in-house team.

- **Slow Innovation**: Difficult to adopt modern DevOps, microservices, and AI without re-architecting applications.

**Ideal Use Cases**

- Government facilities with classified workloads
- Hospitals managing regulated medical records
- Manufacturing with tightly coupled machinery interfaces

---

## Cloud-Native Architecture

Cloud-native refers to applications and services designed specifically for the cloud environment, leveraging its elasticity, distributed nature, and rich service offerings.

**Advantages**

- **Rapid Scalability**: Auto-scaling services can instantly adjust to user demand.
- **Global Reach**: Deploy resources in Azure regions worldwide to reduce latency and ensure redundancy.
- **Built-in Services**: Databases, AI, IoT, networking, security, and more available out-of-the-box.
- **Automation and DevOps**: Templates (ARM/Bicep), pipelines (Azure DevOps/GitHub Actions), and CI/CD processes are native to the ecosystem.

Example ARM snippet for deploying a serverless Azure Function:

```
{
"type": "Microsoft.Web/sites",
"apiVersion": "2021-02-01",
"name": "[parameters('functionAppName')]",
"location": "[parameters('location')]",
"kind": "functionapp",
"properties": {
"siteConfig": {
"appSettings": [
{
"name": "FUNCTIONS_WORKER_RUNTIME",
"value": "node"
}
]
}
}
}
```

### Challenges

- **Vendor Lock-in**: Services are tightly coupled with the cloud provider's APIs and SDKs.
- **Data Residency**: Hard to guarantee that data never crosses borders, even with region-specific deployment.
- **Predictable Costing**: While usage-based pricing is attractive, long-running or data-heavy workloads may become expensive.

### Ideal Use Cases

- SaaS startups launching globally
- Web and mobile applications with unpredictable traffic
- AI/ML workloads requiring high-performance compute

---

## Hybrid Architecture

Hybrid architecture integrates both on-premises and cloud infrastructure, aiming to provide flexibility, compliance, and scalability.

### Advantages

- **Balance of Control and Flexibility**: Critical workloads stay on-prem while scalable workloads run in the cloud.

- **Gradual Migration**: Legacy apps can remain untouched while cloud-native services handle modernization efforts.

- **Enhanced DR and HA**: Use Azure Site Recovery to replicate on-prem workloads for failover.

- **Unified Identity and Access**: Azure AD Connect synchronizes on-prem AD with cloud services.

- **Cost Optimization**: Retain stable workloads on-prem and offload dynamic workloads to the cloud.

Example DR topology:

- SQL Server on-prem with asynchronous replication to Azure SQL Managed Instance

- Azure Load Balancer in front of both environments

- Azure Traffic Manager directing users based on availability

**Challenges**

- **Complex Management**: Requires coordination across two infrastructure sets.

- **Security Posture Management**: Ensuring consistent policies across cloud and on-prem.

- **Network Complexity**: Requires well-architected VPN or ExpressRoute connectivity.

- **Tool Fragmentation**: Hybrid tooling must support legacy and cloud-native environments.

### Tools That Enable Hybrid Success

| Need | Azure Solution |
| --- | --- |
| Unified Management | Azure Arc |
| Secure Connectivity | ExpressRoute, VPN Gateway |
| Identity Federation | Azure AD Connect |
| DR and Backup | Azure Site Recovery, Azure Backup |
| Compliance Enforcement | Azure Policy, Blueprints |
| Monitoring and Alerts | Azure Monitor, Log Analytics |

### Ideal Use Cases

- Enterprises with existing infrastructure investment
- Regulated industries (healthcare, finance)
- Organizations pursuing cloud adoption at their own pace
- Smart cities and industrial IoT with edge compute needs

---

## Architecture Comparison: A Practical View

### Scenario 1: E-Commerce Platform

- **On-Prem Only**: Risk of downtime, limited capacity during sales events

- **Cloud-Native**: Elastic scaling, global content delivery, optimized checkout via Azure CDN

- **Hybrid**: Order processing system on-prem for compliance, front-end hosted in Azure App Services

**Scenario 2: University IT System**

- **On-Prem Only**: Campus resources managed locally, limited collaboration

- **Cloud-Native**: Cloud-hosted student portal, Office 365 integration

- **Hybrid**: Identity managed on-prem with AD Connect to Azure AD, learning management system in Azure with backups hosted locally

**Scenario 3: Healthcare Provider**

- **On-Prem Only**: EHR and imaging data retained locally for privacy

- **Cloud-Native**: Not viable for sensitive data

- **Hybrid**: EHR stored on-prem, Azure used for AI analysis and machine learning on anonymized data, remote clinics connected via Azure Stack Edge

---

## Decision Matrix

| Factor | On-Premises | Cloud-Native | Hybrid |
|---|---|---|---|
| Rapid Deployment | Low | High | Moderate to High |
| Data Sovereignty | High | Low | High |
| Cost Predictability | High | Medium | Medium to High |
| Maintenance Burden | High | Low | Medium |
| Compliance Complexity | Low | High | Medium |
| Scalability | Low | High | High |
| Innovation Enablement | Low | High | High |
| Disaster Recovery Options | Manual | Native | Flexible |

## Trends Toward Hybrid

Modern digital transformation strategies increasingly favor hybrid approaches due to:

- Cloud-native technologies becoming more modular and extensible
- Edge computing's rise in manufacturing, logistics, and agriculture
- AI and data analytics pushing workloads to both edge and cloud
- Global regulations requiring localized data handling

Azure's ecosystem is designed with hybrid in mind. With offerings like Azure Arc, Azure Stack HCI, Azure Sentinel, and Azure AD, enterprises can adopt hybrid models that are secure, compliant, and future-proof.

## Conclusion

There is no one-size-fits-all architecture. Each model—on-premises, cloud-native, and hybrid—offers unique benefits and trade-offs. However, for many organizations, hybrid architecture provides the ideal balance between control and agility, especially in complex or regulated environments.

By leveraging Microsoft Azure's hybrid services, enterprises can preserve existing investments, ensure compliance, and modernize workloads incrementally. The hybrid model not only aligns with operational realities but also provides a strategic advantage in a fast-evolving technology landscape.

The next chapter will focus on preparing your on-premises environment to become part of this hybrid ecosystem, including infrastructure assessments, workload identification, and network design considerations.

# Chapter 3: Preparing Your On-Premises Environment

## Infrastructure Assessment and Readiness

Before integrating on-premises environments with Microsoft Azure in a hybrid architecture, organizations must conduct a thorough infrastructure assessment. This is not simply an inventory exercise—it is a critical planning phase that determines the feasibility, security, performance, and cost of hybrid cloud adoption. Properly assessing infrastructure readiness ensures that the foundation is strong, risks are mitigated, and cloud integration occurs smoothly and strategically.

This section outlines a step-by-step framework to evaluate infrastructure components, tools to assist with assessments, readiness indicators, and common challenges. It also discusses how organizations can align this phase with long-term cloud modernization goals.

### Establishing Assessment Objectives

The goals of an infrastructure assessment should be clear from the outset. Objectives typically include:

- Identifying assets eligible for hybrid deployment
- Evaluating performance, security, and compliance posture
- Understanding dependencies across applications and systems

- Estimating cloud resource sizing and cost
- Identifying legacy systems requiring modernization
- Determining licensing, support, and hardware lifecycle status

A successful assessment will result in a strategic roadmap, clearly delineating what stays on-prem, what moves to the cloud, and how both environments will interact.

---

## Inventory of Existing Resources

Begin by cataloging all IT assets. This includes:

- **Servers** (physical and virtual)
- **Operating Systems** and versions
- **Applications** and databases
- **Storage devices and volumes**
- **Network devices and configuration**
- **Security infrastructure** (firewalls, antivirus, policies)
- **Monitoring and management tools**

Tools like **Microsoft Assessment and Planning (MAP) Toolkit**, **Azure Migrate**, **System Center Configuration Manager (SCCM)**, and **PowerShell scripts** can automate much of this discovery.

Example PowerShell command to list installed software on a server:

```
Get-WmiObject -Class Win32_Product | Select-Object Name, Version
```

This data helps determine compatibility with Azure services, dependencies, and the overall health of the environment.

---

## Infrastructure Health and Performance Analysis

After inventorying assets, assess the performance of your infrastructure. The following metrics should be gathered:

- **CPU and memory usage**
- **Disk I/O and utilization**
- **Network throughput and latency**
- **Application response times**
- **Peak and average loads**

Azure Migrate's **Discovery and Assessment** tool can analyze VM utilization patterns to recommend optimal Azure VM sizes, predict costs, and suggest right-sizing for workloads.

**Example: Azure Migrate Workflow**

1. Deploy the Azure Migrate appliance in your environment.
2. Perform automatic discovery of VMs and servers.
3. Create assessment groups (e.g., by department, function, or app).
4. Run performance-based assessments.
5. Export reports and visualize sizing recommendations.

---

## Application Dependency Mapping

Understanding how applications interact is critical for avoiding disruptions during hybrid deployment. Dependency mapping involves:

- Identifying internal and external connections
- Detecting database and storage interactions
- Mapping authentication and directory services usage

Azure Migrate integrates with dependency visualization tools to create a **map of service-to-service communication**, ideal for identifying workloads that must be migrated together or left intact on-premises.

Dependency example:

- Application Server A communicates with Database Server B on TCP port 1433.
- Application A depends on a local file share.
- Application A authenticates against on-prem Active Directory.

If Application A is moved to Azure while leaving B on-prem, you must ensure latency, DNS resolution, firewall rules, and security policies still permit communication.

## Network Assessment

Networking is a cornerstone of hybrid integration. You must understand current topologies and prepare them for connectivity with Azure.

Areas to evaluate:

- **IP address management**: Are there overlapping subnets that will conflict with Azure VNets?
- **Bandwidth**: Is your WAN/Internet capacity sufficient for hybrid scenarios?
- **Firewall rules and NAT configurations**
- **VPN/ExpressRoute readiness**
- **Routing configurations and dynamic protocols like BGP**

Use the **Azure Network Performance Monitor** or tools like **iPerf** to evaluate throughput, jitter, and latency.

Sample command to test bandwidth to Azure using PowerShell:

```
Test-NetConnection -ComputerName <AzureVMIPAddress> -Port 443
```

---

## Storage and Backup Systems

Assess the current storage stack and backup strategy. Evaluate:

- Storage types: SAN, NAS, DAS
- File system formats and mount points

- Growth trends and capacity planning
- Storage redundancy and replication
- Backup frequency and RTO/RPO objectives
- Compatibility with Azure File Sync, Azure Backup, or Azure Blob Storage

Organizations should consider replacing legacy backup systems with Azure-native solutions where possible, ensuring greater resilience and scalability.

## Security and Compliance Readiness

A hybrid deployment introduces new security considerations. Organizations must assess:

- Current patching and vulnerability management status
- Antivirus and endpoint protection deployment
- Encryption protocols for data in transit and at rest
- Authentication mechanisms (e.g., Kerberos, NTLM)
- Logging and auditing configurations
- Compliance mandates (e.g., ISO, GDPR, HIPAA)

Use **Microsoft Defender for Endpoint** and **Microsoft Secure Score** to gain insight into on-prem endpoint security posture and compare against cloud requirements.

## Identity Infrastructure Assessment

Hybrid environments depend heavily on identity synchronization and federated authentication.

Evaluate:

- Active Directory Domain Services (AD DS) health
- Forests, trusts, and OU structure
- Password policy and lockout settings
- Readiness for Azure AD Connect
- Group Policy Objects (GPOs) affecting cloud capabilities

Azure AD Connect pre-checks include:

- Schema compatibility
- Network connectivity to Azure
- Attribute filtering rules
- Synchronization conflicts

Run the following command to validate AD health:

```
dcdiag /v /c /d /e
```

## Application Readiness

Some applications are better suited for hybrid or cloud environments. Evaluate each app for:

- Cloud compatibility
- Licensing model (perpetual vs. subscription)
- OS and runtime dependencies
- Statefulness (stateless apps are easier to scale/move)
- Interoperability with APIs and modern authentication
- Containerization potential (Docker, Kubernetes)

Azure's **App Service Migration Assistant** and **Azure App Containerization Tool** can assess compatibility and recommend next steps.

---

## Cost and Licensing Considerations

Evaluate the current cost of running infrastructure on-prem, including:

- Hardware refresh cycles
- Software licenses (Windows Server, SQL Server)
- Maintenance contracts
- Power, cooling, and rack space

Then, compare projected Azure costs using the **Azure Pricing Calculator** and **Azure TCO Calculator**. These tools provide side-by-side comparisons between on-prem and Azure pricing models.

---

## Readiness Indicators

A greenlight to proceed with hybrid deployment includes:

- Accurate and complete inventory
- Stable and documented network topology
- Mapped dependencies with minimal latency requirements
- Healthy and secure domain environment
- Documented storage and backup needs
- Clean and compliant security posture
- Financial feasibility validated

If significant gaps exist, remediation steps should be included in the roadmap before integration begins.

## Common Challenges and Pitfalls

| Challenge | Impact | Mitigation |
|---|---|---|
| Incomplete inventory | Missed dependencies, failed migrations | Use automated discovery tools |
| Network bottlenecks | Poor performance of hybrid apps | Validate capacity, use ExpressRoute |
| Unpatched systems | Increased security risks | Implement patching strategy before integration |
| Legacy identity models | SSO failures, sync issues | Modernize AD and plan for Azure AD Connect |
| Incompatible apps | Migration delays | Refactor or leave on-prem in initial phases |

## Building the Hybrid Readiness Report

A complete assessment culminates in a **Hybrid Readiness Report**, which should include:

- Asset inventory
- Dependency diagrams
- Performance metrics and sizing recommendations
- Security gap analysis
- Network topology diagrams
- Cost comparisons and ROI estimates
- Remediation actions and timelines

This report will guide the rollout of Azure hybrid solutions and serve as a baseline for continuous improvement.

---

## Conclusion

Infrastructure assessment and readiness are critical first steps in hybrid cloud adoption. Skipping or rushing through this phase can result in technical debt, downtime, and security vulnerabilities. A thorough and structured evaluation enables smooth integration, informed decision-making, and a long-term strategy that aligns with business goals.

As we proceed to the next section, we will explore how to choose the right workloads to migrate or extend into Azure, and how to prioritize these based on value, complexity, and business impact.

# Choosing Workloads to Migrate or Extend

Selecting which workloads to migrate or extend to the cloud is one of the most critical strategic decisions in any hybrid cloud initiative. This decision must be guided by a framework that balances business value, technical feasibility, operational complexity, compliance requirements, and long-term digital transformation goals.

Not every workload is suitable for migration to Azure in its current state. Some are better left on-premises, others should be extended with cloud-native capabilities, and some may require complete re-architecture to take full advantage of cloud scalability and services.

This section provides a comprehensive methodology for evaluating and selecting workloads, assessing technical readiness, determining business impact, and deciding between migration, extension, or retention. It also covers Azure tools that support this evaluation, and real-world migration scenarios to illustrate the process in practice.

## Strategic Workload Evaluation Framework

A structured approach to evaluating workloads ensures consistency, objectivity, and alignment with organizational goals. The following criteria can be used:

### 1. Business Criticality

- How essential is the workload to daily operations?
- What is the financial or reputational impact if the workload is unavailable?
- Is the workload customer-facing or internal?

### 2. Compliance Requirements

- Does the workload contain sensitive data (PII, PHI, PCI)?
- Are there regulations that restrict where data can be stored or processed?
- Can the application meet its compliance needs in Azure?

### 3. Technical Complexity

- Is the workload composed of tightly coupled components?

- Does it rely on legacy platforms, custom integrations, or proprietary hardware?

- Are there specific OS, storage, or runtime dependencies?

**4. Performance and Latency Sensitivity**

- Are there latency constraints (e.g., real-time analytics, manufacturing control)?

- Is the workload I/O bound or compute intensive?

- Would latency increase if moved to the cloud?

**5. Scalability and Elasticity Needs**

- Does the workload experience seasonal or unpredictable demand spikes?

- Would auto-scaling improve performance or cost efficiency?

- Can the workload benefit from Azure services like autoscaling, load balancing, or serverless execution?

**6. Modernization Potential**

- Is the application monolithic or microservices-based?

- Can it be containerized and run in Kubernetes?

- Is there a roadmap to refactor it using Azure App Services, Functions, or Logic Apps?

## Categorizing Workloads

Based on the evaluation, workloads typically fall into one of the following categories:

**Migrate**

- "Lift and shift" approach for workloads with minimal dependencies or modernization needs.
- Best suited for VMs, line-of-business (LOB) apps, and systems that must be moved quickly due to data center exits or hardware refresh cycles.

**Extend**

- Integrate Azure services with existing on-prem workloads without moving the entire stack.
- Common for analytics, AI, reporting, offloading backups, or using cloud-based APIs.

**Refactor**

- Rewriting or re-architecting applications to take full advantage of cloud-native services.
- Suitable for apps with modernization objectives, especially those needing rapid scaling or agility.

**Retain**

- Workloads that must remain on-premises due to regulatory, latency, or technical constraints.
- Often integrated with cloud via Azure Arc for unified governance and policy management.

---

## Example Assessment Table

| Workload Name | Business Criticality | Compliance Sensitivity | Technical Complexity | Recommendation |
|---|---|---|---|---|
| HR Portal | High | Medium | Medium | Migrate |
| CCTV Archive | Medium | High | Low | Retain |
| Reporting App | High | Low | Medium | Extend |
| E-Commerce | High | Medium | High | Refactor |

---

## Azure Migrate and Workload Discovery

Azure Migrate is a central hub for discovering, assessing, and migrating workloads. It offers the following features:

- Discovery of on-prem VMware, Hyper-V, and physical servers
- Dependency mapping
- Performance-based sizing recommendations
- Cost estimation

• Integration with tools like Data Migration Assistant and App Service Migration Assistant

**Sample Workflow**

1. Deploy Azure Migrate appliance in the data center.
2. Discover workloads using agentless or agent-based methods.
3. Create assessments grouped by application or business unit.
4. Analyze dependency diagrams to determine workload interrelationships.
5. Generate cost and sizing reports.

Example: Assessing a 10-VM SharePoint farm reveals dependencies on SQL Server, file shares, and Active Directory. Azure Migrate recommends migrating all components together or extending only the front-end.

---

## Prioritizing Workloads

Once workloads are evaluated and categorized, prioritize them for migration or extension using criteria such as:

• **Quick wins**: Low complexity and high business value (e.g., file servers to Azure Files).

• **High ROI**: Costly workloads that would benefit from cloud elasticity (e.g., reporting services during quarterly financial closings).

• **Modernization candidates**: Monolithic apps with frequent change cycles that would benefit from CI/CD pipelines.

Start with pilot workloads to test governance, monitoring, identity, and networking strategies before full-scale rollout.

## Common Workload Types and Azure Fit

| Workload Type | Azure Service(s) | Recommended Action |
|---|---|---|
| Web applications | Azure App Services, Front Door | Refactor/ Migrate |
| Virtual desktops | Azure Virtual Desktop (AVD) | Migrate |
| Databases (SQL Server) | Azure SQL Managed Instance, SQL Database | Migrate/ Extend |
| File servers | Azure Files, Azure File Sync | Migrate/ Extend |
| Backup & archival | Azure Backup, Blob Storage (Cool/Archive tiers) | Extend |
| ERP systems | Azure VMware Solution, Azure Arc-enabled VMs | Retain/Extend |
| Legacy apps (COBOL/.NET) | Azure App Services (Windows), Containers, Azure Arc | Retain/ Refactor |
| Data analytics | Azure Synapse, Azure Data Factory, Power BI | Extend/ Refactor |
| AI/ML workloads | Azure Machine Learning, Azure Kubernetes Service (AKS) | Refactor |
| IoT/Edge applications | Azure Stack Edge, Azure IoT Hub | Extend |

## Technical and Financial Feasibility

Before migrating or extending, confirm that the target Azure services meet performance and cost expectations.

### Performance Estimation

Use tools like:

- **Azure Monitor**: For existing cloud workloads
- **PerfMon, iPerf, NetMon**: For on-prem metrics
- **Azure TCO Calculator**: Compare total cost of ownership
- **Azure Pricing Calculator**: Estimate running costs based on region and service tier

### Licensing Considerations

- Use **Azure Hybrid Benefit** to reduce licensing costs on Windows Server and SQL Server.
- Consider **reserved instances** for workloads with steady usage.
- Evaluate **BYOL (Bring Your Own License)** models for third-party software.

---

## Governance and Security Planning

Workload migration or extension must be paired with planning for:

- **Azure Policy and Blueprints** to enforce governance
- **Role-Based Access Control (RBAC)** models to manage permissions

- **Identity federation** using Azure AD and Conditional Access
- **Monitoring strategy** using Azure Monitor and Log Analytics

Example: An application with high data sensitivity requires that its Azure storage is encrypted with customer-managed keys and monitored for anomalous access.

---

## Organizational Readiness

Technical readiness must be matched by organizational preparedness:

- Is the operations team trained on Azure monitoring and backup tools?
- Do developers have CI/CD pipelines integrated with Azure DevOps or GitHub Actions?
- Are helpdesk and support teams prepared for hybrid troubleshooting?
- Are business stakeholders aware of cutover plans and potential disruptions?

---

## Sample Migration Roadmap

**Phase 1** – Assessment and Planning

- Run Azure Migrate
- Identify quick wins

- Evaluate security policies

**Phase 2** – Pilot Migrations

- Migrate non-critical workloads
- Test connectivity, performance, and backup

**Phase 3** – Progressive Rollout

- Migrate prioritized apps
- Extend backup and monitoring

**Phase 4** – Optimization

- Apply reserved instances
- Implement autoscaling
- Modernize legacy workloads

---

## Conclusion

Choosing which workloads to migrate or extend is a strategic decision that affects cost, agility, compliance, and innovation. By applying a rigorous evaluation framework, using tools like Azure Migrate, and aligning decisions with business priorities, organizations can ensure that their hybrid cloud initiatives deliver maximum value with minimal risk.

In the next section, we'll explore how to design a network architecture that supports hybrid integration—including connectivity, DNS, routing, and security across both cloud and on-premises infrastructure.

# Network Design for Hybrid Integration

A robust and secure network design is fundamental to the success of any hybrid cloud deployment. Whether extending services from an on-premises data center to Microsoft Azure or setting up multi-site and multi-cloud architectures, the networking layer serves as the connective tissue. It must provide reliable, low-latency, secure connectivity while supporting complex routing, traffic segmentation, and integrated monitoring.

This section outlines the key components of network design for hybrid environments. We will explore connectivity options such as VPN and ExpressRoute, virtual network (VNet) design, DNS integration, IP addressing, name resolution, routing architecture, security controls, and high availability. Special attention will be given to design patterns that balance cost, performance, and manageability.

---

## Core Principles of Hybrid Network Design

When designing networks for hybrid cloud, follow these guiding principles:

- **Connectivity First**: Establish secure, performant links between on-prem and Azure.
- **Separation of Concerns**: Use segmentation (VNets, subnets, NSGs) to isolate workloads.
- **Resiliency and Redundancy**: Avoid single points of failure at all layers.
- **Scalability**: Plan IP addressing and topology for future growth.

- **Security by Design**: Include encryption, firewalls, and micro-segmentation from the start.

- **Visibility**: Ensure traffic flow is observable with telemetry and diagnostics.

---

## Connectivity Options

Azure provides multiple options to connect on-prem environments to the cloud.

### Site-to-Site VPN

Site-to-site VPNs offer a quick and cost-effective way to establish secure IPsec tunnels between on-prem and Azure virtual networks.

- **Encryption**: Uses IKEv2/IPsec for tunneling.

- **Throughput**: Up to 1.25 Gbps (with HighPerformance SKU).

- **Redundancy**: Active-standby configuration possible.

Ideal for:

- Small and medium businesses

- Development and testing environments

- Backup/failover links

Configuration steps:

1. Create a **gateway subnet** in the VNet.

2. Deploy a **VPN Gateway**.
3. Define a **local network gateway** representing on-prem.
4. Establish the **connection** and configure IPsec/IKE settings.

Sample PowerShell to create a connection:

```
New-AzVirtualNetworkGatewayConnection -Name
"OnPremVPN" `

-ResourceGroupName "HybridRG" `

-Location "eastus" `

-VirtualNetworkGateway1 $azureGateway `

-LocalNetworkGateway2 $onPremGateway `

-ConnectionType IPsec `

-SharedKey "yourSecretKey"
```

**Azure ExpressRoute**

ExpressRoute establishes a private, dedicated connection between your on-premises infrastructure and Azure.

- **No public internet** involvement
- **Up to 100 Gbps** throughput
- **SLA-backed** uptime and performance
- **Multiple peering options**: Private, Microsoft, and public

Ideal for:

- Enterprises with compliance needs
- High-throughput or latency-sensitive workloads
- Backup avoidance of the public internet

Design considerations:

- Plan for **dual ExpressRoute circuits** for redundancy.
- Integrate with **ExpressRoute Global Reach** for branch-to-branch connectivity.
- Use **Route Filters** to control BGP advertisements.

---

## Virtual Network Design in Azure

Azure Virtual Networks (VNets) are the foundation of networking within Azure. Design VNets to reflect organizational structure, isolation needs, and scalability goals.

**Key Concepts**

- **VNet**: Analogous to a traditional on-prem network.
- **Subnets**: Logical subdivisions of a VNet.
- **NSGs**: Network Security Groups applied to subnets or NICs.
- **UDRs**: User-defined routes for controlling traffic flows.

- **Peering**: Connect VNets within or across regions without a gateway.

### Subnet Planning

Segment workloads by function:

- Subnet-01: Web Servers (DMZ)
- Subnet-02: App Servers
- Subnet-03: Databases
- Subnet-04: Bastion and management

Ensure subnet sizes allow for horizontal scaling. Avoid using /30 or /29 unless required for routing.

---

## IP Address Management

Use non-overlapping IP address spaces across on-prem and Azure to avoid routing conflicts.

- Reserve private address ranges: 10.0.0.0/8, 172.16.0.0/12, or 192.168.0.0/16.
- Document IP allocations to prevent collisions.
- Avoid reusing subnets across environments.
- Plan for address expansion (e.g., move from /24 to /22 if needed).

---

## DNS Integration

Reliable name resolution is critical for hybrid workloads. Azure supports multiple DNS models.

### Options

1. **Azure-provided DNS**

    ○ Automatic resolution of Azure resources within a VNet.

    ○ No resolution for on-prem assets.

2. **Custom DNS Servers**

    ○ Configure your own DNS servers (Windows DNS, BIND).

    ○ Allows resolution of both on-prem and Azure FQDNs.

3. **DNS Forwarding**

    ○ Use DNS forwarders in Azure (typically IaaS VMs).

    ○ Forward requests between Azure and on-prem.

Example DNS forwarder configuration on a Windows Server:

```
Add-DnsServerForwarder -IPAddress 10.0.0.10
```

Recommendation:

- Use **conditional forwarders** to direct queries between environments.

- Ensure firewall rules allow DNS (UDP/TCP 53) communication across VPN/ExpressRoute.

---

## Routing Architecture

Routing in hybrid environments must account for multiple entry and exit points, latency, and traffic direction.

### Default Routing Behavior

- Azure automatically injects system routes.
- UDRs can override default behavior.

### Common Routing Scenarios

- **Force Tunnel**: All traffic (including internet) routes back through on-prem.
- **Split Tunnel**: Only specific traffic (e.g., internal IP ranges) routes to on-prem.
- **Branch-to-Branch via Azure**: Use Azure Virtual WAN or ExpressRoute Global Reach.

Example UDR (User-Defined Route):

```
New-AzRouteConfig -Name "ToOnPrem" -AddressPrefix "10.1.0.0/16" -NextHopType "VirtualNetworkGateway"
```

## Security Controls

Network security is layered and involves segmentation, filtering, and encryption.

### Network Security Groups (NSGs)

- Apply at subnet or NIC level.
- Define inbound/outbound rules by protocol, port, and source/destination.
- Combine with **Application Security Groups (ASGs)** for grouping by workload.

Example NSG rule:

```
az network nsg rule create \
—resource-group HybridRG \
—nsg-name WebNSG \
—name AllowHTTPS \
—priority 100 \
—direction Inbound \
—access Allow \
—protocol Tcp \
—destination-port-ranges 443 \
—source-address-prefixes Internet
```

**Azure Firewall**

- Centralized, stateful firewall-as-a-service.
- Supports NAT, DNAT, and FQDN filtering.
- Integrates with Azure Monitor for logging.

**DDoS Protection**

- Automatically protects public IPs in Azure.
- DDoS Standard offers additional telemetry and SLA.

---

## High Availability and Redundancy

Design the network to withstand failures at any point.

- Use **multiple VPN tunnels** or **dual ExpressRoute circuits.**
- Design **hub-and-spoke architectures** for regional redundancy.
- Deploy **Azure Bastion** for secure remote access without public IPs.
- Implement **Load Balancers** (Standard, Global) for traffic distribution.

---

## Monitoring and Troubleshooting

Use Azure-native tools to diagnose and observe network performance.

**Tools**

- **Network Watcher**: Includes IP Flow Verify, Connection Monitor, NSG Diagnostics.
- **Traffic Analytics**: Visualize flow logs to understand traffic patterns.
- **Log Analytics**: Aggregate and query logs for firewall, NSG, and VM traffic.

Example query for denied traffic:

```
AzureDiagnostics
| where Category == "NetworkSecurityGroupRuleCounter"
| where action_s == "Deny"
| summarize count() by SourceIP_s, DestinationIP_s, TimeGenerated
```

---

## Hybrid Network Design Patterns

**Pattern 1: Hub-and-Spoke**

- Central hub VNet with shared services (DNS, firewall, Bastion).
- Spoke VNets for workloads, peered to the hub.

- On-prem connects to hub via VPN/ExpressRoute.

**Pattern 2: Mesh Topology**

- VNets directly peered with one another.
- Less scalable for large deployments.

**Pattern 3: Virtual WAN**

- Managed hub-and-spoke model.
- Integrates VPN, ExpressRoute, SD-WAN with unified policies.

---

## Conclusion

Designing the network for hybrid integration is a foundational step that impacts every layer of the stack—performance, security, scalability, and resilience. A well-designed hybrid network ensures seamless communication between on-premises systems and Azure services, supporting your broader hybrid architecture with reliability and efficiency.

With the right connectivity, segmentation, and monitoring in place, organizations can securely extend their environments into Azure and confidently run hybrid workloads.

In the next section, we will cover identity and access management, focusing on how to extend your on-premises Active Directory into Azure AD and maintain a consistent, secure identity experience across environments.

# Identity and Access Management with Azure AD

In hybrid cloud environments, identity and access management (IAM) is both a cornerstone of security and a fundamental enabler of productivity. The ability to authenticate, authorize, and audit users and devices across both on-premises and cloud resources is essential to ensure consistent experiences, robust security posture, and simplified IT operations. Azure Active Directory (Azure AD) plays a critical role in extending traditional on-premises identity solutions into the cloud, creating a unified identity platform that supports hybrid workloads, modern authentication, and secure collaboration.

This section explores the key concepts, tools, and practices involved in integrating on-premises Active Directory (AD) with Azure AD, managing hybrid identities, enabling secure access to resources, and implementing governance and monitoring for access control. It also covers design patterns for different identity federation models, MFA, Conditional Access, and privileged identity management in hybrid contexts.

## Goals of Hybrid Identity

The primary objectives of hybrid identity management include:

- **Single Sign-On (SSO)**: Allow users to sign in once and access both cloud and on-premises resources without re-authenticating.

- **Unified Identity**: Provide a single identity across platforms for consistent access control and policy enforcement.

- **Modern Authentication Support**: Enable OAuth, SAML, and OpenID Connect to support cloud-native apps.

- **Security**: Apply advanced access controls, such as Conditional Access and Multi-Factor Authentication (MFA).

- **Compliance**: Enforce identity-based governance and auditability across all services.

---

## Azure AD vs. Active Directory

| Feature | Active Directory (On-Prem) | Azure Active Directory (Cloud) |
|---|---|---|
| Protocols Supported | Kerberos, NTLM, LDAP | SAML, OAuth, OpenID Connect, WS-Fed |
| Device Management | Group Policy, AD-joined devices | Intune, Azure AD Join, Conditional Access |
| Application Integration | Legacy Windows apps | SaaS apps, Web APIs, Microsoft 365 |
| User Provisioning | Manual, Group Policy | Self-service, dynamic groups, SCIM |
| Federation Support | ADFS | Native and third-party federation |
| External Identities | Complex setup | Azure AD B2B, B2C support |

While AD is optimal for traditional domain-joined Windows environments, Azure AD excels at enabling identity for modern, cloud-first applications.

## Hybrid Identity Architecture

Hybrid identity links the on-premises AD environment with Azure AD using synchronization and optional federation.

### Azure AD Connect

Azure AD Connect is the core tool that enables hybrid identity. It synchronizes user accounts, groups, contacts, and optional passwords from on-prem AD to Azure AD.

**Key features:**

- Password hash synchronization (PHS)
- Pass-through authentication (PTA)
- Federation with Active Directory Federation Services (ADFS)
- Seamless Single Sign-On (SSO)
- Filtering (by OU, domain, attributes)
- Password writeback

**Installation prerequisites:**

- Windows Server 2016 or later
- .NET Framework 4.8
- Enterprise Admin permissions
- A verified domain in Azure AD

**Deployment process:**

1. Download and install Azure AD Connect.
2. Choose synchronization method (PHS/PTA/ADFS).
3. Configure sync scope (OU, domain).
4. Enable optional features (writeback, SSO).
5. Run initial sync and monitor health.

Sample PowerShell command to verify sync status:

```
Get-ADSyncScheduler
```

---

## Authentication Models

### Password Hash Synchronization (PHS)

- Syncs password hashes from on-prem AD to Azure AD.
- Enables cloud authentication.
- Simplest and most commonly recommended model.
- Supports SSO with Seamless SSO enabled.

### Pass-Through Authentication (PTA)

- Authenticates users directly against on-prem AD in real time.
- Passwords are not stored in the cloud.
- Ideal for compliance scenarios where hashes cannot be in Azure.

**Federation (ADFS)**

- Uses on-prem ADFS servers to authenticate users.
- Supports advanced policies and custom claims.
- Complex to maintain and generally being phased out in favor of PHS/PTA.

**Recommendation**: Use PHS unless specific business or regulatory requirements dictate otherwise.

## Seamless Single Sign-On

Seamless SSO provides silent authentication for domain-joined devices inside the corporate network without needing to re-enter credentials.

**Enable Seamless SSO with Azure AD Connect:**

- Uses a computer account called AZUREADSSOACC in AD.
- Kerberos authentication via user's Windows login.
- No additional agents required.

Verify Seamless SSO configuration:

Get-ADComputer -Filter 'Name -like "AZUREADSSOACC"' -Property servicePrincipalName

## Azure AD Join vs Hybrid Azure AD Join

### Azure AD Join

- Used for cloud-native or personal devices.
- Devices are joined to Azure AD only.
- Ideal for BYOD and Intune-managed endpoints.

### Hybrid Azure AD Join

- Devices are joined to both AD and Azure AD.
- Enables Conditional Access, Intune policies, and device-based authentication.
- Automatically configured via GPO and Azure AD Connect.

---

## Conditional Access

Conditional Access policies in Azure AD enforce contextual access rules based on user, location, device, application, and risk signals.

Examples:

- Require MFA when accessing Microsoft 365 from outside the corporate network.
- Block legacy authentication protocols.
- Enforce compliant device checks via Intune.

**Components:**

- Assignments (users/groups, cloud apps)
- Conditions (location, device state, risk)
- Access controls (grant, block, session limits)

Sample PowerShell to list existing policies:

```
Get-AzureADMSConditionalAccessPolicy
```

---

## Multi-Factor Authentication (MFA)

MFA strengthens authentication by requiring additional verification methods:

- Microsoft Authenticator app
- SMS/phone call
- Hardware tokens
- FIDO2 security keys

**Deployment options:**

- Per-user MFA
- Conditional Access MFA
- Azure AD Security Defaults (recommended for small orgs)

Enable Security Defaults via Azure Portal → Azure AD → Properties → Manage Security Defaults.

---

## Privileged Identity Management (PIM)

PIM provides just-in-time (JIT) access to Azure AD roles and resources. It reduces the risk of standing administrative privileges.

**Features:**

- Time-bound role activation
- Approval workflows
- Justification and MFA requirements
- Audit logs and alerts

**Enable PIM:**

1. Navigate to Azure AD → PIM.
2. Assign eligible roles.
3. Define activation settings and access reviews.

---

## Access Reviews and Identity Governance

Identity governance ensures that the right users have the right access to the right resources, and only for as long as necessary.

**Capabilities:**

- Access reviews for Azure AD roles and groups
- Entitlement management
- Terms of use and consent workflows

Automate periodic access reviews using Microsoft Graph or Azure Portal.

---

## Monitoring and Auditing

Maintaining visibility into authentication activities is crucial for security and compliance.

**Key Tools:**

- **Azure AD Sign-In Logs**: Tracks successful and failed login attempts.
- **Audit Logs**: Captures changes to identities and configurations.
- **Microsoft Sentinel**: Cloud-native SIEM for identity-based threat detection.

Example Kusto Query in Log Analytics:

```
SigninLogs

| where ResultType != 0

| summarize count() by UserPrincipalName, ResultDescription, bin(TimeGenerated, 1h)
```

---

## Common Challenges and Solutions

| Challenge | Description | Mitigation |
| --- | --- | --- |
| Duplicate UPNs | Same username exists in multiple forests | Standardize on a single UPN suffix |
| Sync errors | Attribute mismatch or data corruption | Use Azure AD Connect Health reports |
| MFA fatigue | Too many prompts leading to risky behavior | Implement MFA only via Conditional Access |
| Admin sprawl | Too many users with permanent global admin rights | Use PIM with JIT access |

## Best Practices

- Use **PHS with Seamless SSO** as the default authentication model.
- Limit global administrators to no more than 5 people.
- Use **PIM and access reviews** to govern high-privilege roles.
- Block legacy authentication protocols to prevent password spraying attacks.
- Deploy **MFA for all users**, especially admins and external collaborators.
- Regularly review **audit logs and sign-in data** for anomalies.
- Establish an **identity lifecycle process** integrated with HR systems.

## Conclusion

Implementing a secure and scalable identity and access management strategy is crucial to a successful hybrid cloud deployment. Azure Active Directory enables organizations to extend their on-premises identity into the cloud while adopting modern security practices like MFA, Conditional Access, and least-privilege access. By centralizing identity and enforcing policy across hybrid workloads, organizations can improve user experience, enhance security, and support compliance mandates more efficiently.

In the next chapter, we will focus on how to connect your on-premises environment to Azure, exploring VPN Gateway, ExpressRoute, hybrid network topologies, and best practices for secure, resilient hybrid connectivity.

# Chapter 4: Connecting On-Premises to Azure

## Using VPN Gateway and ExpressRoute

Establishing secure, reliable, and performant connectivity between on-premises data centers and Azure is a foundational step in building a hybrid cloud infrastructure. Azure provides two primary solutions for creating such connectivity: **VPN Gateway** and **ExpressRoute**. Both offer distinct advantages and serve different use cases depending on bandwidth requirements, latency sensitivity, regulatory compliance, and cost considerations.

This section dives deep into both connectivity options, how they work, setup procedures, use cases, and best practices for deploying them in a production-grade hybrid environment.

---

### Understanding VPN Gateway

Azure VPN Gateway connects on-premises networks to Azure through **Site-to-Site (S2S)** VPNs using **IPsec/IKE** protocols. It supports **point-to-site** configurations as well, which are ideal for remote access by users or small branches. VPN Gateway is the go-to solution for organizations looking for a quick, cost-effective way to establish hybrid connectivity without needing dedicated networking infrastructure.

**Features:**

- IPsec/IKE encryption ensures secure tunnels.
- Supports BGP for dynamic routing.

- Can be deployed in active-active configurations for high availability.
- Integrates with Network Security Groups (NSGs), route tables, and Azure Firewall.

**Typical Use Cases:**

- Development/test workloads.
- Small to medium-sized branch offices.
- Initial hybrid cloud pilot projects.
- Disaster recovery configurations.

---

## Understanding ExpressRoute

Azure **ExpressRoute** provides a private, dedicated connection between on-premises infrastructure and Microsoft's Azure data centers via a connectivity provider. It bypasses the public internet, delivering **greater reliability, speed, and security**. ExpressRoute is especially useful for mission-critical workloads that require consistent high performance and regulatory compliance.

**Features:**

- Layer 3 connectivity between your on-premises network and Microsoft Cloud through a connectivity provider.
- SLA-backed performance and uptime.

- Dual circuits for high availability.
- Supports global reach to connect different sites across Azure regions.

**Typical Use Cases:**

- Large enterprise workloads with high throughput requirements.
- Regulatory and compliance-sensitive industries like finance or healthcare.
- SAP, SQL Server, and other latency-sensitive enterprise applications.
- Backup and disaster recovery at scale.

---

## VPN Gateway vs. ExpressRoute Comparison

| Feature | VPN Gateway | ExpressRoute |
|---|---|---|
| Medium | Internet | Private circuit |
| Latency | Variable | Predictable, low |
| Bandwidth | Up to 10 Gbps (with aggregation) | Up to 100 Gbps |
| SLA | Basic | High (99.95% or more) |
| Security | Encrypted | Physically isolated from the public internet |
| Cost | Lower | Higher |

Organizations may start with VPN and later transition to ExpressRoute as their needs evolve, or they may use both for a resilient hybrid setup.

## Architecture Overview

In a hybrid architecture:

- VPN Gateways are deployed in Azure Virtual Network (VNet).
- On-premises devices like Cisco ASA or Fortinet appliances establish the tunnel.
- ExpressRoute uses a circuit established through partners like Equinix or AT&T.
- Redundant paths, failover routes, and traffic inspection are built into the architecture.

## Step-by-Step Guide: Setting Up a Site-to-Site VPN Gateway

### Create a Virtual Network

az network vnet create \

—name myHybridVNet \

—resource-group myResourceGroup \

—address-prefix 10.1.0.0/16 \

—subnet-name GatewaySubnet \

—subnet-prefix 10.1.255.0/27

1.

**Create the VPN Gateway**

```
az network public-ip create \
—resource-group myResourceGroup \
—name myVNetGatewayIP \
—allocation-method Dynamic
az network vnet-gateway create \
—name myVNetGateway \
—resource-group myResourceGroup \
—vnet myHybridVNet \
—public-ip-address myVNetGatewayIP \
—gateway-type Vpn \
—vpn-type RouteBased \
—sku VpnGw1 \
—no-wait
```

2.

**Configure the Local Network Gateway**

```
az network local-gateway create \
—resource-group myResourceGroup \
—name myOnPremGateway \
—gateway-ip-address <OnPrem-Public-IP> \
```

—local-address-prefixes <OnPrem-Address-Space>

3.

**Establish the Connection**

az network vpn-connection create \

—name myVPNConnection \

—resource-group myResourceGroup \

—vnet-gateway1 myVNetGateway \

—local-gateway2 myOnPremGateway \

—shared-key 'YourSharedKeyHere'

4.

5. **On-Premise Configuration**

○ Configure your VPN device using Microsoft's generated configuration templates.

○ Use IPsec/IKEv2 with the same shared key and parameters.

---

## Step-by-Step Guide: Setting Up ExpressRoute

1. **Work with a Connectivity Provider**

○ Engage an ExpressRoute partner to provision a private circuit.

○ Providers include Equinix, BT, Verizon, and others.

- Choose either Layer 2 or Layer 3 connectivity.

**Create an ExpressRoute Circuit**

az network express-route circuit create \

—name myExpressRouteCircuit \

—resource-group myResourceGroup \

—location eastus \

—bandwidth 200 \

—provider "Equinix" \

—peering-location "Silicon Valley" \

—sku-tier Standard \

—sku-family MeteredData

2.

**Obtain Service Key**

az network express-route circuit show \

—name myExpressRouteCircuit \

—resource-group myResourceGroup \

—query "serviceKey"

3.

- Provide this serviceKey to the provider to establish connectivity.

**Configure Peering**

az network express-route peering create \

—circuit-name myExpressRouteCircuit \

—name AzurePrivatePeering \

—resource-group myResourceGroup \

—peering-type AzurePrivatePeering \

—peer-asn 10001 \

—primary-peer-address-prefix "10.0.0.0/30" \

—secondary-peer-address-prefix "10.0.0.4/30" \

—vlan-id 200

4.

5. **Link to Virtual Network via Gateway**

   ○ Provision a virtual network gateway of type ExpressRoute.

   ○ Use az network vnet-gateway create with—gateway-type ExpressRoute.

   ○ Establish a connection between the gateway and ExpressRoute circuit.

---

## Best Practices for Hybrid Connectivity

- **Redundancy**: Always design with high availability in mind. Use active-active VPNs or dual ExpressRoute circuits across diverse providers.

- **Latency Testing**: Validate end-to-end latency and throughput before moving production workloads.

- **Security Controls**: Layer firewalls and NSGs to enforce traffic inspection. Use Azure Firewall or NVA appliances.

- **DNS Integration**: Ensure hybrid DNS resolution works with Azure Private DNS Zones or by forwarding queries to on-prem DNS servers.

- **Monitoring**: Set up alerts in Azure Monitor for BGP session changes, packet drops, or throughput thresholds.

---

## Troubleshooting Common Issues

- **Tunnel Not Establishing**: Check for mismatched IPsec/IKE parameters.

- **Packet Loss**: Validate MTU settings and inspect any intermediate NAT devices.

- **Routing Conflicts**: Use BGP for dynamic routing but validate route advertisements on both sides.

- **Gateway Throughput Limits**: Scale up to higher VPN Gateway SKUs or ExpressRoute tiers for increased performance.

## Hybrid Connectivity Scenarios

1. **Headquarters with Branches**:

○ Use ExpressRoute for HQ, VPNs for branches.

○ Aggregate into a hub-and-spoke model using Azure Virtual WAN.

2. **DR Site Integration**:

○ Use VPNs with automated failover to Azure.

○ Combine with Azure Site Recovery for seamless replication and switchover.

3. **Global Enterprises**:

○ Employ Global Reach with ExpressRoute to interconnect regional offices via Azure.

---

## Final Thoughts

Azure VPN Gateway and ExpressRoute are essential tools in enabling hybrid cloud connectivity. Choosing the right solution depends on your organization's requirements for performance, compliance, scalability, and budget. Often, a combined approach offers the best of both worlds—starting with VPN for agility and scaling to ExpressRoute for production-grade workloads.

Hybrid connectivity is more than just a network link—it's a strategic investment in cloud transformation. Thoughtful planning, rigorous implementation, and ongoing monitoring are key to unlocking the full value of hybrid cloud computing.

## Configuring Hybrid Networking

Establishing a well-architected hybrid networking configuration is critical for enabling seamless communication between on-premises and Azure environments. Beyond just linking networks, hybrid networking ensures scalability, security, and operational consistency across both infrastructures. This section explores the design principles, technical configurations, and key services required to implement robust hybrid networking with Azure.

### Key Design Principles for Hybrid Networking

When planning a hybrid networking setup, several architectural principles should guide your decisions:

- **Security-first approach**: All communication must be encrypted and tightly controlled.
- **High availability**: Network components should not become single points of failure.
- **Scalability**: The architecture must support growth in users, devices, and services.
- **Performance optimization**: Network paths should be optimized for latency-sensitive traffic.
- **Simplicity in management**: Centralized tools should monitor and control all networking resources.

Hybrid networking is not a one-size-fits-all solution. Organizations must tailor implementations based on their goals, size, regulatory needs, and existing infrastructure.

## Core Components of Hybrid Networking in Azure

1. **Azure Virtual Network (VNet)**
   A VNet is a logical isolation of the Azure cloud dedicated to your subscription. It's similar to a traditional on-premises network, but with Azure's scalability and redundancy.
2. **Subnets and Route Tables**
   Subnets help segment VNets, and route tables (UDRs) control how traffic is routed within the VNet and to external resources like on-prem environments.
3. **Network Security Groups (NSGs)**
   NSGs act like firewalls at the subnet or NIC level. They filter traffic based on source/destination IP, port, and protocol.
4. **VPN Gateway / ExpressRoute Gateway**
   These components link Azure with on-premises networks via encrypted tunnels or dedicated connections.
5. **Azure DNS or Private DNS Zones**
   Proper name resolution is critical in a hybrid setup. Azure DNS zones and custom DNS forwarding rules ensure resolution across networks.
6. **Firewall/NVA Solutions**
   Azure Firewall, or third-party NVAs, can be used for deep packet inspection, traffic filtering, and perimeter control.

## Network Topologies for Hybrid Environments

Depending on scale and complexity, different topologies may apply:

**Basic Site-to-Site**

- Azure VNet connects directly to on-premises via VPN Gateway.
- Best for small/medium businesses.

**Hub-and-Spoke**

- A central hub VNet contains the VPN/ExpressRoute gateway, firewall, and shared services (e.g., DNS, AD).
- Spoke VNets host workloads and connect to the hub via peering.

**Virtual WAN**

- Azure Virtual WAN simplifies large-scale hybrid networking.
- Uses a global transit network architecture with branches connected to the hub through SD-WAN or VPN.

---

## Step-by-Step: Building a Hub-and-Spoke Hybrid Network

This guide assumes you're setting up a secure, scalable network using the **Hub-and-Spoke** model.

**1. Create the Hub Virtual Network**

az network vnet create \

—name HubVNet \

—resource-group HybridRG \

—location eastus \

—address-prefix 10.0.0.0/16 \

—subnet-name GatewaySubnet \

—subnet-prefix 10.0.0.0/24

**2. Add a Spoke Virtual Network**

az network vnet create \

—name SpokeVNet1 \

—resource-group HybridRG \

—location eastus \

—address-prefix 10.1.0.0/16 \

—subnet-name AppSubnet \

—subnet-prefix 10.1.0.0/24

**3. Peer Hub and Spoke**

az network vnet peering create \

—name HubToSpoke1 \

—resource-group HybridRG \

—vnet-name HubVNet \

—remote-vnet SpokeVNet1 \

—allow-vnet-access

az network vnet peering create \

—name SpokeToHub1 \

—resource-group HybridRG \

—vnet-name SpokeVNet1 \

—remote-vnet HubVNet \

—allow-vnet-access

**4. Create Route Tables and UDRs**

Create a route table and associate it with the Spoke subnet to force traffic through the firewall in the Hub.

az network route-table create \

—name SpokeRouteTable \

—resource-group HybridRG

az network route-table route create \

—resource-group HybridRG \

—route-table-name SpokeRouteTable \

—name DefaultRouteToFirewall \

—address-prefix 0.0.0.0/0 \

—next-hop-type VirtualAppliance \

—next-hop-ip-address 10.0.1.4

Attach the route table:

az network vnet subnet update \

—vnet-name SpokeVNet1 \

—name AppSubnet \

—resource-group HybridRG \

—route-table SpokeRouteTable

## Configuring DNS in a Hybrid Setup

To enable seamless communication, on-prem and Azure-hosted workloads must resolve each other via DNS.

- **Option 1**: Use a DNS forwarder in Azure that forwards queries to on-prem DNS.
- **Option 2**: Configure on-prem DNS to forward *.azure.local to a forwarder VM in Azure.
- **Option 3**: Use Azure Private DNS Zones and link them to VNets.

Example to link a private DNS zone:

az network private-dns zone create \

—resource-group HybridRG \

```
—name corp.local

az network private-dns link vnet create \

—resource-group HybridRG \

—zone-name corp.local \

—name VNetLink \

—virtual-network HubVNet \

—registration-enabled true
```

## Configuring BGP and Custom Routes

When using ExpressRoute or VPN with BGP, Azure dynamically learns and advertises routes. Ensure BGP ASN numbers don't conflict and define route filters to control advertisement.

To enable BGP on VPN:

```
az network vnet-gateway update \

—name myVNetGateway \

—resource-group HybridRG \

—enable-bgp true \

—asn 65010
```

Use **route filters** with ExpressRoute to control Microsoft peering:

```
az network route-filter create \

—name myRouteFilter \

—resource-group HybridRG
```

az network route-filter rule create \

—resource-group HybridRG \

—filter-name myRouteFilter \

—name AllowAzureServices \

—access Allow \

—route-filter-rule-type Community \

—communities 12076:5010

---

## Enforcing Security with NSGs and Azure Firewall

### Deploy Azure Firewall to Hub

az network firewall create \

—name HubFirewall \

—resource-group HybridRG \

—location eastus \

—vnet-name HubVNet

1.

### Create Rules for Hybrid Traffic

az network firewall network-rule create \

—firewall-name HubFirewall \

—collection-name HybridRules \

—name AllowOnPrem \

—resource-group HybridRG \

—rule-type NetworkRule \

—priority 100 \

—action Allow \

—rule-name AllowHybrid \

—protocols Any \

—source-addresses 10.1.0.0/16 \

—destination-addresses 10.0.0.0/16 \

—destination-ports 80 443

1.

2. **Associate Route Tables to Redirect Traffic to Firewall**

Use UDRs in spoke VNets to send traffic through the Azure Firewall in the hub.

---

## Best Practices for Hybrid Networking Configuration

- **Address Space Planning**: Avoid overlapping IP ranges across on-prem and Azure. Use well-defined CIDR blocks.

- **Segment Critical Workloads**: Use subnets and NSGs to isolate sensitive systems.

- **Leverage Infrastructure as Code**: Use ARM, Bicep, or Terraform to define and track all networking configurations.

- **Enable Diagnostics**: Configure NSG Flow Logs, Firewall Logs, and Traffic Analytics.

- **Test Failover Paths**: Simulate outages to ensure VPN failover, route resiliency, and performance under load.

- **Control East-West Traffic**: Use Azure Firewall or NVA to inspect lateral traffic between subnets and spokes.

---

## Advanced Scenarios

### Multi-Region Hybrid Deployment

Deploy hub-and-spoke architecture in multiple Azure regions. Use Global VNet Peering to connect hubs and replicate security and routing configurations.

### Dual Connectivity

Use both ExpressRoute and VPN as redundant paths. Configure BGP weights to prioritize one over the other, ensuring automatic failover.

### SD-WAN Integration

Integrate with SD-WAN vendors like Cisco Viptela or Fortinet to create intelligent branch-to-Azure connections via Azure Virtual WAN.

---

### Summary

Configuring hybrid networking is about more than simply linking Azure to an on-prem environment. It requires a layered approach encompassing virtual network design, routing strategies, DNS planning, security enforcement, and ongoing monitoring. With proper planning and execution, hybrid networking becomes a robust foundation enabling cloud transformation, supporting legacy systems, and future-proofing enterprise IT operations.

Hybrid connectivity is the circulatory system of modern digital transformation—delivering resilience, performance, and control at enterprise scale.

## Securing Hybrid Connectivity

Securing hybrid connectivity between on-premises environments and Azure is paramount to maintaining the integrity, confidentiality, and availability of enterprise systems and data. With multiple points of integration, diverse protocols, and a mix of public and private paths, the hybrid model introduces new security challenges that must be mitigated through layered, defense-in-depth strategies.

This section provides a comprehensive guide to securing the network paths between Azure and on-premises environments, including identity-based access, encryption mechanisms, traffic control, logging, and advanced threat protection.

---

### Security Threat Landscape in Hybrid Connectivity

Before implementing security controls, it's important to understand the potential threats that may target hybrid networks:

- **Man-in-the-middle (MITM) attacks** over public VPN tunnels.
- **BGP hijacking or misconfiguration** in ExpressRoute circuits.
- **Unauthorized access** due to improper identity management or shared secrets.
- **Lateral movement** once a system is compromised.
- **Data exfiltration** over inadequately secured network paths.
- **DNS poisoning** in name resolution services bridging on-prem and cloud.
- **Misrouted traffic** due to incorrect route tables or UDR configurations.

Understanding these risks provides a foundation for enforcing comprehensive security controls across hybrid network layers.

## Encryption and Tunnel Integrity

At the core of hybrid connectivity are VPN tunnels or dedicated ExpressRoute circuits. Both must be secured with encryption and key management strategies.

### Site-to-Site VPN Encryption

Azure VPN Gateways use **IPsec/IKEv2** for encryption. Ensure that only strong ciphers are used and shared keys are rotated regularly.

Example of recommended IPsec/IKE parameters:

```
{
"ikeEncryption": "AES256",
"ikeIntegrity": "SHA256",
"dhGroup": "DHGroup14",
"ipsecEncryption": "AES256",
"ipsecIntegrity": "SHA256",
"pfsGroup": "PFS14"
}
```

Use these settings in the local VPN device and match them in the Azure configuration.

Azure CLI to update connection:

```
az network vpn-connection ipsec-policy add \
—name MyVPNConnection \
—resource-group MyRG \
—ipsec-encryption AES256 \
—ipsec-integrity SHA256 \
—ike-encryption AES256 \
—ike-integrity SHA256 \
—dh-group DHGroup14 \
—pfs-group PFS14 \
—sa-lifetime 3600 \
```

—sa-max-size 102400000

### ExpressRoute Security

ExpressRoute traffic is not encrypted by default because it uses a private path. However, **encryption should still be enforced at the application or transport layer** (e.g., TLS 1.2+), especially for sensitive or regulated data.

## Access Control and Identity Management

### Role-Based Access Control (RBAC)

Azure RBAC should be used to manage access to networking resources. Always assign users and services the **least privilege** required to perform tasks.

Use custom roles to fine-tune permissions:

```
{
"Name": "Custom Network Operator",
"IsCustom": true,
"Actions": [
"Microsoft.Network/*/read",
"Microsoft.Network/virtualNetworks/write",
"Microsoft.Network/vpnGateways/*"
],
"NotActions": [],
```

"AssignableScopes": ["/subscriptions/xxxxxxxx-xxxx-xxxx-xxxx-xxxxxxxxxxxx"]

}

**Network Access via Conditional Access**

Use **Conditional Access** in Azure AD to control who can access hybrid-connected services. Rules can be applied based on:

- Device compliance
- Location
- Risk level
- Sign-in behavior

Example: Require MFA for users accessing hybrid resources outside the corporate network.

---

## Firewalling and Traffic Filtering

### Azure Firewall

Azure Firewall is a cloud-native, stateful firewall. Deploy it in the hub network to inspect all ingress, egress, and lateral traffic.

Create rulesets to allow only required traffic:

az network firewall network-rule create \

—firewall-name MyFirewall \

—resource-group MyRG \

—collection-name AllowHybridTraffic \

—name AllowADDSync \

—rule-name AllowLDAPS \

—priority 100 \

—action Allow \

—rule-type NetworkRule \

—protocols TCP \

—source-addresses 10.0.0.0/16 \

—destination-addresses 192.168.1.0/24 \

—destination-ports 636

**Network Security Groups (NSGs)**

NSGs provide stateless traffic filtering at the subnet or NIC level. Create granular rules to restrict traffic.

Example:

az network nsg rule create \

—resource-group MyRG \

—nsg-name SpokeNSG \

—name AllowOnPremInbound \

—protocol Tcp \

—priority 200 \

—source-address-prefixes 192.168.1.0/24 \

—destination-port-ranges 443 \

—access Allow \

—direction Inbound

---

## DNS and Name Resolution Security

DNS is a critical but often overlooked component of hybrid security.

- Use **Azure Private DNS Zones** instead of public zones for internal names.
- Configure **split-brain DNS** so on-prem resolves internal domains and Azure resolves external ones securely.
- Deploy **DNS forwarders** in Azure (using a VM with DNS role or NVA) that only forward queries over secure paths.

Always monitor DNS logs for signs of DNS tunneling or poisoning attacks.

---

## Logging and Monitoring for Hybrid Security

Visibility is essential to hybrid security. Use these tools and services:

**Azure Monitor and Network Watcher**

- Enable **NSG flow logs** to audit allowed/denied traffic.

- Use **Traffic Analytics** for visualizations and anomaly detection.

```
az network watcher flow-log configure \
—resource-group MyRG \
—nsg MyNSG \
—enabled true \
—retention 30 \
—storage-account MyStorage \
—log-version 2
```

**Azure Sentinel**

Use Azure Sentinel for SIEM capabilities. Correlate events across hybrid systems, detect anomalies, and respond with automated playbooks.

Example Playbook: Detect BGP route injection and trigger alert with remediation script.

---

## BGP and Route Advertisement Hardening

When using BGP in ExpressRoute or VPN, enforce the following:

- Use **route filters** to only advertise required prefixes.
- Avoid accepting routes from unknown ASNs.
- Enforce **prefix limits** and **maximum path checks** on your on-prem routers.

- Log all BGP advertisements and session changes for auditing.

---

## Secure Application Access

Use **Azure Private Link** or **Service Endpoints** to ensure that Azure services (e.g., Storage, SQL Database) are only accessible via private IPs.

Example: Secure an Azure SQL Database with Private Link

az network private-endpoint create \

—name MySqlPrivateEndpoint \

—resource-group MyRG \

—vnet-name HubVNet \

—subnet Subnet1 \

—private-connection-resource-id "/subscriptions/.../sqlServers/MySqlServer" \

—group-id sqlServer \

—connection-name SqlPrivateLink

---

## Zero Trust Principles in Hybrid Networking

Implement Zero Trust with these pillars:

1. **Verify explicitly** – Always authenticate and authorize.
2. **Use least privilege** – Limit access to only what is needed.
3. **Assume breach** – Monitor, log, and contain threats continuously.

Use tools such as Microsoft Defender for Cloud, Conditional Access, and Azure Policy to enforce Zero Trust principles across the hybrid network.

---

## Compliance and Governance

Ensure hybrid connectivity complies with internal policies and external regulations:

- Use **Azure Policy** to audit or deny non-compliant resources.
- Enable **resource locks** on critical components like gateways and firewalls.
- Store **network activity logs** in immutable storage for audit trails.

Example Policy: Enforce that all VPN gateways use RouteBased routing

```
{
"if": {
"allOf": [
{
"field": "type",
"equals": "Microsoft.Network/virtualNetworkGateways"
},
{
```

```
"field": "Microsoft.Network/virtualNetworkGateways.vpnType",
"notEquals": "RouteBased"
}
]
},
"then": {
"effect": "deny"
}
}
```

## Summary

Securing hybrid connectivity is a multidimensional task involving encryption, identity access control, traffic filtering, threat detection, and governance enforcement. Organizations must approach hybrid security as an evolving discipline that requires continuous validation and improvement.

The hybrid world blurs the boundaries of network perimeters, demanding a mindset shift to Zero Trust, continuous monitoring, and proactive remediation. With the right controls and architecture, hybrid connectivity can become not just secure, but a competitive advantage.

# Monitoring and Troubleshooting Connectivity

Ensuring reliable, performant, and secure hybrid cloud connectivity requires continuous monitoring and effective troubleshooting capabilities. In complex hybrid environments where traffic flows between on-premises data centers and Azure over VPN or ExpressRoute, visibility into network health, latency, packet loss, and tunnel integrity becomes critical. Misconfigurations, degraded tunnels, or routing anomalies can cause outages or data bottlenecks—issues that must be detected and resolved quickly.

This section explores the full lifecycle of hybrid connectivity observability—covering design-time validation, runtime monitoring, alerting, and root cause analysis.

---

## Principles of Connectivity Monitoring

Monitoring hybrid connectivity should be guided by the following principles:

- **End-to-end visibility**: Monitor the full traffic path from on-premises to Azure services and back.

- **Proactive alerts**: Identify issues before they affect users with intelligent thresholds and anomaly detection.

- **Performance metrics**: Measure latency, throughput, packet drops, jitter, and tunnel uptime.

- **Correlation**: Combine logs and metrics from Azure, on-premises appliances, and external ISPs.

- **Automation**: Remediate common issues using workflows, scripts, and Azure Logic Apps.

---

## Azure Monitoring Tools Overview

Azure provides a rich set of monitoring and diagnostics tools specifically suited for hybrid networking:

| Tool | Purpose |
|---|---|
| **Network Watcher** | Monitor, diagnose, and gain insights into Azure networking |
| **Azure Monitor** | Collect metrics, logs, and events for custom dashboards and alerts |
| **Log Analytics** | Query telemetry data using Kusto Query Language (KQL) |
| **Azure Metrics Explorer** | Visualize time-series metrics |
| **Azure Sentinel** | SIEM solution with built-in analytics for hybrid environments |

## Enabling Network Watcher

Before you can use Network Watcher features, it must be enabled in the region hosting your resources.

az network watcher configure \

—locations eastus \

—resource-group MyRG \

—enabled true

Use the az network watcher list command to validate active instances.

## Key Metrics to Monitor

1. **VPN Gateway Metrics**

   ○ Tunnel status

   ○ Bytes sent/received

   ○ Tunnel uptime/downtime

   ○ P2S and S2S connection counts

2. **ExpressRoute Metrics**

   ○ BGP availability

   ○ Circuit provisioning state

   ○ Ingress/egress bytes

   ○ Route flaps

3. **Virtual Network Metrics**

   ○ Packet drops

   ○ SNAT port usage

   ○ Route table propagation

4. **Firewall and NSG Logs**

   ○ Allowed/denied flows

   ○ Traffic per port/protocol

- ○ Lateral movement patterns

---

## Capturing VPN Gateway Metrics

You can configure Azure Monitor to collect and alert on VPN metrics.

```
az monitor metrics alert create \

—name VPNDownAlert \

—resource-group MyRG \

—scopes /subscriptions/<sub-id>/resourceGroups/MyRG/providers/Microsoft.Network/virtualNetworkGateways/MyGateway \

—condition "avg TunnelStatus == 0" \

—description "Alert when VPN tunnel goes down" \

—action-group MyAlertGroup
```

This rule triggers an alert when a VPN tunnel becomes unavailable.

---

## Viewing Logs with Log Analytics

Enable diagnostic settings on networking resources to route logs to Log Analytics:

```
az monitor diagnostic-settings create \

—name VNetGatewayLogs \

—resource /subscriptions/<sub-id>/resourceGroups/MyRG/providers/Microsoft.Network/virtualNetworkGateways/MyGateway \
```

```
—workspace MyLogAnalyticsWorkspace \
—logs '[{"category":"GatewayDiagnosticLog","enabled":true}]' \
—metrics '[{"category":"AllMetrics","enabled":true}]'
```

Query VPN logs using KQL:

```
AzureDiagnostics
| where ResourceType == "VIRTUALNETWORKGATEWAYS"
| where Category == "GatewayDiagnosticLog"
| where TunnelStatus_s == "Disconnected"
| summarize count() by bin(TimeGenerated, 5m), TunnelName_s
```

## NSG Flow Logs and Traffic Analytics

NSG Flow Logs capture allowed and denied traffic at the NIC or subnet level. Enable them as follows:

```
az network watcher flow-log configure \
—nsg MyNSG \
—resource-group MyRG \
—enabled true \
—storage-account MyStorage \
—retention 30
```

You can visualize this data with **Traffic Analytics**, a feature of Network Watcher that processes NSG logs and provides insights into:

- Top talkers
- Traffic hotspots
- Unused rules
- Protocol distribution

This helps to identify misrouted or unexpected traffic within your hybrid network.

## Using Connection Monitor

**Connection Monitor** enables end-to-end connection testing from Azure to on-prem or vice versa. It checks reachability, latency, and packet loss.

Example: Monitor HTTP connectivity from a VM in Azure to an on-prem endpoint.

```
az network watcher connection-monitor create \
—name HybridHttpMonitor \
—resource-group MyRG \
—location eastus \
—source-resource /subscriptions/<sub-id>/resourceGroups/MyRG/providers/Microsoft.Compute/virtualMachines/AzureVM \
—dest-address onprem.contoso.local \
—dest-port 80 \
—protocol Http \
```

```
—interval 60
```

## Diagnosing VPN and ExpressRoute Issues

### VPN Tunnel Down

- **Check shared key**: Mismatched PSK will prevent tunnel establishment.
- **Review IPsec/IKE policies**: Ensure both ends match exactly.
- **Validate on-prem device logs**: Look for Phase 1/2 negotiation failures.
- **Use Network Watcher IP Flow Verify**:

```
az network watcher ip-flow-verify \
—resource-group MyRG \
—direction Inbound \
—protocol TCP \
—local 10.0.0.4 \
—remote 192.168.1.5 \
—local-port 443 \
—remote-port 56000 \
—nic-id <nic-id>
```

**ExpressRoute BGP Down**

- **Check peering configuration**: Are ASNs and subnets correct?
- **Verify router health**: Contact provider if required.
- **Use Route Viewer**: In the portal, inspect advertised routes.
- **Correlate logs**: Use Sentinel to match BGP logs with routing tables.

---

## Automating Troubleshooting with Logic Apps

Use Azure Logic Apps to create automatic remediation workflows:

Example: Restart VPN Gateway when Tunnel Down alert triggers

1. Create an alert rule on TunnelStatus == 0
2. Trigger a Logic App that:
    - Authenticates with Azure
    - Calls the az network vnet-gateway reset command

---

## Hybrid Troubleshooting Case Studies

**Case Study 1: Intermittent Packet Loss Over VPN**

**Symptoms:**

- Users report slow application response.
- NSG logs show bursty traffic.

**Resolution**:

- Increased P2S scale-out units.
- Enabled VPN diagnostics, found IKEv2 rekey issues.
- Rotated keys and increased IPsec SA lifetime.

**Case Study 2: ExpressRoute Circuit Disconnected**

**Symptoms**:

- Azure resources unreachable from HQ.
- BGP peering down.

**Resolution**:

- Confirmed provider had router upgrade outage.
- Switched traffic to failover VPN route.
- Alerting now includes ExpressRoute metrics and provider status API.

---

## Best Practices for Monitoring and Troubleshooting

- **Baseline your environment**: Know what "normal" looks like for latency, routes, and logs.

- **Enable diagnostic logs** on all critical networking components.

- **Build layered alerts**: Don't rely on a single signal (e.g., use metrics + logs + flow data).

- **Use Azure Workbooks** to create visual dashboards for hybrid connectivity KPIs.

- **Keep an incident playbook** with known issues, escalation paths, and remediation scripts.

---

## Summary

Robust monitoring and troubleshooting practices ensure that hybrid connectivity remains resilient, performant, and secure. Azure's built-in tools—combined with well-defined metrics, automated alerting, and diagnostic logging—empower organizations to detect, diagnose, and resolve issues quickly.

By treating observability as a first-class citizen in hybrid architecture, you not only reduce downtime and improve user experience but also gain operational confidence in managing the complexity of modern distributed systems.

# Chapter 5: Hybrid Identity and Security

## Azure Active Directory Hybrid Identity Options

Hybrid identity is a cornerstone of modern enterprise infrastructure, enabling organizations to bridge their on-premises identity systems with cloud-based services securely and reliably. Microsoft Azure Active Directory (Azure AD) offers a variety of hybrid identity options that provide flexible authentication, single sign-on (SSO), and unified access control across cloud and on-premises resources.

This section provides a deep dive into the hybrid identity models supported by Azure AD, including their architectural patterns, configuration steps, pros and cons, and best practices for real-world enterprise deployments.

---

### What Is Hybrid Identity?

Hybrid identity refers to an identity management model in which users, groups, and credentials exist in both on-premises directories (typically Active Directory Domain Services, or AD DS) and cloud directories (Azure AD). These directories are synchronized or federated to allow a seamless and secure identity experience across environments.

The goal is to provide a **single user identity** across cloud and on-premises platforms while maintaining **security**, **manageability**, and **compliance**.

---

## Azure AD Hybrid Identity Models

Microsoft supports three main models for hybrid identity:

| Hybrid Identity Model | Description | Authentication Location |
|---|---|---|
| Password Hash Sync (PHS) | Syncs password hashes from AD to Azure AD | Azure AD |
| Pass-through Authentication (PTA) | Authenticates against on-prem AD in real time | On-premises |
| Federation (AD FS) | Uses Active Directory Federation Services to authenticate users | On-premises |

Each model has different benefits, infrastructure requirements, and use cases.

---

## Password Hash Synchronization (PHS)

PHS is the most commonly recommended approach. It syncs user accounts and password hashes from on-prem AD to Azure AD using **Azure AD Connect**.

**Key Benefits:**

- Simple to configure and maintain
- No dependency on on-premises availability during authentication
- Supports SSO and modern authentication
- Compatible with Conditional Access and Identity Protection

**Configuration Steps:**

1. **Install Azure AD Connect** on a domain-joined server.
2. Select **"Password Hash Synchronization"** as the sign-in method.
3. Choose the OU filtering and attribute mapping settings.
4. Schedule periodic sync or configure staging mode for validation.
5. Monitor sync using Azure AD Connect Health.

Azure CLI to verify user authentication method:

Get-AzureADUser -ObjectId user@domain.com | Select-Object -Property UserPrincipalName, DirSyncEnabled

**Considerations:**

- Password hashes are irreversibly encrypted before upload.
- Does not support smart card or certificate-based authentication directly.
- Recommended default for most organizations unless specific needs dictate otherwise.

---

## Pass-through Authentication (PTA)

PTA allows Azure AD to validate passwords against on-prem AD in real time, without storing password hashes in the cloud.

**How It Works:**

- Azure AD Connect installs an **authentication agent** on one or more domain-joined servers.
- When a user logs in, Azure AD sends a request to the agent to validate the credentials.
- The result is passed back securely to Azure AD.

**Benefits:**

- Credentials never stored in the cloud
- Supports real-time user lockouts and password policies
- Allows integration with legacy password filters

**High Availability:**

Multiple PTA agents can be installed for redundancy. Azure will automatically failover if one agent becomes unavailable.

Install-AzureADConnectAuthenticationAgent

Check PTA agent status:

Get-ADSyncAuthAgent

**Considerations:**

- Requires persistent outbound connectivity from the agent to Azure AD.

- Authentication depends on on-prem availability—useful in scenarios with strong compliance restrictions.

- Does not support legacy clients (e.g., Office 2010) unless modern auth fallback is configured.

---

## Federation with Active Directory Federation Services (AD FS)

Federation provides a way to delegate authentication entirely to on-premises infrastructure.

**Architecture:**

- Users are redirected to the AD FS endpoint for login.

- AD FS validates credentials and issues SAML tokens.

- Azure AD trusts tokens from AD FS.

**Use Cases:**

- Organizations that require custom authentication policies

- Certificate-based smart card auth

- Support for third-party identity providers

**Federation Components:**

- AD FS servers

- Web Application Proxies (WAP)
- Azure AD as relying party

Federation metadata configuration via PowerShell:

```
Set-MsolDomainAuthentication `
-DomainName contoso.com `
-FederationBrandName "Contoso Federated" `
-Authentication Federated `
-PassiveLogOnUri https://fs.contoso.com/adfs/ls/ `
-SigningCertificate "MIID..." `
-IssuerUri https://fs.contoso.com/adfs/services/trust
```

**Considerations:**

- Highest complexity and cost to deploy
- Requires proper certificate and token management
- Best suited for large enterprises with advanced security requirements

---

## Choosing the Right Identity Model

| Criteria | Recommended Model |
|---|---|
| Simplicity | PHS |
| Real-time auth with no cloud password copy | PTA |
| Smart card or certificate auth | Federation |
| High compliance environments | PTA or Federation |
| Legacy support | Federation (with fallback) |

Microsoft's official guidance is to prefer **PHS** unless there's a specific need for real-time or federated authentication.

---

## Coexistence and Migration Strategies

Organizations often need to transition from federation to cloud-based models. Azure supports staged migrations:

- **Staged rollouts**: Enable PHS for select groups while federation remains for others.
- **Cloud fallback**: Enable PHS or PTA alongside AD FS to allow fallback during outages.
- **Monitor authentication traffic**: Use Azure AD sign-in logs and AD FS logs to determine usage patterns.

Example: Switch from federation to PHS with staged rollout

Set-MsolDomainAuthentication -DomainName contoso.com -Authentication Managed

---

## Azure AD Connect Health

Use **Azure AD Connect Health** to monitor the status of synchronization, PTA agents, and AD FS servers.

Capabilities:

- Alerts for sync failures
- Performance metrics
- Token issuance logs
- Security insights

Enable via PowerShell:

Install-Module -Name "AzureADConnectHealth"

Register-AzureADConnectHealthADDSAgent

View logs in the Azure portal under **Azure AD Connect Health.**

## Integrating with Azure Services

Once hybrid identity is enabled, users gain access to a broad set of Azure capabilities:

- **Single Sign-On (SSO)**: Seamless login to Microsoft 365, Azure, and SaaS apps.
- **Conditional Access**: Apply policies based on location, risk, or device.
- **Azure AD B2B/B2C**: Extend authentication to partners and consumers.

- **Identity Protection**: Detect leaked credentials, suspicious sign-ins, and risky users.

Example: Require MFA for external logins

```
New-AzureADMSConditionalAccessPolicy `
-DisplayName "MFA for External Users" `
-Conditions @{ Users = @{ IncludeGuestsOrExternalUsers = "guest"; IncludeRoles = @(); }; Applications = @{ IncludeApplications = @("All"); }; } `
-GrantControls @{ Operator = "OR"; BuiltInControls = @("mfa") } `
-State "enabled"
```

---

## Security and Compliance Considerations

- **Audit identity logs** regularly using Log Analytics or Sentinel.
- **Enable password protection policies** in Azure AD to block weak or leaked passwords.
- **Use Privileged Identity Management (PIM)** to restrict admin access with just-in-time elevation.
- **Review synchronization scope**: Ensure only required users and attributes are synced to minimize exposure.
- **Maintain password change synchronization** policies with user education.

---

## Summary

Azure AD's hybrid identity solutions enable secure, unified authentication across cloud and on-premises resources. Whether using password hash sync for simplicity, pass-through for compliance, or federation for advanced scenarios, organizations can meet diverse identity needs while maintaining governance and control.

The key to success lies in aligning the chosen model with organizational requirements, security posture, and technical capabilities—while continuously monitoring and adapting as needs evolve. With hybrid identity in place, the path to cloud transformation becomes secure, seamless, and user-friendly.

# Implementing Conditional Access and MFA

Conditional Access (CA) and Multi-Factor Authentication (MFA) are two of the most powerful security features available in Azure Active Directory (Azure AD) for managing access to hybrid and cloud resources. They provide dynamic, context-aware controls to protect corporate identities and data from threats, both internal and external. These capabilities are fundamental to a Zero Trust security model and form the backbone of identity protection in hybrid environments.

This section provides an in-depth walkthrough of designing, configuring, and managing Conditional Access and MFA in Azure AD, with real-world considerations and practical implementation examples.

## What Is Conditional Access?

Conditional Access is a policy-based approach to securing access to resources. It evaluates a wide range of conditions before granting access and can enforce controls like MFA, app restrictions, or session limitations based on those conditions.

**Core Components of Conditional Access:**

- **Assignments**: Define **who, what**, and **when** policies apply.
  - **Users and groups**
  - **Cloud apps or actions**
  - **Conditions** (e.g., device platform, location, risk level)
- **Access Controls**: Define **what happens** when conditions are met.
  - Require MFA
  - Require compliant device
  - Block access
  - Use session controls (e.g., limited session duration)

---

## What Is Multi-Factor Authentication?

MFA requires users to provide two or more forms of verification to prove their identity. Azure AD supports:

- Microsoft Authenticator app (push notifications)
- OATH tokens
- SMS or phone call
- FIDO2 security keys
- Temporary Access Pass (TAP)

By enforcing MFA, you significantly reduce the risk of account compromise—even if credentials are stolen.

---

## Prerequisites for Conditional Access and MFA

1. **Azure AD Premium P1 or P2 license** for Conditional Access.
2. **Users must be synchronized** to Azure AD if using hybrid identity.
3. **Authentication methods** must be configured in the Azure AD portal.

Verify available licenses:

```
Get-AzureADSubscribedSku | Where-Object {$_.SkuPartNumber -like "*P1*"}
```

---

## Creating a Basic Conditional Access Policy

Let's walk through a policy that enforces MFA for all users accessing the Azure Portal.

**Steps:**

1. Navigate to **Azure AD > Security > Conditional Access > New Policy**.
2. Name the policy: Require MFA for Azure Portal.
3. Assign to: All Users (exclude break-glass accounts).
4. Cloud apps: Select "Microsoft Azure Management".
5. Conditions: None (apply globally).
6. Grant controls: Require multi-factor authentication.
7. Enable policy: On.

**Equivalent PowerShell Example:**

```
Connect-AzureAD

New-AzureADMSConditionalAccessPolicy `

-DisplayName "Require MFA for Azure Portal" `

-State "enabled" `

-Conditions @{

Users = @{

IncludeUsers = @("All");

ExcludeUsers = @("<BreakGlassAccount>")

};

Applications = @{

IncludeApplications = @("797f4846-ba00-4fd7-ba43-dac1f8f63013") # Azure Management
```

```
}
}`
-GrantControls @{
Operator = "OR";
BuiltInControls = @("mfa")
}
```

## Common Conditional Access Use Cases

### 1. Block Access from Risky Countries

Block access to corporate resources from countries where your business does not operate.

Condition:

Locations: Include "All Locations"

Exclude: Named Locations > “Corporate Countries”

Control:

Grant Access: Block

### 2. Require Compliant Devices

Only allow access from devices that meet compliance policies in Intune.

Control:

Grant Access: Require device to be marked as compliant

### 3. High-Risk Sign-ins

Automatically enforce MFA or block access for users flagged as high-risk by Microsoft Defender for Identity.

Condition:

Sign-in risk level: High

Control:

Grant Access: Require MFA or Block Access

---

## Designing Conditional Access Policies

Follow a structured approach:

1. **Plan**: Understand user roles, applications, and threat landscape.
2. **Pilot**: Apply policies to test groups or environments.
3. **Monitor**: Use the "Report-only" mode to evaluate impact.
4. **Refine**: Iterate based on telemetry.
5. **Enforce**: Apply policies in full enforcement mode.

**Policy layering** is recommended. For example:

- Base policy for all users: MFA required.
- Admins: Require compliant device + MFA.
- External users: Limited access + MFA + session timeouts.

---

## Implementing MFA in Hybrid Environments

If using **Azure AD Password Hash Sync** or **PTA**, users can be prompted for MFA during cloud authentication.

**MFA Options:**

| Method | Use Case | Secure? | Usability |
|---|---|---|---|
| Microsoft Authenticator | General users | High | Easy |
| FIDO2 Key | Admins, high-risk users | Very High | Medium |
| Phone/SMS | Backup | Medium | High |

**Register MFA Methods:**

Users can register their MFA methods via:

- https://aka.ms/mfasetup
- MySecurityInfo portal

Admin view to audit registered MFA methods:

```
Get-MgUserAuthenticationMethod -UserId user@domain.com
```

## MFA Registration Policy

To enforce MFA registration before a user can proceed:

1. Navigate to **Azure AD > Security > Authentication Methods > Registration Campaign**.
2. Enable policy.
3. Target to selected or all users.

4. Define authentication methods to register.

This ensures MFA setup becomes part of the onboarding process.

---

## Secure MFA Implementation Practices

- **Exclude emergency access accounts** from CA policies.
- **Enforce MFA for admin roles** such as Global Administrator, Conditional Access Administrator, Security Administrator.
- **Rotate authenticator apps** for admins every 90 days.
- **Avoid reliance on SMS/phone for admins** due to SIM-swap vulnerabilities.
- **Monitor sign-in logs** for unexpected MFA prompts or bypass attempts.

---

## Monitoring and Troubleshooting

Azure AD provides rich telemetry through the **Sign-in logs** and **Audit logs**.

Example KQL query in Log Analytics:

```
SigninLogs

| where ConditionalAccessStatus == "failure"

| summarize count() by ResultDescription, UserPrincipalName
```

You can also view **policy decisions** per sign-in:

- Go to **Azure AD > Sign-in logs**
- Select a log entry
- Expand **Conditional Access** to see which policies were evaluated, and their results

---

## Automating MFA and CA with Graph API

Organizations can programmatically manage MFA and CA policies using Microsoft Graph.

Example: Enable MFA registration campaign via Graph:

PATCH https://graph.microsoft.com/beta/policies/authenticationMethodsPolicy

```
{
"registrationEnforcement": {
"mode": "enabled",
"includeTargets": [
{
"id": "all_users",
"targetType": "group"
}
]
}
```

```
}
```

## Real-World Scenarios and Recommendations

**Scenario: Remote Work Transition**

**Solution**: Implement Conditional Access to allow only trusted devices and enforce MFA for unmanaged endpoints.

- CA Policy 1: Trusted device required for Exchange Online
- CA Policy 2: Session control for SharePoint Online (read-only)

**Scenario: Contractors and Partners**

**Solution**: Use guest access policies combined with session limits.

- CA Policy: External users > Require MFA + block download via session control

**Scenario: Privileged Role Protection**

**Solution**: Require compliant device + MFA + just-in-time access via PIM

## Summary

Conditional Access and MFA are no longer optional—they are critical layers of protection in the hybrid identity model. They enable dynamic access control policies that adapt to changing risk and business needs, while reducing friction for legitimate users. When implemented effectively, they enhance security posture without compromising usability.

Organizations that fully leverage Conditional Access and MFA position themselves to combat modern identity threats and support secure, scalable hybrid operations.

# Hybrid Security Best Practices

As organizations adopt hybrid cloud architectures, the attack surface expands across on-premises data centers and cloud environments. To effectively protect users, data, and applications, a holistic security strategy that spans both realms is essential. This is where hybrid security best practices come into play—serving as a blueprint for building a strong, adaptive, and resilient security posture across your enterprise infrastructure.

This section explores best practices that unify traditional IT security with cloud-native principles, incorporating identity protection, encryption, endpoint hardening, network security, threat detection, logging, compliance, and automation.

---

## Embrace Zero Trust Security Principles

The foundational security model for hybrid environments is **Zero Trust**, which shifts the mindset from "trust but verify" to "never trust, always verify."

**Core Pillars of Zero Trust:**

1. **Verify explicitly** – Always authenticate and authorize based on all available data.
2. **Use least privileged access** – Limit user and workload access to what is strictly necessary.

3. **Assume breach** – Design systems with containment and recovery in mind.

**Implementation Tips:**

- Apply Conditional Access policies at every entry point.
- Segment internal networks and restrict lateral movement.
- Use Just-In-Time (JIT) access for administrative tasks.
- Monitor continuously with identity and endpoint telemetry.

---

## Secure Identity and Access Management (IAM)

Identity is the new perimeter in a hybrid world. A compromised identity can provide attackers with access to both cloud and on-prem systems.

**Best Practices:**

- Enforce MFA for **all users**, especially privileged roles.
- Use **Privileged Identity Management (PIM)** to provide time-bound admin access.
- Audit **sign-ins and authentication attempts** regularly.
- Apply **role-based access control (RBAC)** across Azure resources.

Example: Enable PIM for Azure subscription owners

Enable-AzPIMSubscription -ResourceId "/subscriptions/xxxxxxxx-xxxx-xxxx-xxxx-xxxxxxxxxxxx"

**Hybrid Directory Sync Considerations:**

- Limit sync scope to **essential users and groups**.
- Exclude sensitive objects like break-glass accounts.
- Sync only required attributes—avoid unnecessary exposure.

---

## Harden Endpoints and Devices

In a hybrid model, endpoints access both cloud and on-prem resources. Endpoint hardening is vital for stopping threats at the edge.

**Recommendations:**

- Enforce **device compliance policies** via Microsoft Intune.
- Require **BitLocker encryption** for all endpoints.
- Disable **legacy authentication protocols** (e.g., POP, IMAP).
- Implement **Endpoint Detection and Response (EDR)** with Microsoft Defender for Endpoint.

Use Intune to require compliance:

```
New-DeviceCompliancePolicy -Platform Windows10 -RequireEncryption $true -MinimumPasswordLength 8
```

## Encrypt Data at Rest and In Transit

Data must be encrypted across its entire lifecycle to prevent unauthorized access or tampering.

**For On-Premises:**

- Use **BitLocker** or third-party encryption on disks and servers.
- Secure databases with **Transparent Data Encryption (TDE)**.

**For Azure:**

- Enable **encryption at rest** with Microsoft-managed or customer-managed keys (CMK).
- Enforce **TLS 1.2 or higher** for data in transit.
- Use **Azure Key Vault** to manage secrets and certificates.

Example: Enable customer-managed encryption on a storage account

```
az storage account update \
—name mystorageaccount \
—resource-group myrg \
—encryption-key-source Microsoft.Keyvault \
```

—encryption-key-vault-properties keyName=mykey keyVaultUri=https://myvault.vault.azure.net/

## Strengthen Network Security

Hybrid networks introduce complexity. Implement layered network security across virtual and physical boundaries.

**Azure-Specific Best Practices:**

- Use **NSGs** to restrict subnet and NIC-level traffic.
- Deploy **Azure Firewall** or **NVA appliances** for perimeter defense.
- Set up **UDRs (User Defined Routes)** to steer traffic through inspection points.
- Leverage **Private Endpoints** and **Service Endpoints** to access Azure services securely.

**On-Premises Considerations:**

- Disable unused ports and protocols.
- Isolate critical infrastructure into protected VLANs.
- Monitor inter-segment traffic with IDS/IPS systems.

Example: Configure a UDR to route traffic through Azure Firewall

az network route-table route create \

—resource-group myrg \

—route-table-name myroute \

—name ToFirewall \

—address-prefix 0.0.0.0/0 \

—next-hop-type VirtualAppliance \

—next-hop-ip-address 10.0.1.4

## Centralize Logging and Threat Detection

Visibility is critical to securing hybrid environments. Logs must be collected, analyzed, and retained to detect threats early.

**Tools to Use:**

- **Azure Monitor and Log Analytics** for metrics and logs
- **Microsoft Sentinel** for SIEM/SOAR
- **Microsoft Defender for Cloud** for continuous assessment and threat protection

**Best Practices:**

- Enable **diagnostic settings** on all Azure resources.
- Ingest **on-prem logs** into Azure Monitor or Sentinel via agents or Syslog connectors.
- Monitor for **anomalous activity** across identity, network, and data layers.

KQL query example for failed sign-ins:

SigninLogs

| where ResultType != 0

| summarize Count = count() by UserPrincipalName, ResultDescription

---

## Protect Against Advanced Threats

Sophisticated attacks such as ransomware, phishing, and supply chain compromises target hybrid environments aggressively.

**Recommendations:**

- Enable **Microsoft Defender for Identity** to detect lateral movement and domain compromises.
- Use **Safe Links and Safe Attachments** in Defender for Office 365.
- Apply **adaptive risk policies** with Conditional Access based on real-time signals.

Use Defender for Identity to detect reconnaissance:

- Monitor for **enumeration of domain controllers**.
- Detect **pass-the-hash or pass-the-ticket** attacks.

---

## Establish Backup and Recovery Plans

A robust backup and recovery strategy ensures operational continuity in case of disaster, ransomware, or human error.

**Hybrid Backup Strategy:**

- Use **Azure Backup** for VMs, SQL, and file shares.
- For on-premises systems, use **Azure Backup Server** or third-party agents.
- Protect against deletion with **soft delete and immutability**.

Example: Enable soft delete for Azure Backup vault

az backup vault backup-properties set \

—name myvault \

—resource-group myrg \

—soft-delete-feature-state Enabled

Ensure regular **disaster recovery drills** and validate restore points.

## Maintain Regulatory Compliance

Security is tightly coupled with compliance in hybrid infrastructures.

**Steps to Ensure Compliance:**

- Map your controls to regulatory frameworks using **Azure Policy Initiatives**.
- Use **Compliance Manager** in Microsoft 365 for gap analysis and documentation.
- Retain logs according to legal and business needs.

- Monitor **data residency** and sovereignty across regions.

Example: Assign built-in initiative for ISO 27001

```
az policy assignment create \
—name "ISO27001Compliance" \
—scope "/subscriptions/xxxxx" \
—policy-set-definition "a8e07156-65f3-4c41-a3a3-6b0c5efc0c2b"
```

## Automate and Enforce with Policy and Code

Manual configuration does not scale. Use **Infrastructure as Code (IaC)** and **policy-as-code** for consistent enforcement.

**Tools to Adopt:**

- **Azure Bicep** or **ARM templates** for infrastructure deployment
- **Terraform** for multi-cloud and on-prem integration
- **Azure Policy** to audit and enforce configuration standards

Use Azure Policy to deny non-encrypted storage creation:

```
{
"if": {
"allOf": [
{
```

```
"field": "type",
"equals": "Microsoft.Storage/storageAccounts"
},
{
"field": "Microsoft.Storage/storageAccounts.supportsHttpsTrafficOnly",
"equals": false
}
]
},
"then": {
"effect": "deny"
}
}
```

## Regularly Review and Test Your Security Posture

Security is not set-and-forget. Perform regular reviews and assessments.

- Run **Microsoft Secure Score** and address recommendations.
- Conduct **penetration tests** and red team exercises.

- Use **Azure Security Benchmark** to evaluate your configuration.
- Review **role assignments and privileged access** monthly.

Automate reports with Azure Graph API and Logic Apps for governance dashboards.

---

### Summary

Securing a hybrid cloud environment is a multi-dimensional challenge that requires strategy, tooling, and discipline. From identity to infrastructure, and from policies to practices, every layer must be designed with security in mind. By adopting these best practices, organizations can not only reduce risk but also build a proactive, resilient security posture that supports innovation and scalability.

Ultimately, hybrid security is about achieving **balance**—leveraging the flexibility and agility of the cloud while retaining the control and assurance of on-premises systems. Through continuous improvement and automation, hybrid security becomes a strategic enabler, not just a defensive necessity.

## Integration with Microsoft Defender

Integrating Microsoft Defender with hybrid environments is critical for implementing a cohesive, enterprise-grade security posture. Microsoft Defender provides advanced threat protection across identities, endpoints, data, applications, and infrastructure—both on-premises and in the cloud. When integrated correctly, Defender offers deep insights, real-time alerts, automated responses, and continuous risk assessment across your hybrid environment.

This section outlines how Microsoft Defender integrates with hybrid infrastructures, including step-by-step configurations, real-world use cases, monitoring capabilities, and incident response strategies.

## Defender for Identity (formerly Azure ATP)

**Microsoft Defender for Identity** is a cloud-based security solution that helps protect on-premises Active Directory by detecting suspicious activities, compromised identities, and advanced persistent threats.

**Capabilities:**

- Detects pass-the-hash, brute force, and reconnaissance attacks.
- Monitors lateral movement and privilege escalation.
- Provides detailed timelines and attacker maps.

**Architecture:**

- Lightweight sensors installed on domain controllers.
- Data sent to the Defender for Identity cloud service for analysis.

**Deployment Steps:**

1. Install the sensor on all domain controllers.
2. Connect Defender for Identity to your Microsoft 365 security portal.
3. Configure email notifications and SIEM integration.

PowerShell to verify sensor status:

```
Get-Service AzureAdvancedThreatProtectionSensor
```

Use the Microsoft 365 Defender portal to view suspicious activities and investigate identity-based threats in real time.

## Defender for Endpoint

**Microsoft Defender for Endpoint** provides EDR (Endpoint Detection and Response) for both Windows and non-Windows systems, delivering endpoint visibility across hybrid environments.

**Key Features:**

- Behavioral-based, heuristic detection.
- Attack surface reduction (ASR) rules.
- Integration with Microsoft Threat Intelligence.
- Automated investigation and response (AIR).

**Hybrid Integration:**

- Enroll on-prem Windows Servers using Group Policy or Microsoft Endpoint Manager.
- Enroll Azure VMs using Defender for Servers (see below).
- Include non-Windows devices using platform-specific agents.

Example of onboarding a Windows Server via Group Policy:

1. Download onboarding package from Microsoft 365 Defender.
2. Use Group Policy to deploy the script and configuration.
3. Verify onboarding:

```
sc query sense
```

After deployment, use the security portal to monitor alerts, isolate devices, and run live response sessions.

---

## Defender for Servers (Part of Defender for Cloud)

**Microsoft Defender for Servers** extends endpoint protection into the hybrid ecosystem by integrating directly with your Azure and on-prem server workloads.

**Benefits:**

- Unified threat protection for IaaS VMs (Linux and Windows).
- Integration with Microsoft Defender for Endpoint.
- File integrity monitoring (FIM).
- Log analytics and security recommendations.

**Setup via Azure:**

1. Navigate to **Microsoft Defender for Cloud**.
2. Enable **Microsoft Defender for Servers** under environment settings.
3. Azure Arc is required for onboarding non-Azure servers.

Example: Enable Defender for Servers Plan 2 for a subscription

```
az security pricing create \
—name VirtualMachines \
—tier Standard \
—resource-type Microsoft.Compute \
—subscription <subscription-id>
```

**Azure Arc for On-Premises Servers:**

To manage and protect non-Azure servers, integrate with **Azure Arc**.

1. Install the Azure Connected Machine agent.
2. Register the machine with Azure Arc.
3. Apply Defender for Servers protection.

```
az connectedmachine connect—resource-group HybridRG—name OnPremServer01
```

---

## Defender for Cloud Apps (formerly MCAS)

**Microsoft Defender for Cloud Apps** enables visibility, control, and protection for SaaS and on-prem apps.

**Use Cases:**

- Discover shadow IT.
- Enforce Conditional Access policies for third-party apps.

- Monitor app usage across cloud and on-prem traffic.

**Hybrid Use:**

- Deploy log collectors to capture on-prem firewall and proxy logs.
- Identify risky app behaviors and enforce real-time session control.

Configure log collector:

1. Create a log collector VM.
2. Configure syslog ingestion or firewall log parsing.
3. Upload logs to Defender for Cloud Apps.

Integration with Conditional Access:

```
New-AzureADMSConditionalAccessPolicy `

-DisplayName "Restrict Cloud App Sessions" `

-Conditions @{ Applications = @{ IncludeApplications = @("<app-id>") } } `

-SessionControls @{ CloudAppSecurity = @{ Mode = "monitorOnly" } } `

-GrantControls @{ Operator = "OR"; BuiltInControls = @("mfa") }
```

## Defender for Cloud Integration

**Microsoft Defender for Cloud** offers continuous assessment and threat protection for hybrid environments spanning Azure, AWS, GCP, and on-premises.

**Features:**

- Secure Score recommendations.
- Just-In-Time (JIT) VM access.
- Regulatory compliance dashboards.
- Integration with Azure Policy and Azure Sentinel.

**Hybrid Onboarding with Azure Arc:**

- Use Azure Arc to onboard on-prem servers.
- Enable Defender for Servers to extend protection.
- Use security recommendations to harden hybrid resources.

Use Azure Policy to auto-deploy Defender:

```
az policy assignment create \
—name "DeployDefenderForServers" \
—scope "/subscriptions/<sub-id>" \
—policy-set-definition "DefenderForServersPolicy"
```

## Security Alerts and Incident Correlation

All Defender components feed alerts into **Microsoft 365 Defender**, which correlates signals across identity, email, endpoint, and cloud workloads.

**Features:**

- Unified incidents.
- Automated investigation and response (AIR).
- Threat analytics reports.
- Attack simulation and training.

Example: Respond to an incident across hybrid identities

1. Alert from Defender for Identity detects lateral movement.
2. Defender for Endpoint confirms unusual process execution.
3. Incident is correlated in M365 Defender.
4. Use live response to collect forensic data or isolate host.

Use KQL in Microsoft Sentinel to analyze attack chains:

```
SecurityIncident

| where Title contains "lateral movement"

| join kind=inner (

DeviceNetworkEvents

| where RemotePort == 445

) on $left.Entities[0].Name == $right.DeviceName
```

## Best Practices for Defender Integration in Hybrid Environments

1. **Centralize management** through the Microsoft 365 Defender portal.
2. **Onboard all identities**—including guest users—into Defender for Identity.
3. **Enable Auto-IR** to isolate high-risk endpoints automatically.
4. **Segment alert rules** to classify incidents by hybrid zones (on-prem, Azure, multi-cloud).
5. **Use tags** to distinguish between Azure and Arc-connected resources.

---

## Automation and Response with Logic Apps

Integrate Defender alerts into **Azure Logic Apps** or **Microsoft Sentinel Playbooks** for automated response.

Example: Auto-isolate device on high-severity alert

1. Alert triggers Sentinel Playbook.
2. Playbook calls Defender for Endpoint API.
3. Device is isolated pending investigation.

POST https://api.securitycenter.microsoft.com/api/machines/{machineId}/isolate

Authorization: Bearer <token>

---

## Licensing and Planning Considerations

Ensure you have the appropriate licenses for full Defender functionality:

| Defender Product | License Required |
| --- | --- |
| Defender for Identity | Microsoft 365 E5 or standalone |
| Defender for Endpoint | Microsoft Defender for Endpoint P1/P2 |
| Defender for Servers | Azure Defender for Servers Plan 1/2 |
| Defender for Cloud Apps | Microsoft 365 E5 Security |
| Defender for Cloud | Azure subscription with Defender plans |

Evaluate your organization's needs and assign licenses based on user roles and workload criticality.

---

## Summary

Microsoft Defender's suite of solutions offers comprehensive protection across hybrid environments, blending native Azure security with on-premises defense. By integrating Defender for Identity, Endpoint, Cloud, and Apps, organizations can achieve unified threat detection, faster response times, and actionable insights into their security posture.

In a hybrid world where threats span both local data centers and the cloud, Defender becomes a central pillar of enterprise cybersecurity—helping organizations move from reactive defense to proactive, intelligent protection. With proper integration and continuous tuning, Defender empowers security teams to stay ahead of evolving threats across every domain.

# Chapter 6: Data Management in Hybrid Cloud

## Hybrid Storage Solutions (Azure File Sync, Blob Storage)

Data lies at the heart of all modern applications, making its availability, accessibility, and integrity essential in any IT strategy—especially in hybrid cloud environments. Managing storage in a hybrid model presents unique challenges: maintaining performance, ensuring security, managing replication, and preserving compliance while seamlessly bridging on-premises systems and cloud-native platforms.

Azure offers several hybrid-friendly storage solutions, most notably **Azure File Sync** and **Azure Blob Storage**, each of which enables organizations to modernize storage without discarding existing investments. This section provides a comprehensive exploration of how these solutions are architected, deployed, and managed within hybrid infrastructures.

---

### Understanding the Hybrid Storage Landscape

Hybrid cloud storage allows organizations to extend or replicate on-premises storage capabilities to the cloud, offering:

- **Cloud-scale capacity** without physical infrastructure expansion.
- **Tiered storage**, combining high-performance local access with long-term cloud archiving.

- **Data redundancy and resilience** across multiple geographies.

- **Centralized policy enforcement and security**.

Traditional file servers and network shares often need modernization, but complete cloud migration may not be feasible due to latency-sensitive workloads or compliance requirements. Hybrid solutions fill this gap effectively.

## Azure File Sync Overview

**Azure File Sync** transforms Windows Servers into a fast, local cache for Azure Files shares. It allows organizations to retain their on-prem file server experience while benefiting from centralized cloud-based file management.

**Core Capabilities:**

- **Multi-site sync**: Share data across multiple branch offices.

- **Cloud tiering**: Frequently used files stay local, older files are tiered to Azure.

- **Backup integration**: Protect data using Azure Backup.

- **Disaster recovery**: Deploy a new server and sync data from the cloud.

**Architecture:**

- Azure File Share (cloud file system)

- Windows Server 2012 R2 or later with Azure File Sync agent
- Sync group configuration (links File Share to on-prem server endpoints)

---

## Deploying Azure File Sync

**Prerequisites:**

- Azure subscription with a storage account and File Share
- Windows Server with access to the internet
- Server registered with Azure File Sync service

**Step-by-Step Setup:**

1. **Create a Storage Account**

```
az storage account create \
—resource-group HybridRG \
—name hybridfilestore \
—sku Standard_LRS \
—kind StorageV2 \
—location eastus
```

1. **Create a File Share**

az storage share create \

—account-name hybridfilestore \

—name sharedocs \

—quota 100

1. **Install Azure File Sync Agent** Download the agent from Microsoft and install on the file server. During installation, you'll register the server with Azure.
2. **Create a Sync Group** Navigate to **Azure File Sync > Sync groups** in the portal.

- Create a sync group linking the storage account and File Share.

- Add a server endpoint pointing to the local path (e.g., D:\SharedDocs).

1. **Enable Cloud Tiering (Optional)**

Cloud tiering can be enabled to offload less-used files:

Set-FileSyncTieringPolicy `

-Path "D:\SharedDocs" `

-VolumeFreeSpacePercent 20 `

-MinimumFileAgeDays 30

---

## Azure Blob Storage in Hybrid Scenarios

**Azure Blob Storage** is Microsoft's object storage solution for unstructured data such as documents, images, videos, and backups.

It is highly scalable, durable, and cost-efficient, making it ideal for hybrid backup, archiving, and analytics.

**Key Features:**

- Hot, Cool, and Archive tiers for cost optimization
- Native HTTPS and encryption support
- Integration with Azure Data Factory, Synapse, and Logic Apps
- Immutable storage support (WORM)

**Use Cases:**

- Backup and restore targets
- Media storage and distribution
- Large-scale data ingestion
- Archiving compliance data

---

## Mounting Blob Storage via Azure Blobfuse

Blobfuse is an open-source virtual file system driver that allows you to mount Azure Blob Storage as a file system in Linux.

**Blobfuse Example on Linux:**

1. **Install prerequisites:**

```
sudo apt-get update

sudo apt-get install blobfuse fuse
```

1. **Configure credentials** in a file:

```
accountName myblobaccount

accountKey <your-account-key>

containerName mycontainer
```

1. **Mount the Blob container:**

```
mkdir /mnt/blob

blobfuse /mnt/blob—config-file=/path/to/fuse_connection.cfg -o attr_timeout=240 -o entry_timeout=240 -o negative_timeout=120
```

This allows hybrid workloads to interact with Blob Storage as a mountable resource, enabling efficient data movement and access from on-prem systems.

---

## Managing Data Lifecycle and Tiers

To optimize cost and performance, Azure Storage offers **lifecycle management policies** for both File and Blob storage.

**Example Policy: Move blobs to cool storage after 30 days**

```
{

"rules": [

{
```

```
"name": "archiveOldBlobs",
"enabled": true,
"type": "Lifecycle",
"definition": {
"filters": {
"blobTypes": ["blockBlob"],
"prefixMatch": ["logs/"]
},
"actions": {
"baseBlob": {
"tierToCool": {
"daysAfterModificationGreaterThan": 30
}
}
}
}
}
]
}
```

Apply using Azure CLI:

```
az storage account management-policy create \
—account-name hybridfilestore \
—resource-group HybridRG \
—policy @policy.json
```

## Backup and Disaster Recovery with Hybrid Storage

Hybrid storage must support robust **backup and DR** mechanisms.

**For Azure File Sync:**

- Use **Azure Backup** to back up File Shares directly—no need for additional software.
- Recovery can be point-in-time or file-level.

```
az backup protection enable-for-azurefileshare \
—vault-name myRecoveryVault \
—resource-group HybridRG \
—storage-account hybridfilestore \
—azure-file-share sharedocs \
—policy-name DefaultPolicy
```

**For Blob Storage:**

- Enable **soft delete** to protect against accidental deletion.

- Use **object versioning** for long-term change tracking.
- Replicate data across regions with **RA-GRS** (Read-access geo-redundant storage).

---

## Security Best Practices

Hybrid storage solutions must be secured both at rest and in transit.

**Azure File Sync:**

- Use **private endpoint access** to storage accounts.
- Restrict access using **shared access signatures (SAS)** or **Azure RBAC**.
- Enable **Azure Defender for Storage** to detect threats like data exfiltration or malware.

**Blob Storage:**

- Enable **encryption with customer-managed keys (CMK)**.
- Use **immutable storage** for regulatory data.
- Monitor access using **storage logs and alerts**.

Example: Enable soft delete for blob storage

az storage blob service-properties delete-policy update \

—account-name hybridfilestore \

```
—enable true \
—days-retained 30
```

## Monitoring and Troubleshooting

Azure provides robust monitoring tools for hybrid storage:

- **Azure Monitor**: Collects metrics such as file share usage, request latency, and throttling.
- **Log Analytics**: Ingests diagnostics from storage accounts and sync agents.
- **Azure Backup Reports**: Provides insights into backup jobs and failures.

Example KQL query to view storage access logs:

```
StorageBlobLogs
| where OperationName == "GetBlob"
| summarize count() by RequesterIpAddress, Resource, TimeGenerated
```

## Real-World Use Cases

### Branch Office File Sharing

Use Azure File Sync to synchronize data across multiple branch offices and centralize storage management in Azure.

#### Cloud Backup Target

Migrate your Veeam, Commvault, or custom backup software to use Azure Blob Storage (via REST or Blobfuse) as the backend, reducing tape and local storage dependency.

#### Archival Storage for Compliance

Store unstructured records (e.g., legal or medical documents) in Blob Archive Tier with WORM retention for compliance with standards like HIPAA or GDPR.

### Summary

Hybrid storage solutions such as Azure File Sync and Blob Storage enable organizations to bridge on-premises performance with cloud scalability and resilience. They support a broad range of use cases—file sharing, data archiving, backups, and application data ingestion—while offering deep integration with Azure's security, compliance, and automation tools.

By deploying these technologies strategically, organizations can modernize their storage infrastructure, reduce operational overhead, and prepare for a fully cloud-optimized future—without sacrificing the performance or control offered by on-premises systems.

## Data Replication and Backup Strategies

Data replication and backup are essential pillars of any hybrid cloud strategy. In a hybrid environment, data often resides in both on-premises and cloud systems, requiring consistent synchronization, redundancy, and recovery mechanisms to maintain availability, integrity, and resilience. The ability to recover from accidental deletion, hardware failure, or ransomware attacks depends on how well these strategies are implemented.

This section explores various replication and backup models supported by Azure and how they can be integrated with on-premises infrastructure. We'll examine techniques for file-level, block-level, and object-level replication; describe best practices; and provide examples for designing reliable backup workflows that span hybrid boundaries.

## Defining the Difference: Replication vs. Backup

Though often used interchangeably, replication and backup serve different purposes:

- **Replication** is the real-time or scheduled copying of data from one location to another, intended for availability and performance.

- **Backup** is a point-in-time copy of data, typically optimized for long-term retention and recovery.

**Key Differences:**

| Aspect | Replication | Backup |
|---|---|---|
| Purpose | High availability | Disaster recovery / data retention |
| Frequency | Near real-time / continuous | Scheduled |
| Storage Location | Usually same or secondary site | Isolated storage |
| Retention | Limited | Configurable (days to years) |
| Use Cases | Failover, load balancing | Recovery, auditing, ransomware |

## Azure Replication Technologies

Azure offers multiple services to support replication across different workloads:

### 1. Azure Site Recovery (ASR)

Azure Site Recovery provides **real-time replication** of on-premises VMs or Azure VMs to a secondary region or to Azure itself.

**Use Cases:**

- Disaster recovery for Hyper-V, VMware, and physical servers.
- VM replication between Azure regions.

**How It Works:**

- ASR replicates the disk-level data to Azure Storage.
- Supports failover and failback scenarios.
- Integration with Azure Automation for runbooks.

**Example: Enable ASR for a Hyper-V VM**

```
Set-AzRecoveryServicesAsrProtectionDirection `
-PrimaryProtectionContainer $PrimaryContainer `
-RecoveryProtectionContainer $RecoveryContainer `
-RecoveryAzureStorageAccountId $StorageAccountId
```

## 2. Geo-Redundant Storage (GRS)

GRS is a replication option for Azure Storage accounts, automatically replicating data across two geographically distant Azure regions.

**Options:**

- **LRS**: Locally-redundant (3 copies in one region)
- **ZRS**: Zone-redundant (across zones in one region)
- **GRS**: Geo-redundant (primary + secondary region)
- **RA-GRS**: GRS with read-access to the secondary

**Configuring GRS:**

```
az storage account update \
—name myaccount \
—resource-group myrg \
—sku Standard_GRS
```

Use RA-GRS for read-only access to secondary replicas for reporting or backup testing.

---

### 3. SQL Server Replication

SQL Server supports several replication strategies that can be extended to Azure environments:

- **Transactional Replication**: For near real-time consistency.
- **Merge Replication**: Bi-directional sync for mobile/ disconnected apps.
- **Always On Availability Groups**: High availability and disaster recovery.

Azure also supports replication to **Azure SQL Managed Instance** or **SQL Database** using tools like **Data Migration Assistant** and **Azure Data Sync**.

---

## Backup Strategies for Hybrid Environments

Backups are the last line of defense in a hybrid model. Microsoft provides a full suite of backup solutions tailored to hybrid needs.

## Azure Backup Overview

Azure Backup is a cloud-native service for protecting workloads like:

- Azure VMs
- SQL databases
- Azure Files
- On-prem physical and virtual machines

## On-Prem Integration with Azure Backup Server (MABS)

Azure Backup Server (based on DPM) enables backup of:

- Bare metal systems
- Exchange, SQL Server, SharePoint
- Files and folders
- VMware and Hyper-V VMs

Backups are stored **locally and/or in Azure**, supporting offline seeding via Data Box.

### Example: Configure MABS Vault

az backup vault create \

—resource-group myrg \

—name myRecoveryVault \

—location eastus

Register the server and configure retention policies (e.g., 30 days daily, 12 months monthly, 7 years yearly).

## Implementing a Tiered Backup Plan

A robust hybrid backup architecture includes multiple layers:

1. **Local backups** for fast recovery
2. **Cloud backups** for durability and offsite protection
3. **Archive tiering** for long-term retention

**Recommended Policy Structure:**

| Backup Type | Frequency | Retention |
|---|---|---|
| Daily Incremental | Daily | 30 days |
| Weekly Full | Weekly | 3 months |
| Monthly | Monthly | 12 months |
| Yearly | Yearly | 7+ years |

**Using Lifecycle Policies with Blob Storage:**

```
{
"rules": [
{
"name": "archiveAfter90Days",
"enabled": true,
"definition": {
```

```
"filters": {
"blobTypes": ["blockBlob"],
"prefixMatch": ["backup/"]
},
"actions": {
"baseBlob": {
"tierToArchive": {
"daysAfterModificationGreaterThan": 90
}
}
}
}
}
]
}
```

## Backup for Specialized Workloads

### SQL Server on Azure VM:

Use Azure Backup to back up SQL databases natively, with point-in-time restore.

```
az backup protection enable-for-sql-db \
```

—vault-name myVault \

—resource-group myrg \

—server-name mysqlvm \

—database-name prodDB \

—policy-name DefaultPolicy

**SAP HANA:**

Azure Backup supports agentless backups for SAP HANA on Azure VMs with integrated scheduling and recovery.

**Azure Files:**

File shares can be protected using snapshot-based backups via Recovery Services Vault.

---

## Security and Compliance Considerations

Hybrid backup and replication strategies must align with compliance frameworks such as ISO 27001, GDPR, HIPAA, etc.

**Best Practices:**

- **Enable encryption** at rest and in transit.
- **Use private endpoints** for backup traffic.
- **Enable soft delete** to protect against ransomware.
- **Isolate backup credentials and roles** using Azure RBAC.

- **Audit backup operations** using diagnostic logs.

Enable soft delete for Recovery Services Vault:

```
az backup vault backup-properties set \
—name myVault \
—resource-group myrg \
—soft-delete-feature-state Enabled
```

## Monitoring and Alerts

Use Azure Monitor and built-in alerts to track backup health and job statuses.

**Metrics to Monitor:**

- Backup success/failure rates
- Job duration and timeouts
- Storage consumption growth
- Recovery point status

Sample KQL query for backup failure analysis:

```
AzureDiagnostics
| where Category == "AzureBackupReport"
| where OperationName == "BackupItemOperation"
| where Status_s == "Failed"
```

```
| summarize count() by Resource, ResultDescription
```

Integrate alerts with **Logic Apps** or **ServiceNow** for automated ticketing and escalation.

## Real-World Scenarios

### Scenario 1: Multi-Site File Server Backup

An enterprise with regional offices uses Azure File Sync and backs up each file share to a centralized Azure vault. This ensures file availability at the edge and centralized recovery capability.

### Scenario 2: Legacy App Backup to Azure

A legacy Windows 2008 server running an internal app is protected using Azure Backup Server. Cloud storage reduces local hardware dependency and provides compliance support.

### Scenario 3: Critical VM Replication with ASR

A business-critical on-prem VM is replicated to Azure using ASR. In case of site failure, the VM can be spun up in Azure within minutes.

## Summary

Effective replication and backup strategies form the backbone of any resilient hybrid infrastructure. They ensure that data remains accessible, recoverable, and protected across on-premises and cloud environments. Microsoft's ecosystem of tools—Azure Site Recovery, Azure Backup, MABS, Storage Replication, and more—offers the flexibility and scalability needed for modern enterprises.

By adopting a layered and policy-driven approach, organizations can not only meet SLAs and compliance requirements but also gain the agility to scale protection in line with growth and evolving threats. In hybrid cloud architecture, backup and replication are not just safeguards—they are enablers of business continuity and operational excellence.

## Using Azure Data Box and Import/Export

In hybrid cloud environments, transferring large datasets between on-premises infrastructure and Azure can be a challenging task—especially when the data exceeds the capacity of typical network connections or when time constraints and data sensitivity are critical factors. Microsoft Azure addresses this challenge with **Azure Data Box** and **Import/Export** services, designed to facilitate high-volume, secure, and efficient data transfers.

This section explores the architecture, use cases, security mechanisms, setup procedures, and real-world implementations of Azure Data Box and Import/Export services. We will dive into best practices and technical guidance for integrating these services into enterprise-scale hybrid cloud workflows.

### Introduction to Azure Data Box Family

The **Azure Data Box family** provides physical and virtual appliances for transferring terabytes to petabytes of data to Azure. Instead of relying solely on network-based transfers, these services offer **offline data ingestion**, ideal for:

- Initial cloud seeding during migration.
- Disaster recovery data ingestion.

- Periodic bulk uploads from remote or disconnected sites.
- Long-term cold storage archiving.

**Types of Data Box Devices:**

| Product | Capacity | Connectivity | Use Case |
|---|---|---|---|
| Data Box | ~80 TB usable | 1/10 GbE | Mid-size bulk data ingestion |
| Data Box Heavy | ~800 TB usable | 40 GbE | Massive data transfer workloads |
| Data Box Disk | 8 TB (x5 disks) | USB 3.1 | Smaller, distributed data sets |
| Data Box Gateway | Virtual Appliance | Network over SMB/NFS | Continuous transfer over WAN |

## Use Cases for Azure Data Box

1. **Cloud Migration**: Transfer existing file shares, databases, or VM images from on-prem to Azure.
2. **Data Center Consolidation**: Migrate data before decommissioning or repurposing hardware.
3. **Media and Entertainment**: Upload video archives, raw footage, or post-production content.
4. **Healthcare and Research**: Move large genomics datasets or diagnostic imaging repositories.
5. **Backup Seeding**: Upload the first full backup to Azure without saturating network bandwidth.

## Security Model

Azure Data Box and Import/Export services employ a strong **defense-in-depth** security model:

- **AES-256 bit encryption** at rest and in transit.
- **TPM-based hardware protection** on Data Box devices.
- **Role-based access control (RBAC)** for device ordering and usage.
- **Automatic data erasure** post-upload, following NIST 800-88 guidelines.

Access to each device is controlled via an **activation key**, ensuring only authorized users and systems can decrypt and interact with the device.

---

## Setting Up an Azure Data Box Transfer

### Step 1: Create a Data Box Order

```
az databox job create \
—name mydataboxjob \
—resource-group myrg \
—location eastus \
—sku DataBox \
—transfer-type ImportToAzure \
```

—contact-name "John Smith" \

—street-address "123 Enterprise Dr" \

—postal-code "90210" \

—country "USA" \

—phone-number "+1-555-1234"

**Step 2: Configure Storage Accounts**

You must specify one or more target storage accounts (Blob, File, or Managed Disks) for the data.

az databox job update \

—name mydataboxjob \

—resource-group myrg \

—details
destinationAccountDetails='[{"storageAccountId":"/subscriptions/xxxx/resourceGroups/myrg/providers/Microsoft.Storage/storageAccounts/mystorage"}]'

**Step 3: Receive and Connect the Device**

- Data Box arrives with all network and storage components embedded.
- Connect via RJ-45 or SFP+ based on bandwidth requirements.
- Configure static IP or DHCP as needed.

**Step 4: Copy Data to Device**

Use tools like **Robocopy**, **AzCopy**, or **rsync** to stage data.

Example with Robocopy:

```
robocopy D:\Media E:\Staging\Media /MIR /MT:8
```

**Step 5: Return Device and Track Upload**

Once copying is complete and device is deactivated, ship it back. Azure ingests data and deletes the contents post-validation.

---

## Azure Import/Export Service

Azure Import/Export is a **disk-based** alternative for transferring smaller datasets using customer-supplied encrypted disks.

**Features:**

- Supports BitLocker-encrypted HDDs or SSDs (2.5" or 3.5" SATA).
- Data upload to Azure Blob Storage or File Storage.
- Ideal for smaller migrations, forensic data, or legal archives.

---

## Using the Import Service

**Step 1: Create an Import Job**

```
az import-export job create \
```

—name diskjob01 \

—resource-group myrg \

—location eastus \

—storage-account mystorage \

—job-type Import \

—return-address "123 Enterprise Dr, NY" \

—return-contact-name "Jane Doe"

**Step 2: Prepare Disks**

Use the **WAImportExport tool** to encrypt and write data to the disks.

WAImportExport.exe PrepImport /sk:<storage-key> /d:D /Data:D:\MyData /LogDir:C:\Logs /DestAccount:mystorage

**Step 3: Ship Disks**

Send encrypted disks to the Microsoft-specified data center. Tracking and status updates are available via the Azure portal.

## Automating and Monitoring Transfers

Azure Data Box integrates with **Azure Monitor**, **Log Analytics**, and **Service Health** for operational visibility.

**Monitor Status with CLI:**

az databox job show \

—name mydataboxjob \

—resource-group myrg

Use **activity logs and diagnostic settings** to audit device usage, completion, and ingestion success.

---

## Best Practices for Hybrid Data Transfers

1. **Plan for lead time**: Device shipping and ingestion may take days.
2. **Group data logically**: Avoid splitting datasets across different devices or jobs.
3. **Use retry-capable tools**: AzCopy and Robocopy can resume failed transfers.
4. **Secure your staging environment**: Only trusted systems should handle sensitive data pre-transfer.
5. **Track compliance**: Maintain logs of what was transferred, when, and by whom.

---

## Real-World Examples

### Case 1: National Broadcaster Seeding Petabyte Archive

A television network used Data Box Heavy to migrate over 2 PB of historical footage to Azure Blob Storage, reducing migration time from months (over network) to days.

**Case 2: Remote Research Facility Syncing Periodically**

A genetics research group uses Data Box Disk monthly to deliver 10 TB of raw DNA data to Azure due to limited internet bandwidth at their rural lab.

**Case 3: Legal eDiscovery via Import Service**

A law firm shipped encrypted SSDs with scanned evidence documents to Azure, enabling analysis via Azure Cognitive Search and Logic Apps.

---

### Summary

Azure Data Box and Import/Export services empower hybrid organizations to manage large-scale, secure data transfers without relying exclusively on bandwidth-heavy or time-consuming network uploads. These solutions are especially valuable when dealing with initial cloud seeding, remote operations, or compliance-driven environments.

With robust security, automated workflows, and flexible deployment models, these services make data mobility a seamless part of hybrid cloud strategy—eliminating bottlenecks and enabling faster time-to-value for data-intensive workloads.

## Data Compliance and Sovereignty

Data compliance and sovereignty are critical considerations in the design and operation of hybrid cloud environments. As organizations manage data across both on-premises infrastructure and public cloud platforms like Microsoft Azure, they must ensure that data handling practices align with legal, regulatory, and industry standards. Failure to do so can result in severe penalties, reputational damage, and loss of customer trust.

This section explores the key principles of data compliance and sovereignty, outlines Microsoft Azure's built-in tools and services to support regulatory requirements, and offers strategic guidance on architecting a hybrid data environment that respects data locality, privacy, security, and auditability.

## Defining Compliance and Data Sovereignty

- **Compliance** refers to adhering to rules and regulations that govern how data must be stored, processed, accessed, and deleted. These can be industry-specific (e.g., HIPAA, PCI-DSS) or geographically scoped (e.g., GDPR, CCPA).

- **Data Sovereignty** involves ensuring that data remains within the borders of the jurisdiction it originates from and is subject to the local laws of that region.

In hybrid environments, where data can reside in multiple physical and logical locations, achieving compliance and sovereignty requires intentional planning, appropriate tooling, and continuous monitoring.

## Key Regulatory Frameworks and Their Requirements

Understanding the scope and requirements of common regulations is foundational for compliant hybrid design:

| Regulation | Scope | Key Requirements |
|---|---|---|
| **GDPR** (EU) | Personal data of EU residents | Data minimization, user consent, breach reporting, data localization |
| **HIPAA** (US) | Health data (PHI) | Encryption, access controls, audit trails, Business Associate Agreements |
| **CCPA** (California) | Personal data of California residents | Disclosure, right to delete, opt-out of sale |
| **ISO 27001** | Global (Information Security) | Risk assessments, controls, policies, continuous improvement |
| **FedRAMP** | US Federal systems | Security controls, audits, continuous monitoring |

## Azure's Compliance Offerings

Microsoft Azure provides a broad array of built-in compliance capabilities:

### Microsoft Compliance Manager

A centralized dashboard that maps your organization's controls against over **350 compliance frameworks**.

- Pre-built assessments (e.g., NIST, GDPR, ISO)
- Control implementation guidance
- Evidence upload and tracking

**Azure Policy**

Enables governance through enforcement of compliance rules across subscriptions and resource groups.

Example: Enforce that all resources are deployed only in EU regions

```
{
"if": {
"not": {
"field": "location",
"in": ["northeurope", "westeurope"]
}
},
"then": {
"effect": "deny"
}
}
```

**Compliance Certifications**

Azure holds numerous certifications, including:

- ISO 27001, 27018
- SOC 1, 2, and 3

- FedRAMP High, Moderate, Low
- HITRUST
- PCI-DSS Level 1

These certifications provide customers with assurance that Azure services are built with security and compliance in mind.

## Architecting for Data Sovereignty

Ensuring data sovereignty in a hybrid model requires controlling where data is **stored, processed, backed up, and transmitted**.

**Key Principles:**

1. **Regional Resource Deployment**
    - Use Azure regions aligned with your jurisdiction.
    - Example: Only deploy to "westeurope" and "northeurope" for EU-bound data.
2. **Data Residency Labels**
    - Tag resources with metadata indicating jurisdiction (e.g., dataRegion = "EU").
3. **Use Azure Availability Zones Within Country Borders**
    - For high availability without cross-border data movement.
4. **Avoid Multi-Region Services When Not Required**

- ○ Some services replicate data across regions (e.g., GRS). Opt for **LRS or ZRS** if regional boundaries are essential.

```
az storage account create \
—name securestoreeu \
—resource-group rg-eu \
—location westeurope \
—sku Standard_ZRS
```

---

## Encryption and Access Controls

Encryption is essential for ensuring data privacy and meeting compliance requirements.

**Encryption Best Practices:**

- Enable **encryption at rest** using **Customer-Managed Keys (CMK)** from Azure Key Vault.
- Enforce **encryption in transit** using TLS 1.2 or above.
- Use **Double Encryption** (encryption at both application and storage layers).

```
az keyvault key create \
—vault-name myVault \
—name myComplianceKey \
—protection software
```

**Access Control Best Practices:**

- Apply **least privilege access** using RBAC or Azure AD roles.
- Monitor privileged roles with **Azure AD Privileged Identity Management**.
- Use **Conditional Access** policies to restrict access by location, device compliance, or user risk.

---

## Logging, Auditing, and Monitoring

Regulations often require full traceability of data access and handling events.

**Tools to Implement:**

1. **Azure Monitor** and **Activity Logs**
   - Capture all management operations and resource access.
2. **Azure Diagnostic Logs**
   - Enable for individual services (e.g., Storage, Key Vault, SQL).
3. **Microsoft Sentinel**
   - SIEM tool for real-time threat detection and audit log correlation.

Example: Enable diagnostics on a storage account

```
az monitor diagnostic-settings create \

—resource /subscriptions/xxxx/resourceGroups/rg-eu/providers/Microsoft.Storage/storageAccounts/securestoreeu \

—name enable-logging \

—workspace myLogAnalyticsWorkspace \

—logs '[{"category":"StorageRead","enabled":true}]'
```

## Backup and Retention Policies

Long-term retention and timely deletion are critical components of compliance.

**Implementing Retention:**

- Use **Azure Backup** with custom retention policies.
- Configure **Blob Lifecycle Management** to auto-delete or archive.

**Implementing Legal Hold:**

- For compliance scenarios like litigation or investigations, use **Immutable Blob Storage**.

```
az storage container immutability-policy create \

—account-name securestoreeu \

—container-name auditlogs \

—policy-mode Locked \
```

—period 365

## Data Subject Rights (DSRs) and Privacy

Frameworks like GDPR require organizations to respond to **Data Subject Rights** requests, such as:

- Right to access
- Right to delete
- Right to correct
- Right to port data

Azure provides tools and APIs to help identify and act on personal data stored in services like:

- Azure SQL
- Azure Blob
- Microsoft 365 (via Compliance Center)

Use **Microsoft Purview** to classify and label personal data across hybrid sources, automate tagging, and ensure audit trails for DSR actions.

## Hybrid Data Sovereignty Considerations

**On-Prem Integration:**

- Ensure backups from on-prem systems to Azure are routed and stored in compliant regions.

- Use **Azure ExpressRoute** or **VPN Gateways** with forced tunneling to control data paths.

**Third-Party and SaaS Systems:**

- Ensure SaaS apps that interface with Azure or on-prem storage comply with your data policies.
- Perform **Data Protection Impact Assessments (DPIA)** before onboarding new apps.

**Azure Stack Integration:**

- For high-security or ultra-sovereign workloads, Azure Stack Hub allows you to run Azure services **entirely on-premises** under your control.

---

## Real-World Examples

### Financial Institution in the EU

A bank implemented Azure Policy to restrict all data storage to EU regions, enforced encryption with CMK via Key Vault, and used Azure Monitor and Sentinel for auditing access logs. Data Box was used for initial seeding under full compliance with GDPR guidelines.

### Healthcare Provider in the US

To meet HIPAA requirements, a healthcare provider used Azure Blueprint for HIPAA/HITRUST, locked down access using PIM, stored patient data on encrypted disks, and maintained audit logs in immutable blob containers with 7-year retention.

## Summary

Data compliance and sovereignty are foundational to trust and legal standing in a hybrid cloud strategy. Azure offers an extensive portfolio of tools—ranging from Policy and Key Vault to Purview and Sentinel—that empower organizations to build compliant systems without sacrificing performance or scalability.

By designing for region-specific deployment, enforcing strict access and encryption policies, and implementing continuous auditability, organizations can confidently operate across jurisdictions while adhering to evolving global standards. In today's hybrid world, compliance isn't just about avoiding penalties—it's about creating responsible, resilient, and future-ready data environments.

# Chapter 7: Managing Hybrid Applications

## Application Migration and Refactoring

In the context of hybrid cloud computing, managing applications—both legacy and modern—is a critical component. Many enterprises rely on applications that have been running on-premises for years, often built using older technology stacks, while also seeking to embrace the scalability, agility, and advanced services provided by cloud platforms like Microsoft Azure. This section focuses on the strategies, tools, and best practices for migrating and refactoring applications in a hybrid cloud environment using Azure.

### Understanding Application Portfolios

Before undertaking any migration or refactoring effort, organizations must first perform a comprehensive application portfolio assessment. This includes categorizing applications into groups such as:

- **Retain:** Continue running on-premises without modification.
- **Rehost (Lift-and-Shift):** Move to Azure VMs with minimal changes.
- **Refactor:** Modify code to better align with cloud-native principles.
- **Rearchitect:** Redesign for scalability, performance, or maintainability using cloud services.

- **Replace:** Substitute with SaaS or COTS (Commercial Off-The-Shelf) solutions.

This classification informs the hybrid strategy by aligning business needs with technical feasibility and investment priorities.

## Application Migration Strategies

Azure supports a wide range of migration paths that can accommodate various types of workloads and levels of cloud readiness. These strategies typically include:

### Rehosting (Lift-and-Shift)

This is often the fastest migration path, particularly suited for applications that are stable but require minimal cloud optimization. Azure Migrate is the go-to tool for rehosting:

```
# Example PowerShell command using Azure Migrate for server discovery

Import-Module Az.Migrate

Start-AzMigrateServerDiscovery -ProjectName "HybridAppMigrate" -ResourceGroupName "HybridRG"
```

**Pros:**

- Minimal code changes
- Quick time to cloud

**Cons:**

- Misses out on cloud-native benefits

- Higher operational overhead compared to PaaS

### Refactoring

This strategy involves minor code and configuration changes to take better advantage of Azure services, such as moving from a self-hosted SQL Server to **Azure SQL Database**, or from a local file system to **Azure Blob Storage**.

```
// Example: Using Azure Blob Storage SDK in a refactored .NET app

BlobServiceClient blobServiceClient = new BlobServiceClient(connectionString);

BlobContainerClient containerClient = blobServiceClient.GetBlobContainerClient("appdata");

BlobClient blobClient = containerClient.GetBlobClient("config.json");

await blobClient.UploadAsync(fileStream, true);
```

Refactoring is ideal for applications that need performance boosts or improved maintainability without a full rewrite.

### Rearchitecting

For mission-critical applications that must scale and evolve rapidly, rearchitecting to microservices or serverless computing is preferred. Tools like **Azure Functions**, **App Service**, and **Azure Kubernetes Service (AKS)** play a central role.

### Replacing

Replacing legacy applications with SaaS alternatives (like replacing an on-prem CRM with **Dynamics 365**) can offload infrastructure management and bring quick wins.

## Hybrid Deployment Patterns

In a hybrid environment, you may need to run parts of your application on-premises while others reside in Azure. Here are common patterns:

- **Split-Tier:** UI and app logic in Azure, database on-premises.

- **Bursting:** Compute-intensive workloads burst to Azure during peak demand.

- **Data Gravity Compliance:** Keep data on-prem for compliance while apps run in Azure.

- **Edge-Connected:** Use **Azure Stack Edge** for low-latency, on-site processing connected to Azure for long-term storage and analysis.

## Tools for Migration and Refactoring

Azure provides a rich toolset to support your hybrid application journey:

- **Azure Migrate** – Assess and migrate VMs, databases, and apps

- **Azure App Service Migration Assistant** – Move web apps to Azure App Service

- **Data Migration Assistant (DMA)** – Evaluate and migrate databases

- **Visual Studio + Azure SDK** – Refactor and redeploy apps with minimal effort

- **Azure DevOps** – CI/CD pipelines to automate hybrid deployments

## Case Study: Hybrid Migration of an Inventory System

A manufacturing firm had a legacy inventory management system built in .NET Framework 4.5 using SQL Server 2012. They needed better uptime, global access, and analytics integration.

**Steps Taken:**

1. **Assessment:** DMA showed compatibility with Azure SQL.
2. **Database Migration:** Used DMA to migrate schema and data.
3. **App Migration:** Used App Service Migration Assistant to move the web app to Azure App Service.
4. **Refactoring:** Modified connection strings and added blob storage for media files.
5. **Hybrid Access:** VPN Gateway established for secure on-prem connectivity to Azure services.

Post-migration, downtime reduced by 80%, and the team could integrate Azure Synapse Analytics for real-time reporting.

## Refactoring Legacy Monoliths

Monolithic applications pose challenges due to tight coupling and difficult scaling. Here's how to gradually refactor a monolith in a hybrid scenario:

1. **Identify Domains:** Use Domain-Driven Design (DDD) to break down responsibilities.
2. **Strangle Pattern:** Incrementally replace monolith modules with microservices.
3. **Service Mesh:** Use **Azure Service Fabric** or **AKS with Istio** to manage service discovery, routing, and resilience.
4. **Shared Identity:** Ensure seamless access using **Azure AD** B2C or hybrid identity options.

�# Example AKS deployment snippet for a microservice

apiVersion: apps/v1

kind: Deployment

metadata:

name: inventory-service

spec:

replicas: 3

selector:

matchLabels:

app: inventory

template:

metadata:

labels:

app: inventory

spec:

containers:

- name: inventory

image: myregistry.azurecr.io/inventory:latest

ports:

- containerPort: 80

## �DevOps Considerations in Hybrid Environments

Hybrid applications require consistent build, test, and deployment strategies. Azure DevOps or GitHub Actions should integrate both on-prem and cloud resources using secure agents and artifacts.

- **CI/CD Pipelines:** Deploy code to Azure and on-prem targets.
- **Infrastructure as Code:** Use **Bicep** or **Terraform** for consistent deployments.
- **Release Gates:** Introduce approvals, canary releases, and blue-green deployments even in hybrid settings.

�# Example GitHub Actions workflow for hybrid CI/CD

jobs:

build-and-deploy:

runs-on: ubuntu-latest

steps:

- uses: actions/checkout@v2

- name: Build and test

run: dotnet build && dotnet test

- name: Deploy to Azure

uses: azure/webapps-deploy@v2

with:

app-name: 'hybrid-inventory-app'

publish-profile: ${{ secrets.AZURE_WEBAPP_PUBLISH_PROFILE }}

## ⟐Monitoring and Observability

Applications running across cloud and on-prem need unified monitoring:

- **Azure Monitor** and **Application Insights** for telemetry
- **Log Analytics** to query across hybrid environments
- **Azure Arc** to manage and monitor non-Azure resources

⟐// Sample Kusto Query for hybrid log analytics

Heartbeat

| where TimeGenerated > ago(1h)

| summarize count() by Computer, OSName

## ◈Security in Hybrid Applications

Ensure secure communication, data protection, and identity management:

- Use **Azure Key Vault** for secrets management
- Apply **Conditional Access** and **MFA**
- Enable **Microsoft Defender for Cloud** for threat detection

## Conclusion

Managing applications in a hybrid cloud requires thoughtful planning, effective tooling, and a strong understanding of both legacy and modern paradigms. By leveraging Azure's hybrid capabilities—from migration tools to container orchestration—you can modernize applications incrementally and securely. Organizations that build agility into their application lifecycle across environments are better positioned to innovate, scale, and respond to market demands.

The following sections will cover how Azure Kubernetes Service on Azure Stack HCI enables deeper hybrid flexibility, and how CI/CD pipelines can be adapted to seamlessly handle the complexity of hybrid operations.

# Using Azure Kubernetes Service (AKS) on Azure Stack HCI

Azure Kubernetes Service (AKS) on Azure Stack HCI brings the power of container orchestration to your on-premises infrastructure while maintaining consistent tooling and management through Azure. By bridging the gap between cloud-native and traditional environments, AKS on Azure Stack HCI enables enterprises to deploy and manage Kubernetes workloads locally, reduce latency, maintain data sovereignty, and address compliance requirements—all while leveraging a hybrid cloud strategy.

This section explores how AKS on Azure Stack HCI works, how to deploy and manage it, best practices for operation, and real-world hybrid architecture scenarios.

## What Is Azure Stack HCI?

Azure Stack HCI is a hyperconverged infrastructure solution that combines software-defined compute, storage, and networking on validated hardware. It integrates tightly with Azure services, enabling hybrid capabilities such as backup, monitoring, and VM replication.

AKS on Azure Stack HCI extends this further by enabling containerized workloads to run within the local data center using a Kubernetes environment that aligns with AKS in the cloud.

Key features include:

- Consistent Kubernetes experience across cloud and on-prem
- Integrated lifecycle management for Kubernetes clusters

- Azure Portal and CLI support for deployment and management

- Support for Windows and Linux containers

- Ability to integrate with Azure Monitor, Azure Arc, and other services

## Benefits of AKS on Azure Stack HCI in Hybrid Applications

1. **Latency-sensitive workloads**: Run applications closer to the users or devices.
2. **Data residency compliance**: Meet industry-specific or geographic data regulations.
3. **Disconnected scenarios**: Operate in environments with limited or no internet connectivity.
4. **Legacy modernization**: Incrementally containerize legacy apps before full cloud migration.
5. **Unified DevOps pipelines**: Maintain consistent deployment practices across environments.

## Prerequisites and System Requirements

Before deploying AKS on Azure Stack HCI, ensure the following requirements are met:

- A valid Azure subscription

- Azure Stack HCI version 21H2 or later

- Windows Admin Center installed and configured

- Hyper-V enabled on the host servers

- A supported hardware configuration
- Internet connectivity for downloading images and accessing Azure services

You must also register Azure Stack HCI and your host with Azure using the AzStackHci and AzAksHci PowerShell modules.

# Register Azure Stack HCI host with Azure

Register-AzStackHCI -SubscriptionId "xxxxx-xxxx-xxxx-xxxx-xxxxxxxx" -ResourceGroupName "HybridRG" -Region "eastus"

# Install AKS on Azure Stack HCI

Install-AksHci

## Deploying AKS on Azure Stack HCI

There are two main deployment options:

- **Using Windows Admin Center (WAC)**: A GUI-based deployment experience.
- **Using PowerShell and CLI**: Offers automation and scripting capabilities.

### Deployment via Windows Admin Center

1. Open WAC and navigate to the Azure Stack HCI cluster.

2. Select "Azure Kubernetes Service" from the extensions.

3. Follow the guided steps:

- ○ Choose the cluster nodes
- ○ Configure storage and networking
- ○ Set up Kubernetes control plane and node pools
- ○ Connect to Azure

4. Complete deployment and validate cluster status

**Deployment via PowerShell**

```
# Set up the AKS-HCI configuration

Set-AksHciConfig -vnetPrefix "192.168.100.0/24" `

-vipPoolStart "192.168.100.100" `

-vipPoolEnd "192.168.100.110" `

-gateway "192.168.100.1" `

-dnsServers "192.168.100.2"

# Create a new Kubernetes cluster

New-AksHciCluster -name "HybridCluster01" -nodeCount 3
```

After deployment, you can interact with the cluster using kubectl, just as with AKS in Azure.

```
kubectl get nodes

kubectl create -f myapp-deployment.yaml
```

## Example Hybrid Scenario: Retail Store Chain

A global retail company runs a centralized inventory management application in Azure, but local stores require low-latency access to pricing and POS services. By deploying microservices on AKS on Azure Stack HCI in each regional data center, they:

- Achieve faster transaction processing
- Meet local data residency laws
- Continue operations even during internet outages

Changes are pushed through a GitOps pipeline using Azure DevOps, and metrics from all edge locations are aggregated in Azure Monitor via Azure Arc.

## Azure Arc Integration

Azure Arc brings Azure management capabilities to non-Azure environments. When integrated with AKS on Azure Stack HCI, Arc enables:

- Centralized policy and RBAC management
- GitOps-based deployment with Flux
- Aggregated monitoring and logging
- Consistent tagging and cost management

az connectedk8s connect—name hybrid-retail-cluster—resource-group HybridRetail

Once connected, you can apply Azure Policies, manage configuration using GitOps, and receive health status updates in Azure.

## Security and Identity Management

Security in a hybrid environment is paramount. AKS on Azure Stack HCI supports:

- Integration with Azure AD for RBAC
- Role-based access control for developers and operators
- Use of Azure Key Vault for managing secrets
- Network isolation and ingress/egress controls
- Private container registries (e.g., Azure Container Registry)

```
# Sample Kubernetes Role for read-only access
kind: Role
apiVersion: rbac.authorization.k8s.io/v1
metadata:
namespace: default
name: readonly
rules:
- apiGroups: [""]
resources: ["pods", "services"]
```

verbs: ["get", "list"]

## Monitoring and Maintenance

For production-ready AKS deployments on Azure Stack HCI, robust monitoring is crucial:

- **Azure Monitor and Container Insights**: Use these tools to visualize metrics and logs from on-prem AKS clusters.
- **Log Analytics Workspace**: Aggregate and query telemetry using Kusto Query Language (KQL).
- **Prometheus and Grafana**: Can be deployed within the cluster for customized dashboards.

```
// Example KQL to show pod memory usage
InsightsMetrics
| where Namespace == "container.azm.ms"
| where Name == "memoryWorkingSetBytes"
| summarize avg(Total) by bin(TimeGenerated, 5m), Computer
```

Regular maintenance tasks include:

- Applying Kubernetes updates
- Monitoring node health
- Backing up cluster configuration
- Rotating secrets and certificates

## CI/CD Integration

Hybrid clusters must integrate seamlessly into enterprise DevOps pipelines. AKS on Azure Stack HCI supports:

- GitHub Actions, Azure Pipelines, Jenkins
- Helm charts for package management
- Automated rollback and canary deployments
- Secret injection from Azure Key Vault or HashiCorp Vault

```
# Example GitHub Actions workflow deploying to hybrid AKS

jobs:

deploy:

runs-on: self-hosted

steps:

- uses: actions/checkout@v2

- name: Set up kubectl

uses: azure/setup-kubectl@v1

with:

version: 'v1.25.2'

- name: Deploy to cluster

run: kubectl apply -f k8s/deployment.yaml
```

## Challenges and Considerations

While AKS on Azure Stack HCI offers flexibility, it also introduces challenges:

- **Operational Overhead**: Requires local IT resources for setup and maintenance
- **Capacity Planning**: Limited by physical infrastructure
- **Connectivity**: Internet access needed for Azure-based services
- **Version Skew**: Keep Kubernetes versions in sync with Azure for consistency

Mitigating these issues involves proper planning, monitoring, and aligning the architecture with business goals.

## Summary and Best Practices

Deploying AKS on Azure Stack HCI in a hybrid cloud model delivers cloud-native capabilities to on-premises environments while maintaining operational consistency and control. For success:

- Leverage Azure Arc for centralized management
- Use Infrastructure as Code to deploy reliably
- Secure clusters with RBAC, Key Vault, and network policies
- Monitor health using Azure-native and open-source tools
- Plan for updates and capacity needs proactively

By combining local processing power with cloud scalability, AKS on Azure Stack HCI empowers organizations to modernize legacy applications, deploy new services, and create resilient, compliant hybrid architectures ready for the future.

## CI/CD Pipelines in Hybrid Environments

Continuous Integration and Continuous Deployment (CI/CD) pipelines are essential for delivering software efficiently, reliably, and securely. In hybrid environments—where workloads are distributed between on-premises infrastructure and cloud platforms like Microsoft Azure—CI/CD becomes more complex but also more impactful. With the right tooling, automation, and architectural practices, organizations can implement pipelines that deploy to both environments seamlessly, enhancing developer productivity and operational resilience.

This section provides a comprehensive guide to building CI/CD pipelines that support hybrid cloud applications. It covers the architecture of hybrid pipelines, integration with Azure DevOps and GitHub Actions, secrets and artifact management, multi-environment deployments, and strategies for observability, security, and rollback.

### Fundamentals of Hybrid CI/CD

Hybrid CI/CD pipelines must account for the nuances of deploying code to heterogeneous environments:

- **Target Environments:** Azure App Services, Azure Kubernetes Service (AKS), Azure Stack HCI, on-prem VMs, IIS servers, containers

- **Connectivity:** Secure access to on-prem infrastructure through VPN, ExpressRoute, or self-hosted agents
- **Toolchain Consistency:** Aligning build tools, testing frameworks, and deployment patterns across environments
- **Security Boundaries:** Managing identity, access, and secrets across cloud and local contexts

Key benefits of hybrid CI/CD pipelines include:

- Faster time-to-market with automation
- Lower risk through frequent, incremental changes
- Unified governance and policy enforcement
- Support for disconnected or latency-sensitive workloads

## Pipeline Architecture Overview

A hybrid CI/CD pipeline generally involves the following stages:

1. **Source Control Integration**
   Monitor Git repositories for changes. Use GitHub, Azure Repos, or Bitbucket.
2. **Build Stage**
   Compile, test, and package the application. This stage runs in the cloud or on self-hosted build agents.
3. **Artifact Storage**
   Store built artifacts in a secure, centralized location. Azure Artifacts, GitHub Packages, or an internal NuGet/NPM registry may be used.

4. **Deployment Stages**
   Deploy artifacts to different environments (dev, QA, staging, prod) across Azure and on-prem.
5. **Post-Deployment Verification**
   Run integration and smoke tests, check logs, and validate telemetry.
6. **Monitoring and Feedback Loop**
   Integrate with Azure Monitor, Application Insights, and Log Analytics for health insights.

## Using Azure DevOps in Hybrid CI/CD

Azure DevOps provides a complete solution with Git repositories, CI/CD pipelines, artifact storage, and test plans. It also supports deployment to Azure and on-premises environments using:

- **Microsoft-hosted agents** for cloud resources
- **Self-hosted agents** for on-premises or isolated networks

### Setting Up a Self-Hosted Agent

```
# Download and configure the self-hosted agent

$agentPackage = "https://vstsagentpackage.azureedge.net/agent/3.220.5/vsts-agent-win-x64-3.220.5.zip"

Invoke-WebRequest -Uri $agentPackage -OutFile agent.zip

Expand-Archive -Path agent.zip -DestinationPath C:\azagent

cd C:\azagent
```

.\config.cmd—unattended—url https://dev.azure.com/myorg—auth pat—token <myPAT>—pool "OnPremPool"

.\run.cmd

With this agent registered, Azure DevOps can now deploy to any on-prem server, Azure Stack HCI cluster, or edge device.

**YAML Pipeline Example for Hybrid Deployment**

```
trigger:

branches:

include:

- main

pool:

name: OnPremPool

variables:

buildConfiguration: 'Release'

stages:

- stage: Build

jobs:

- job: BuildApp

steps:

- task: DotNetCoreCLI@2
```

inputs:

command: 'build'

projects: '**/*.csproj'

- stage: Deploy

jobs:

- job: DeployToHybrid

steps:

- task: AzureWebApp@1

inputs:

azureSubscription: 'MyAzureConnection'

appType: 'webApp'

appName: 'hybrid-app-service'

package: '$(System.DefaultWorkingDirectory)/**/*.zip'

- script: |

scp deploy/scripts/setup.ps1 myuser@onpremserver:/scripts/

ssh myuser@onpremserver "powershell -ExecutionPolicy Bypass -File C:\scripts\setup.ps1"

displayName: 'Deploy to On-Prem Server'

## GitHub Actions in Hybrid CI/CD

GitHub Actions also supports hybrid workflows through self-hosted runners. These can be installed on on-prem machines or edge servers.

**Example GitHub Actions Workflow**

```
name: Hybrid CI/CD Pipeline

on:

push:

branches:

- main

jobs:

build:

runs-on: ubuntu-latest

steps:

- uses: actions/checkout@v3

- name: Build and Package

run: dotnet publish -c Release -o ./publish

deploy-cloud:

runs-on: ubuntu-latest

needs: build

steps:

- name: Deploy to Azure App Service

uses: azure/webapps-deploy@v2

with:
```

```
app-name: 'hybrid-cloud-app'

publish-profile: ${{ secrets.AZURE_PUBLISH_PROFILE }}

package: ./publish

deploy-onprem:

runs-on: self-hosted

needs: build

steps:

- name: Copy to On-Prem Server

run: |

cp -r ./publish /var/www/onprem-hybrid-app

systemctl restart hybrid-app.service
```

With this setup, the same source code gets built once and deployed to both environments in parallel.

## Handling Secrets in Hybrid Pipelines

Secure handling of secrets is essential, especially in a hybrid context. Use:

- **Azure Key Vault** for cloud secrets
- **Local secrets management tools** (e.g., HashiCorp Vault, Windows Credential Store) for on-prem
- **Environment variables and pipeline secrets** for injection at runtime

Avoid hardcoding secrets in scripts or codebases.

```
env:

CONNECTION_STRING: ${{ secrets.ONPREM_DB_CONN }}

steps:

- run: ./deploy.sh—conn "$CONNECTION_STRING"
```

Use Azure Key Vault integration with DevOps pipelines for seamless and secure retrieval.

## Deployment Patterns in Hybrid CI/CD

Deployments in hybrid setups often follow patterns that balance risk and flexibility:

- **Blue-Green Deployments**: Maintain two environments and switch traffic between them.
- **Canary Releases**: Gradually roll out changes to a subset of users.
- **Ring-Based Deployments**: Deploy to internal teams first, then to external users.
- **Infrastructure-as-Code (IaC)**: Use Bicep, ARM, or Terraform to manage both Azure and on-prem resources.

### Terraform Example for Dual Targeting

```
provider "azurerm" {

features {}
```

```
}
resource "azurerm_app_service" "example" {
name = "hybridApp"
location = azurerm_resource_group.example.location
resource_group_name = azurerm_resource_group.example.name
app_service_plan_id = azurerm_app_service_plan.example.id
}
# A provisioner for on-prem deployment
resource "null_resource" "onprem_deploy" {
provisioner "remote-exec" {
connection {
type = "ssh"
user = "admin"
host = var.onprem_host
private_key = file("~/.ssh/id_rsa")
}
inline = [
"sudo systemctl restart hybrid-app"
]
}
```

}

## Observability in Hybrid Pipelines

Once code is deployed, it must be observed and verified. Incorporate:

- **Application Insights** for telemetry
- **Azure Monitor Logs** for querying metrics
- **Custom dashboards** in Grafana or Power BI
- **Alerts** via email, Teams, or PagerDuty for critical issues

Establish health probes, logging, and feedback mechanisms in every environment to ensure SLA adherence.

```
requests
| where cloud_RoleName == "hybrid-app"
| summarize avg(duration) by bin(timestamp, 5m)
```

## Rollback and Recovery

CI/CD pipelines should include mechanisms to quickly revert changes:

- Maintain previous versions of artifacts
- Use deployment slots in Azure App Services
- Keep rollback scripts for on-prem infrastructure
- Implement automated snapshots or backups

```
- task: AzureWebApp@1
inputs:
azureSubscription: 'MySub'
appType: 'webApp'
appName: 'hybrid-app'
slotName: 'staging'
package: '$(Build.ArtifactStagingDirectory)/old_release.zip'
```

## Best Practices for Hybrid CI/CD

1. **Unify Pipelines**: Use a single pipeline framework to manage cloud and on-prem targets.
2. **Secure Everything**: Ensure identity, secrets, and access are protected.
3. **Use Tags and Metadata**: Tag environments, commits, and deployments to trace issues.
4. **Test Everywhere**: Run unit, integration, and smoke tests in every environment.
5. **Automate Rollbacks**: Include automatic rollback conditions in your pipelines.
6. **Version Artifacts**: Ensure traceability from commit to deployment.

## Conclusion

Implementing CI/CD pipelines in hybrid environments empowers organizations to deliver software faster and more reliably, regardless of infrastructure location. By leveraging tools like Azure DevOps, GitHub Actions, and Terraform, combined with self-hosted runners and robust security practices, teams can maintain consistent deployment workflows and enforce governance across the entire hybrid estate. With careful planning and automation, CI/CD in hybrid cloud becomes not just feasible—but a strategic enabler of innovation and resilience.

# Managing Legacy and Modern Applications Together

In a hybrid cloud environment, enterprises often face the reality of managing legacy systems alongside modern, cloud-native applications. This duality introduces operational complexity but is also a strategic necessity—legacy applications often contain business-critical functionality, while modern applications offer the agility, scalability, and innovation needed to remain competitive.

This section provides an in-depth exploration of how to manage, integrate, and modernize legacy applications while simultaneously supporting and evolving modern workloads. It includes strategies for interoperability, lifecycle management, security, monitoring, and governance across both types of applications.

## Understanding Legacy and Modern Applications

**Legacy Applications** typically exhibit the following characteristics:

- Monolithic architecture
- Hosted on physical or virtual machines
- Use of older frameworks (e.g., .NET Framework, Java EE)

- Reliance on traditional RDBMS like SQL Server or Oracle
- Limited or no API exposure
- Manual deployment processes

**Modern Applications** are designed for agility and scalability:

- Microservices-based architecture
- Hosted on containers or serverless platforms
- Use of modern frameworks (e.g., .NET Core, Node.js, Python)
- API-first design
- CI/CD enabled
- Deployed on Kubernetes or App Services

In a hybrid environment, both types coexist. Successful management hinges on harmonizing tooling, access, security, and observability across this spectrum.

## Coexistence and Interoperability Strategies

The key to hybrid management is enabling communication and integration between legacy and modern systems without disrupting existing workflows.

**API Wrapping**

Expose legacy application functionality via REST or GraphQL APIs using wrapper services. This allows modern apps to consume legacy logic without modifying the legacy system itself.

```
// .NET Core API Wrapper for a legacy billing system

[ApiController]

[Route("api/[controller]")]

public class BillingController : ControllerBase

{

private readonly ILegacyBillingService _legacyService;

public BillingController(ILegacyBillingService legacyService)

{

_legacyService = legacyService;

}

[HttpGet("{customerId}")]

public IActionResult GetBillingInfo(int customerId)

{

var result = _legacyService.FetchCustomerBilling(customerId);

return Ok(result);

}

}
```

### Message Queues and Event Hubs

Use asynchronous communication to decouple systems. Azure Service Bus, Event Grid, or Kafka can act as intermediaries to enable data exchange between legacy and modern applications without tight coupling.

```
# Azure Event Grid topic deployment (Bicep)

resource eventGridTopic 'Microsoft.EventGrid/topics@2021-12-01' = {

name: 'legacy-integration-topic'

location: resourceGroup().location

properties: {

inputSchema: 'EventGridSchema'

}

}
```

### Database Synchronization

Implement data replication between legacy and modern data stores. Azure Data Factory or SQL replication tools can sync operational data, enabling modern apps to function without direct database dependency.

## Lifecycle Management Across Application Types

Managing the software development lifecycle (SDLC) of both legacy and modern applications requires unified processes with some tailored practices.

### Version Control

Even for legacy apps, introduce Git-based version control where possible. Use monorepos or polyrepos depending on organizational preference.

### Build and Deployment

- **Legacy:** Automate build and deployment using tools like Jenkins, PowerShell scripts, or Azure DevOps pipelines.
- **Modern:** Use containerized builds, Helm charts, and GitOps for rapid deployments.

```
# Azure DevOps YAML for building and deploying a legacy .NET app
trigger:
branches:
include: [main]
pool:
name: OnPremBuildAgent
steps:
- task: UseDotNet@2
inputs:
packageType: 'sdk'
```

```
version: '3.1.x'

- task: VSBuild@1

inputs:

solution: '**/*.sln'

msbuildArgs: '/p:DeployOnBuild=true'

- script: 'xcopy /E /Y "$(Build.ArtifactStagingDirectory)" "\\onpremserver\apps\legacy-app"'
```

**Configuration Management**

Use Azure App Configuration or Consul to manage environment-specific settings across both application types. Avoid hardcoded values and maintain separate config files or secrets for dev, staging, and production environments.

## Security and Access Control

Legacy apps often lack modern authentication mechanisms. Here's how to bridge the gap:

**Azure Active Directory Integration**

Use Azure AD Application Proxy or Azure AD B2C to front legacy applications, allowing users to authenticate with modern OAuth2 or OpenID Connect flows.

```
# Configure Azure AD Application Proxy

New-AzureADApplicationProxyApplication -DisplayName "LegacyERP" `
```

-ExternalUrl "https://erp.contoso.com" `

-InternalUrl "http://erp.internal.contoso.local"

### Conditional Access and MFA

Apply conditional access policies through Azure AD to enforce security for both modern and legacy apps. This includes enforcing Multi-Factor Authentication (MFA), IP restrictions, and device compliance.

### Network Segmentation

Place legacy systems behind private subnets or firewalls and expose them only through secure reverse proxies or VPNs. For modern apps, use NSGs, Azure Firewall, or WAF for controlled access.

## Monitoring and Observability

Observability tools must be able to ingest data from both legacy and modern workloads.

### Legacy Monitoring

Use tools like System Center Operations Manager (SCOM), PerfMon, or Nagios to monitor CPU, memory, and disk metrics.

### Modern Monitoring

Use Azure Monitor, Application Insights, and Log Analytics to collect telemetry from cloud-native apps.

### Centralized Logging

Aggregate logs from all systems into a single platform like Azure Monitor or ELK Stack.

```
// Unified query across modern and legacy logs

union legacyAppLogs, AppTraces

| where TimeGenerated > ago(1h)

| project AppName, Message, Severity, TimeGenerated

| sort by TimeGenerated desc
```

## Performance Optimization

Legacy apps may not scale elastically, but performance tuning can still improve hybrid resilience:

- **Introduce Caching:** Use Azure Cache for Redis to cache common queries.
- **Optimize Queries:** Update legacy stored procedures and indexing strategies.
- **Offload Compute:** Offload batch jobs to Azure Functions or Logic Apps for scalability.

## Modernization Strategy

While coexistence is necessary, long-term modernization should be the goal. Consider:

### Strangler Fig Pattern

Refactor individual features from the monolith into microservices. Route traffic to the new components while gradually deprecating legacy functionality.

### Containerization of Legacy Apps

Package legacy apps into containers to standardize deployment and isolate dependencies. This makes them easier to run in modern orchestration platforms like AKS or Azure Stack HCI.

```
# Dockerfile for legacy .NET Framework app

FROM mcr.microsoft.com/dotnet/framework/aspnet:4.8-windowsservercore-ltsc2019

COPY . /inetpub/wwwroot
```

### SaaS Replacement

Evaluate if legacy functionality can be replaced with SaaS offerings (e.g., Dynamics 365, ServiceNow) to eliminate technical debt.

## Governance and Policy Enforcement

Ensure compliance across environments by enforcing policies through:

- **Azure Policy:** Apply governance to cloud-native components
- **Group Policy/Intune:** Manage configuration of legacy systems

- **Role-Based Access Control:** Define roles and responsibilities clearly across both systems

- **Cost Management Tools:** Track and optimize spend across hybrid environments

## Real-World Scenario: Hybrid Financial Services Platform

A mid-sized bank ran its core banking system on-prem using COBOL and Java EE. As part of its modernization effort:

1. Wrapped the COBOL logic behind RESTful APIs.
2. Introduced Azure-hosted microservices for new features (e.g., digital onboarding, alerts).
3. Used Azure DevOps pipelines to deploy both legacy (via batch scripts) and modern services (via Helm charts).
4. Enabled centralized monitoring using Azure Monitor and integrated SCOM alerts via webhook.

This allowed the bank to continue innovation without risking legacy system stability, while gradually replacing components.

## Best Practices

1. **Don't Rewrite Everything**: Evaluate ROI before modernizing legacy systems.
2. **Embrace Incrementalism**: Use strangler fig or facade patterns.
3. **Centralize Monitoring and Security**: Unify logging, telemetry, and access control.
4. **Automate as Much as Possible**: Use scripts and pipelines even for legacy deployments.
5. **Bridge Through APIs**: Encapsulate legacy logic using

modern interface patterns.

6. **Establish Clear Ownership**: Assign teams to legacy and modern components with coordination protocols.

## Conclusion

Managing legacy and modern applications together in a hybrid environment is a balancing act that requires thoughtful planning, robust tooling, and a commitment to long-term modernization. By enabling integration through APIs, securing access with Azure AD, standardizing deployment via CI/CD, and centralizing monitoring, organizations can maintain stability while enabling innovation. The result is a resilient, flexible hybrid application landscape that supports both continuity and transformation.

# Chapter 8: Automation and Monitoring

## Azure Monitor and Log Analytics

Effective monitoring and observability are fundamental to the successful operation of hybrid cloud environments. As workloads span across on-premises infrastructure and cloud services, organizations need unified monitoring tools to ensure consistent visibility, performance optimization, and rapid troubleshooting. Azure Monitor, combined with Log Analytics, offers a comprehensive platform to collect, analyze, and act upon telemetry data from across the hybrid estate.

This section delves into the architecture, configuration, best practices, and real-world use cases of Azure Monitor and Log Analytics for hybrid cloud scenarios, focusing on how these tools help maintain operational excellence in modern IT environments.

### Overview of Azure Monitor and Log Analytics

**Azure Monitor** is a unified platform for collecting telemetry data from Azure resources, on-premises environments, and other cloud platforms. It enables:

- Infrastructure and application performance monitoring
- Log collection and querying
- Metrics analysis
- Alerts and automation
- Integration with ITSM and incident management platforms

**Log Analytics**, a feature of Azure Monitor, provides a powerful query language (Kusto Query Language, or KQL) for analyzing structured and unstructured log data from diverse sources.

Azure Monitor consists of several key components:

- **Metrics**: Real-time performance data (e.g., CPU, memory, latency)
- **Logs**: Event and diagnostic data collected from VMs, containers, and applications
- **Alerts**: Rules based on metrics or logs that trigger actions
- **Workbooks**: Interactive dashboards for visualization
- **Insights**: Built-in solutions for VMs, containers, networks, and applications

## Architecture in a Hybrid Environment

In a hybrid scenario, telemetry must be collected from both Azure-native services and on-prem resources. The architecture typically includes:

- **Azure Monitor Agent (AMA)** or **Log Analytics Agent** installed on VMs (both Azure and on-prem)
- **Azure Arc** to extend Azure management and monitoring capabilities to non-Azure machines
- **Diagnostic settings** for PaaS services to stream logs to Log Analytics

- **Custom scripts** or APIs to ingest logs from third-party systems

```
# Install Azure Monitor Agent on an on-prem Windows server

$workspaceId = "<LogAnalyticsWorkspaceID>"

$workspaceKey = "<PrimaryKey>"

$agentInstaller = "https://aka.ms/InstallAzureMonitorAgent"

Invoke-WebRequest -Uri $agentInstaller -OutFile "InstallAzureMonitorAgent.exe"

Start-Process .\InstallAzureMonitorAgent.exe -ArgumentList "/workspaceId:$workspaceId /workspaceKey:$workspaceKey /silent" -Wait
```

Using Azure Arc, you can onboard non-Azure machines and containers to Azure Monitor with minimal configuration.

```
az connectedmachine connect—resource-group HybridRG—name legacy-web01—location eastus
```

## Collecting Logs and Metrics

Telemetry sources in a hybrid environment include:

- Azure VMs, App Services, AKS
- On-premises Windows/Linux servers
- Azure Stack HCI clusters
- Network devices via syslog

- Applications instrumented with Application Insights SDK

Azure Monitor can ingest data via:

- Azure Monitor Agent (AMA)
- Diagnostic settings for Azure resources
- REST API for custom log ingestion
- Container insights and Prometheus scraping
- Data connectors (e.g., for Microsoft Defender, Office 365, third-party services)

Logs are ingested into a **Log Analytics Workspace**, where they can be queried using KQL.

```
// Example KQL query to retrieve CPU usage from all connected VMs

Perf

| where ObjectName == "Processor" and CounterName == "% Processor Time"

| summarize avg(CounterValue) by bin(TimeGenerated, 5m), Computer
```

Metrics, meanwhile, are stored in a time-series database and accessed using metric explorer or alerts.

## Visualization with Workbooks and Dashboards

**Azure Workbooks** provide a flexible canvas to build interactive visualizations using metrics and log queries. These can be shared across teams or embedded in Azure dashboards.

```
// VM memory usage over time

Perf

| where ObjectName == "Memory" and CounterName == "Available MBytes"

| summarize avg(CounterValue) by bin(TimeGenerated, 5m), Computer

| render timechart
```

Best practices for building workbooks:

- Use clear and descriptive labels
- Apply filters and parameters for interactivity
- Group data by environment, region, or business unit
- Combine metrics, logs, and alerts in a single view

## Creating and Managing Alerts

Alerts in Azure Monitor can be configured based on metrics or log queries. These alerts can trigger:

- Email, SMS, or push notifications
- Azure Logic Apps or webhooks

- ITSM tool integration (e.g., ServiceNow, PagerDuty)
- Automation runbooks

**Metric-based alerts** are best for near real-time thresholds, while **log-based alerts** offer more flexibility and advanced logic.

```
// Log-based alert query: Detect failed logins on hybrid machines

SecurityEvent

| where EventID == 4625

| summarize count() by Account, Computer, bin(TimeGenerated, 15m)

| where count_ > 5
```

You can manage alert rules programmatically using ARM templates, Bicep, or Terraform for reproducibility.

## Use Cases in Hybrid Environments

### 1. Monitoring Azure Stack HCI Clusters

Install Log Analytics agents on cluster nodes to collect system and application logs. Integrate with Azure Arc for unified management.

- Track node availability
- Monitor storage latency and IOPS
- Visualize CPU/memory usage

**2. Application Performance Monitoring**

Instrument both legacy and modern apps using **Application Insights** to track:

- Request rates, durations, and failures
- Dependency performance (e.g., SQL, HTTP)
- Exception and crash reporting
- User behavior analytics

```
// .NET App Insights Telemetry

TelemetryClient telemetry = new TelemetryClient();

telemetry.TrackEvent("HybridLoginAttempt", new Dictionary<string, string>{{"User", "jdoe"}});

telemetry.TrackException(ex);
```

**3. Hybrid Network Visibility**

Stream NSG flows, firewall logs, and VPN gateway diagnostics to Log Analytics. Correlate with on-prem network device logs to identify bottlenecks and anomalies.

- Detect unusual traffic patterns
- Monitor ExpressRoute and VPN tunnel health
- Alert on dropped packets or failed connections

**4. Compliance and Audit**

Use Log Analytics to build audit trails across systems. Combine Azure Activity Logs with Windows Event Logs and security data to meet regulatory requirements.

- Monitor admin actions
- Track configuration changes
- Validate role-based access enforcement

## Performance and Cost Optimization

Monitoring systems must be efficient and cost-effective. Key considerations include:

- **Data retention settings**: Choose between 30 to 730 days based on compliance needs.
- **Sampling**: Limit the frequency of data collection for high-volume metrics.
- **Query optimization**: Use summarized queries and narrow time ranges.
- **Workspace design**: Use separate workspaces per environment (dev, prod) or department.

Cost management features within Azure Monitor help identify expensive queries or excessive data volumes.

// Identify top queries by data consumption

Usage

| summarize TotalGB = sum(Quantity) by Solution, bin(TimeGenerated, 1d)

| order by TotalGB desc

## Integration with Third-Party Tools

Azure Monitor and Log Analytics support integration with various tools:

- **Grafana**: Native integration for dashboards
- **Power BI**: Export query results for business reporting
- **SIEMs**: Connect to Sentinel, Splunk, or QRadar
- **DevOps tools**: Integrate with Azure Pipelines, GitHub Actions, or Jenkins for feedback loops

You can also export logs via Event Hubs for real-time ingestion into custom systems.

## Security and Access Control

Security is a priority when dealing with telemetry:

- **RBAC**: Use Azure role assignments to control access to Log Analytics workspaces
- **Data masking**: Avoid logging sensitive information (PII, secrets)
- **Secure endpoints**: Use private links or service endpoints for workspace access
- **Audit logs**: Track access to telemetry data

Ensure that on-prem systems sending data to Azure Monitor are protected via VPN or ExpressRoute, and use managed identities where applicable.

## Best Practices

1. **Use Azure Arc for non-Azure resource onboarding**
2. **Centralize telemetry from all environments into unified workspaces**
3. **Adopt a tagging strategy for environment, app, owner, and region**
4. **Automate alert rule deployment using IaC**
5. **Tune data ingestion frequency to balance cost and detail**
6. **Combine metrics and logs for complete observability**
7. **Use workbooks to democratize insights across teams**
8. **Regularly audit access and usage of monitoring resources**

## Conclusion

Azure Monitor and Log Analytics empower organizations to manage complex hybrid environments with a unified, scalable, and intelligent observability platform. By leveraging these tools, IT teams can gain actionable insights, reduce MTTR, enforce compliance, and maintain the high availability and performance of both on-premises and cloud workloads. As hybrid adoption grows, the ability to monitor systems holistically becomes not just an advantage—but a critical necessity.

# Automation with Azure Runbooks and Logic Apps

Automation is the backbone of modern IT operations, enabling teams to manage hybrid cloud environments efficiently and consistently. In the context of Azure, two powerful services—**Azure Automation Runbooks** and **Azure Logic Apps**—stand out as key components for orchestrating workflows, remediating issues, and streamlining repetitive tasks across on-premises and cloud-based systems.

This section explores in detail how to design, implement, and manage automation using Runbooks and Logic Apps in hybrid environments. It includes architectural considerations, practical examples, best practices, and integration strategies to maximize operational efficiency and minimize human error.

## The Role of Automation in Hybrid Cloud

Hybrid cloud introduces complexity due to the presence of multiple environments, diverse platforms, and distributed teams. Manual processes cannot scale in such a scenario. Automation helps in:

- Reducing operational overhead
- Enforcing consistent configurations
- Minimizing downtime and human errors
- Accelerating deployment and maintenance tasks
- Enabling self-healing systems and intelligent workflows

Key hybrid scenarios for automation include:

- Scheduled maintenance tasks across Azure and on-prem
- Auto-remediation of alerts or policy violations
- Routine patching and backup operations
- User onboarding/offboarding workflows
- Secure credential rotation and certificate renewal

## Overview of Azure Automation and Logic Apps

**Azure Automation** offers a cloud-based automation and configuration service that supports:

- **Runbooks**: Scripts (PowerShell, Python) that automate tasks
- **Update management**: Track and deploy OS patches
- **Change tracking**: Monitor file, registry, and software changes
- **Desired State Configuration (DSC)**: Ensure systems maintain specific configurations

**Azure Logic Apps** is a serverless workflow orchestration service that enables the creation of complex workflows through a visual designer. It integrates with:

- Microsoft and third-party services (e.g., Office 365, SAP, ServiceNow)
- On-prem systems via gateways

- RESTful APIs and Azure Functions

These two services complement each other: Logic Apps are ideal for orchestrating business processes and integrating with external services, while Runbooks are best for infrastructure-level automation.

## Creating and Managing Runbooks

Runbooks are the core unit of execution in Azure Automation. They can be authored using:

- PowerShell
- PowerShell Workflow (legacy)
- Python 2 (being phased out)
- Python 3 (via Automation Hybrid Workers)

### Setting Up Azure Automation Account

```
# Create an Automation Account

New-AzAutomationAccount -Name "HybridAutomation" -ResourceGroupName "HybridRG" -Location "eastus"
```

### Sample Runbook: Restart On-Prem VM via Azure Arc

```
workflow Restart-OnPremVM {

param (

[string]$VMName,
```

```
[string]$ResourceGroup

)

InlineScript {

Write-Output "Restarting VM: $using:VMName"

Restart-Computer -ComputerName $using:VMName -Force

}

}
```

This Runbook can be linked to alerts, scheduled to run periodically, or invoked on-demand. When targeting on-prem resources, use **Hybrid Runbook Workers**—local agents that allow runbooks to execute in your private datacenter.

```
# Register a Hybrid Worker

Add-AzAutomationHybridWorkerGroup -ResourceGroupName "HybridRG" `

-AutomationAccountName "HybridAutomation" `

-Name "OnPremWorkers"
```

**Runbook Triggers and Scheduling**

Runbooks can be triggered via:

- **Schedules** (e.g., daily backups)
- **Webhooks** (e.g., called by Logic Apps or alerts)
- **Alerts** (e.g., high CPU)

- **Manual invocation** (e.g., via Azure portal or API)

```
# Create a schedule

$Schedule = New-AzAutomationSchedule
-AutomationAccountName "HybridAutomation" `

-Name "DailyMaintenance" `

-StartTime (Get-Date).AddMinutes(15) -DayInterval 1

# Link schedule to a runbook

Register-AzAutomationScheduledRunbook -
AutomationAccountName "HybridAutomation" `

-ScheduleName $Schedule.Name -RunbookName
"Restart-OnPremVM"
```

## Building Logic Apps for Hybrid Automation

Logic Apps allow you to visually design workflows that span systems, clouds, and services. They are ideal for:

- Approvals and human-in-the-loop processes
- Email or Teams-based alerts and updates
- Multi-step business flows
- Conditional branching and looping

### Sample Workflow: Notify and Remediate Failed Login Attempts

1. **Trigger**: New failed login log entry in Log Analytics

2. **Condition**: If count > 5 within 10 minutes

3. **Actions**:

○ Send email alert to admin

○ Call Azure Runbook to lock the account

```
{
"definition": {
"triggers": {
"When_a_response_to_an_Azure_Log_Analytics_query_is_received": {
"type": "HttpWebhook",
"inputs": {
"uri": "https://query.loganalytics.io/v1/workspaces/xyz...",
"method": "GET",
"authentication": {
"type": "ActiveDirectoryOAuth"
}
}
}
},
"actions": {
```

```
"Send_email": {
"type": "Office365.SendEmail",
"inputs": {
"To": "admin@company.com",
"Subject": "Multiple Failed Login Attempts Detected",
"Body": "More than 5 failed login attempts in 10 minutes."
}
},
"Invoke_Runbook": {
"type": "Http",
"inputs": {
"method": "POST",
"uri": "https://management.azure.com/subscriptions/xxx/resourceGroups/HybridRG/providers/Microsoft.Automation/automationAccounts/HybridAutomation/runbooks/LockUserAccount/run",
"authentication": {
"type": "ManagedServiceIdentity"
}
}
}
```

```
}
}
}
```

This example showcases Logic Apps as an orchestrator that integrates telemetry (Log Analytics), communication (Outlook), and infrastructure automation (Runbooks).

## Integration with On-Prem Systems

To extend automation to on-premises environments:

- Use **Hybrid Runbook Workers** for Runbooks
- Use **On-premises data gateway** for Logic Apps
- Use **Azure Arc-enabled servers** for uniform management

**Use Case: Hybrid Patch Management**

- Logic App triggers on scheduled interval
- Queries Log Analytics for outdated OS versions
- Invokes a Runbook to install patches via Hybrid Worker
- Sends status report to Microsoft Teams

This use case demonstrates hybrid automation at scale while maintaining control and auditability.

## Monitoring and Logging

Automation outputs are stored in job logs, which can be:

- Viewed in the Azure Portal
- Queried in Log Analytics (if linked)
- Exported via REST APIs

```
// Query runbook job status

AzureDiagnostics

| where Category == "JobLogs"

| where Resource == "HybridAutomation"

| summarize count() by ResultType, bin(TimeGenerated, 1h)
```

## Security and Governance

Securing automated workflows is essential:

- Use **Managed Identities** to grant least privilege access
- Store secrets in **Azure Key Vault**
- Audit all automation runs with **Activity Logs**
- Limit access using **RBAC** and **custom roles**
- Implement **approval workflows** where human validation is required

```
# Example: Using Managed Identity with Azure Runbook
```

$Secret = Get-AzKeyVaultSecret -VaultName "HybridVault" -Name "DbPassword"

## Best Practices for Automation

1. **Use Hybrid Workers** to execute tasks inside private networks
2. **Break down complex scripts** into modular Runbooks
3. **Implement error handling** and retries in both Runbooks and Logic Apps
4. **Use version control** (e.g., GitHub integration) for script management
5. **Monitor execution history** for performance tuning and audit
6. **Avoid hardcoded credentials**—use Key Vault
7. **Test automation in dev environments** before promoting to production
8. **Schedule during low-usage windows** to reduce impact

## Real-World Scenario: Retail Chain Infrastructure Maintenance

A global retailer with hundreds of stores used Azure Automation and Logic Apps to manage infrastructure maintenance:

- Each store had on-prem servers running POS software
- Logic Apps monitored CPU, memory, and disk from Log Analytics
- When thresholds exceeded, Runbooks were triggered via Hybrid Workers to:
  - Clear temp files

  - ○ Restart services
  - ○ Notify local staff

- Weekly patching was handled through a scheduled Runbook and update management

This drastically reduced the manual workload and improved SLA compliance.

## Conclusion

Azure Runbooks and Logic Apps are critical tools for enabling enterprise-grade automation in hybrid environments. They empower IT teams to orchestrate complex workflows, respond to incidents automatically, and enforce consistent operations across cloud and on-premises infrastructure. By combining the power of script-driven and event-driven automation, organizations can ensure agility, reduce errors, and establish a robust foundation for modern hybrid operations.

# Integrating On-Prem Tools with Azure Monitoring

As organizations adopt hybrid cloud architectures, a common challenge is unifying observability across both on-premises infrastructure and cloud-native services. While Azure offers robust native monitoring capabilities through Azure Monitor, Application Insights, and Log Analytics, enterprises often have long-standing investments in traditional monitoring tools such as System Center Operations Manager (SCOM), Nagios, Zabbix, Prometheus, or custom-built solutions. Rather than replacing these tools entirely, a more practical and cost-effective approach is to **integrate on-prem**

**tools with Azure monitoring services**, creating a cohesive and centralized monitoring framework.

This section outlines strategies, architectures, and techniques for integrating legacy and third-party monitoring systems with Azure, ensuring complete visibility across the hybrid landscape.

## The Case for Hybrid Monitoring Integration

Enterprises retain on-prem monitoring systems for several valid reasons:

- Regulatory requirements to store data locally
- Deep customization and long-established operational procedures
- High-fidelity, low-latency data collection for critical systems
- Cost optimization, especially in environments with minimal change rates

However, without integration with Azure Monitor, these tools often function in silos. This results in:

- Fragmented visibility and delayed root cause analysis
- Inconsistent alerting and operational response workflows
- Manual correlation between cloud and on-prem metrics
- Inefficient incident management and longer MTTR

Integration resolves these challenges by centralizing telemetry, enabling advanced analytics using Kusto Query Language (KQL), automating remediation, and aligning hybrid operations under a unified governance model.

## Integration Patterns

There are several ways to bridge on-prem monitoring tools with Azure:

1. **Data Forwarding**: Exporting logs, metrics, or alerts from on-prem tools to Azure Monitor or Log Analytics.
2. **API-Based Integration**: Using REST APIs to ingest data into Azure Monitor from third-party tools.
3. **Connector-Based Integration**: Leverage built-in Azure connectors for tools like SCOM, Grafana, or Prometheus.
4. **Gateway/Collector Agents**: Use custom agents or gateways to act as intermediaries.
5. **Azure Arc Integration**: Extend Azure capabilities to non-Azure environments.

These integration patterns are not mutually exclusive and can be combined to achieve the desired outcomes.

## Using Azure Monitor SCOM Connector

System Center Operations Manager (SCOM) remains a widely used enterprise monitoring platform. Microsoft provides a native integration path with Azure Monitor using the **SCOM Management Pack for Azure**.

**Steps:**

1. Install the Azure Management Pack on the SCOM

management server.

2. Configure an Azure Active Directory application with access to your Azure resources.
3. Add your Azure subscription and resource groups in the SCOM Operations Console.
4. Select the Azure services to monitor from within SCOM.
5. Use the management pack views to observe Azure health, availability, and performance.

This allows on-prem administrators to monitor cloud resources alongside traditional infrastructure using familiar SCOM dashboards.

## Forwarding Logs from On-Prem Tools to Log Analytics

### Using Syslog for Linux Servers

Many Linux-based monitoring tools (e.g., Nagios, Zabbix) can forward logs via syslog. You can configure these tools to send logs to a Log Analytics Workspace using the **Log Analytics agent for Linux**.

```
# Install Log Analytics Agent on Linux

wget https://aka.ms/InstallAzureMonitorAgentLinux

bash
InstallAzureMonitorAgentLinux.sh—workspace-id=<workspace-id>—w
```

Update rsyslog.conf to forward logs:

```
*.* @127.0.0.1:25226
```

This enables ingestion of syslog-based alerts, metrics, and events directly into Azure.

#### Using Fluentd or Logstash

For more advanced log routing, tools like **Fluentd** or **Logstash** can be used as intermediaries to transform and forward logs to Azure Monitor.

```
# Fluentd config for forwarding logs to Azure

<match **>

@type azure_loganalytics

workspace_id YOUR_WORKSPACE_ID

shared_key YOUR_SHARED_KEY

log_type customLog

</match>
```

This pattern is useful when integrating multiple tools (e.g., Apache logs, NGINX metrics, MySQL slow queries) into Azure.

### Prometheus Integration

Prometheus is a widely adopted open-source monitoring system, often used in Kubernetes environments.

Azure Monitor provides a **managed Prometheus service** and also supports ingestion of Prometheus metrics from AKS and other clusters via the Azure Monitor OpenTelemetry Distro.

To scrape Prometheus metrics from an on-prem system and push to Azure:

1. Use a Prometheus Exporter (e.g., Node Exporter, MySQL Exporter)
2. Configure Azure Monitor scraping via Azure Monitor for containers
3. Use the **Azure Monitor metrics API** to ingest custom metrics if running outside Kubernetes

Alternatively, if Prometheus is running in a hybrid Kubernetes cluster (e.g., AKS on Azure Stack HCI), Azure Monitor can scrape metrics directly using the built-in support for Prometheus endpoints.

```
# Sample ServiceMonitor resource in AKS for Prometheus metrics collection

apiVersion: monitoring.coreos.com/v1

kind: ServiceMonitor

metadata:

name: node-exporter

spec:

selector:

matchLabels:

app: node-exporter

endpoints:

- port: metrics

interval: 30s
```

## Custom Log Ingestion via REST API

Azure Monitor's HTTP Data Collector API allows ingestion of logs from any source that can perform HTTP POST requests.

### Sample Python Script

```
import requests, datetime, hashlib, hmac, base64

workspace_id = 'your-workspace-id'

shared_key = 'your-shared-key'

log_type = 'CustomAppLogs'

body = '[{ "LogMessage": "App failed to start", "Level": "Error" }]'

rfc1123date = datetime.datetime.utcnow().strftime('%a, %d %b %Y %H:%M:%S GMT')

string_to_hash = 'POST\n{}\napplication/json\nx-ms-date:{}\n/api/logs'.format(len(body), rfc1123date)

bytes_to_hash = bytes(string_to_hash, encoding="utf-8")

decoded_key = base64.b64decode(shared_key)

encoded_hash = base64.b64encode(hmac.new(decoded_key, bytes_to_hash, hashlib.sha256).digest()).decode()

headers = {

'Content-Type': 'application/json',

'Authorization': f'SharedKey {workspace_id}:{encoded_hash}',

'Log-Type': log_type,
```

'x-ms-date': rfc1123date

}

response = requests.post(

f'https://{workspace_id}.ods.opinsights.azure.com/api/logs?api-version=2016-04-01',

data=body,

headers=headers

)

This method enables any tool with scripting capabilities (e.g., PowerShell, Python, Bash) to send logs to Azure.

## Integration with Alerting and Incident Management

Once logs and metrics are centralized in Azure Monitor, you can route alerts to various systems:

- **Email, SMS, push notifications**
- **Microsoft Teams and Slack**
- **ITSM tools** like ServiceNow, PagerDuty, or Opsgenie
- **Automation tools** like Azure Runbooks or Logic Apps

// Sample alert query for high disk usage

Perf

| where ObjectName == "LogicalDisk" and CounterName == "% Free Space"

```
| where CounterValue < 10

| project Computer, InstanceName, TimeGenerated
```

This query can be tied to an alert rule that triggers a Logic App to create an incident in ServiceNow and notify the on-call engineer via Teams.

## Dashboards and Visualizations

Use **Azure Workbooks**, **Power BI**, or **Grafana** to build unified dashboards that blend metrics from both Azure and on-prem systems.

Grafana supports **Azure Monitor** as a native data source, and Workbooks can visualize custom log queries.

```
// Display CPU usage across hybrid infrastructure

Perf

| where CounterName == "% Processor Time"

| summarize avg(CounterValue) by bin(TimeGenerated, 5m), Computer

| render timechart
```

This data can be combined with alerts, user actions, and application performance logs for a comprehensive view.

## Governance and Security

When integrating multiple systems, maintain tight control over access and data flow:

- Use **private endpoints** and **firewalls** to secure log ingestion paths

- Enforce **RBAC** and **Azure Policies** to limit access to monitoring resources

- Use **Azure Key Vault** or **Managed Identities** to secure API keys and credentials

- Enable **log audit trails** to track ingestion, transformation, and access patterns

## Best Practices

1. **Start small**: Integrate critical on-prem tools first, then expand.
2. **Normalize data**: Tag and structure logs for easy querying.
3. **Avoid duplication**: Filter redundant logs to control costs.
4. **Secure endpoints**: Use encryption, firewalls, and IAM best practices.
5. **Visualize strategically**: Build dashboards for different audiences—ops, dev, execs.
6. **Automate remediation**: Couple monitoring with Logic Apps or Runbooks.
7. **Document integrations**: Maintain an integration map for operational transparency.

## Conclusion

Integrating on-prem monitoring tools with Azure Monitor and Log Analytics empowers organizations to establish unified observability across the hybrid estate. It enhances operational insight, streamlines incident response, and enables predictive analytics through advanced query capabilities. Rather than discarding legacy investments, enterprises can modernize their monitoring strategy incrementally—bridging the old and the new in a way that drives resilience, agility, and informed decision-making.

## Unified Operations and Management

In a hybrid cloud architecture, unifying operations and management across disparate environments is essential for maintaining performance, enforcing governance, ensuring compliance, and responding effectively to incidents. The increasing complexity of hybrid ecosystems—where legacy systems coexist with modern cloud-native applications—requires integrated tooling, consistent policies, and cohesive operational processes that span both on-premises and cloud infrastructures.

This section explores how to achieve unified operations and management using Azure's suite of management services, including Azure Arc, Azure Policy, Azure Lighthouse, Azure Monitor, and Azure Automation. It also covers architectural patterns, implementation strategies, and real-world examples to help you build a scalable and cohesive operations model.

### The Case for Unified Management

Hybrid environments often suffer from operational fragmentation due to:

- Different tools used for monitoring and configuration
- Lack of consistent policy enforcement
- Disparate security postures across environments
- Isolated teams managing different platforms

These issues lead to:

- Inconsistent configurations and increased risk
- Inefficient troubleshooting and alert fatigue
- Poor visibility into infrastructure health
- High operational costs

A unified operations approach addresses these problems by enabling centralized visibility, consistent governance, shared automation, and integrated security across all environments.

## Key Principles of Unified Operations

1. **Consistency**: Apply the same policies, monitoring, tagging, and automation regardless of where the resource is located.
2. **Visibility**: Centralize metrics, logs, and insights into a single platform.
3. **Governance**: Enforce compliance and access control through scalable policy management.
4. **Automation**: Reduce manual intervention using workflow orchestration and remediation.
5. **Interoperability**: Seamlessly integrate with third-party tools and APIs.
6. **Security**: Implement unified identity, threat detection, and configuration baselines.

## Azure Arc: The Foundation for Unified Management

Azure Arc extends Azure's management and governance capabilities to non-Azure environments, including on-premises servers, Kubernetes clusters, SQL servers, and third-party clouds.

**Benefits:**

- Register on-prem resources in Azure Resource Manager
- Apply Azure Policy, Defender for Cloud, and role-based access
- Enable telemetry and monitoring through Azure Monitor
- Use GitOps and ARM templates for consistent configuration

### Onboarding a Server with Azure Arc

```
az connectedmachine connect—resource-group "HybridRG" \

—location "eastus" \

—name "onprem-sql01"
```

After registration, the server appears in the Azure Portal like any native resource, allowing management through Azure tooling.

## Centralized Monitoring and Alerting

Azure Monitor consolidates telemetry from:

- Azure resources

- Arc-enabled servers
- Azure Stack HCI
- Containers (AKS, Arc-enabled Kubernetes)
- Applications (via Application Insights)
- Network devices and on-prem VMs (via Log Analytics)

This creates a unified telemetry layer that supports:

- Alert rules based on metrics and logs
- Visual dashboards using Workbooks
- Automated incident response using Logic Apps and Runbooks

```
Heartbeat
| where TimeGenerated > ago(1h)
| summarize heartbeat_count = count() by Computer, bin(TimeGenerated, 5m)
```

This query helps track server availability across your entire hybrid environment.

## Policy and Compliance Management

Azure Policy allows you to define and enforce rules for resource configuration and deployment. Policies can be scoped to subscriptions, management groups, or individual resources.

**Key Capabilities:**

- Enforce naming conventions and tag requirements
- Prevent non-compliant resource types (e.g., public IPs in dev)
- Audit VM configurations (e.g., encryption, backups)
- Deploy security agents automatically

Azure Arc enables policy enforcement on non-Azure servers and Kubernetes clusters, bringing compliance to on-premises and multicloud environments.

```
{
"if": {
"field": "location",
"equals": "eastus"
},
"then": {
"effect": "audit"
}
}
```

This sample policy audits any resources not deployed in the "eastus" region.

### Compliance Dashboards

Use Azure Policy's compliance dashboard to:

- Track adherence across environments
- Identify non-compliant resources
- Trigger remediation tasks (automatic or manual)

## Role-Based Access Control (RBAC)

Unified management requires a consistent access control model. Azure provides RBAC that can be extended to Arc-enabled resources.

- Assign roles at the resource, group, or subscription level
- Use built-in roles (e.g., Reader, Contributor) or define custom ones
- Integrate with Azure AD for identity federation across environments

```
New-AzRoleAssignment -ObjectId "user-object-id" `
-RoleDefinitionName "Virtual Machine Contributor" `
-Scope "/subscriptions/{subscriptionId}/resourceGroups/HybridRG"
```

This ensures that a developer has controlled access to hybrid VMs for debugging purposes.

## Unified Automation and Orchestration

Use Azure Automation and Logic Apps to automate repetitive tasks and respond to events:

- Patch management across cloud and on-prem
- Certificate renewal and rotation
- Resource provisioning workflows
- Auto-remediation of alerts

**Example: Hybrid Patch Management Workflow**

1. Azure Monitor identifies a VM with missing updates
2. Alert triggers a Logic App
3. Logic App calls a Runbook via webhook
4. Runbook initiates update on Arc-enabled server using Hybrid Worker
5. Result is logged in Log Analytics and sent to Teams

This automation eliminates manual intervention, improves compliance, and accelerates response times.

## Azure Lighthouse: Managing at Scale

For service providers or large enterprises managing multiple tenants or business units, Azure Lighthouse enables:

- Cross-tenant management
- Delegated resource access
- Consolidated monitoring and policy enforcement

- RBAC segregation across customers or units

Lighthouse works with Azure Arc, allowing you to manage customer environments—including on-prem resources—at scale through a single pane of glass.

```
{
"properties": {
"authorizations": [
{
"principalId": "admin-id",
"roleDefinitionId": "/providers/Microsoft.Authorization/roleDefinitions/owner"
}
],
"description": "Cross-tenant management"
}
}
```

Lighthouse enhances security and simplifies multi-environment operations.

## Standardizing Configuration and Tagging

Unified operations demand consistent configuration across all resources. This includes:

- Tagging for ownership, cost center, environment

- Configuration baselines for VM images, storage, and network settings

- Enforcement through policies and templates

```
{
"field": "tags['Environment']",
"equals": "Production"
}
```

Apply this policy to ensure that every production resource is tagged properly for cost allocation and compliance audits.

## Integrated Incident Management

With centralized logging and alerting, integrate with incident management tools:

- **ServiceNow**: Auto-create incidents based on Azure Monitor alerts

- **PagerDuty/Opsgenie**: Escalate critical issues

- **Microsoft Teams**: Notify relevant teams with alert context and runbook links

```
# Logic App step: Create ServiceNow incident
{
"type": "ServiceNow.CreateIncident",
"inputs": {
```

```
"short_description": "High CPU on hybrid SQL server",
"priority": "1",
"caller_id": "AzureMonitor"
}
}
```

Automation ensures faster triage and resolution, minimizing business impact.

## Real-World Example: Unified Operations in Manufacturing

A global manufacturing firm implemented unified operations for 250 factories using Azure:

- Registered all plant servers and equipment VMs with Azure Arc
- Centralized logs and metrics in Azure Monitor
- Enforced baseline policies for security agents and updates
- Used RBAC and tagging for environment-specific access control
- Connected Azure Monitor with Logic Apps and PagerDuty for 24/7 incident response
- Created dashboards in Azure Workbooks for leadership visibility

This transformed their siloed IT operations into a modern, scalable, and policy-driven platform.

## Best Practices

1. **Adopt Azure Arc early** to onboard non-Azure resources
2. **Use a centralized Log Analytics workspace** for full visibility
3. **Automate tagging and configuration enforcement** via policy
4. **Standardize alerting thresholds** across environments
5. **Secure identities and credentials** using Azure AD and Key Vault
6. **Document operational workflows and escalations**
7. **Train teams on KQL, RBAC, and policy authoring**
8. **Continuously optimize alerts and dashboards based on usage**

## Conclusion

Unified operations and management are crucial to realizing the full potential of hybrid cloud strategies. Azure provides a mature set of tools that, when used in concert, enable seamless governance, observability, automation, and security across all environments. By integrating on-premises systems with cloud-native practices through Azure Arc, Monitor, Policy, Lighthouse, and Automation, organizations can create a robust, scalable, and resilient operations framework capable of supporting modern business needs well into the future.

# Chapter 9: Real-World Use Cases and Case Studies

## Enterprise Hybrid Deployments

As organizations embrace digital transformation, the transition to hybrid cloud has become a strategic imperative, particularly for large enterprises with complex infrastructure landscapes. These organizations face unique challenges such as legacy system entrenchment, strict regulatory requirements, and the need for global scale. Hybrid cloud allows them to modernize incrementally while preserving existing investments and maintaining control where necessary.

This section explores real-world enterprise hybrid cloud deployments across various industries. It highlights architectures, deployment strategies, operational models, and lessons learned from organizations that have successfully leveraged Microsoft Azure for hybrid transformation. The goal is to provide practical insights for IT leaders, architects, and engineers seeking to replicate these successes within their own environments.

### Characteristics of Enterprise Hybrid Deployments

Enterprise hybrid cloud implementations typically include:

- **Large-scale infrastructure**: Thousands of VMs, applications, and endpoints spread across global data centers and Azure regions.
- **Strict compliance requirements**: Industries such as healthcare, finance, and government must adhere to standards like HIPAA, PCI-DSS, or ISO 27001.

- **Multiple clouds and environments**: Enterprises often operate in multicloud environments alongside hybrid deployments.

- **Legacy modernization mandates**: A mix of mainframes, older ERP systems, and newer microservices must coexist.

- **Governance at scale**: Policy enforcement, cost controls, access management, and operational visibility must scale across hundreds of business units or teams.

Hybrid cloud models provide these enterprises with the flexibility to balance agility with control, leveraging Azure services like Azure Arc, Azure Stack HCI, ExpressRoute, and hybrid identity.

## Case Study 1: Financial Services Firm Modernizing Core Banking

**Background:**

A global financial institution operated core banking workloads on-premises using a mix of mainframes and custom .NET applications hosted on VMware infrastructure. The firm needed to modernize to offer digital services, but regulatory constraints required that certain data remain within the country.

**Hybrid Approach:**

- **Azure Arc** was used to onboard legacy VMs into Azure management for unified policy enforcement.

- **ExpressRoute** established a high-speed private connection between data centers and Azure.

- **Azure Stack HCI** hosted latency-sensitive services in-country, while web front-ends ran in Azure App Service.

- **Azure Key Vault and Defender for Cloud** extended security controls to both environments.

**Outcome:**

- Deployment velocity increased by 4x via Azure DevOps and GitOps pipelines.

- Incident resolution times dropped by 60% through centralized logging.

- The bank remained fully compliant with regional data sovereignty laws.

## Case Study 2: Manufacturing Giant with Smart Factory Initiative

**Background:**

A Fortune 100 manufacturing company embarked on a global smart factory initiative to digitize production lines, reduce downtime, and enable predictive maintenance. However, network constraints and low-latency requirements prevented moving all workloads to the cloud.

**Hybrid Architecture:**

- **Azure Stack Edge** deployed at each plant for edge compute and ML inferencing.

- IoT data from sensors collected by Azure IoT Hub and processed locally, then synced to Azure Data Lake.
- **Azure Arc-enabled Kubernetes** clusters used for standardizing application deployment on-prem and in the cloud.
- **Azure Monitor and Azure Sentinel** used for centralized monitoring and security incident response.

**Outcome:**

- Reduced unplanned downtime by 40% using ML-based failure prediction.
- Improved operational efficiency through real-time dashboards aggregated in Power BI.
- Simplified compliance with global data handling policies.

## Case Study 3: Retail Enterprise Migrating POS Systems

**Background:**

A major retail chain with over 2,000 stores ran its point-of-sale (POS) system locally at each site, supported by a centralized ERP in a private data center. The business needed to enable real-time inventory tracking and customer analytics without replacing its legacy POS software immediately.

**Hybrid Model:**

- POS systems were containerized using Windows containers and hosted on **Azure Stack HCI** clusters per region.
- Data was synchronized in near-real time with Azure SQL Database using **Azure Data Factory** and **Event Grid**.
- The legacy ERP system was refactored gradually and extended with **Azure Functions** to support modern APIs.
- **Azure Virtual WAN** and **Azure Firewall** provided secure inter-store and cloud communication.

**Result:**

- Central inventory visibility enabled just-in-time restocking.
- Loyalty programs integrated with POS systems, improving customer retention.
- Reduced total cost of ownership by 25% through centralized update management.

## Case Study 4: Global Energy Provider Improving Regulatory Compliance

**Background:**

An energy provider managing oil fields and renewable facilities globally needed to comply with evolving carbon reporting standards while integrating field data from remote locations.

**Hybrid Deployment:**

- Deployed **Azure Arc-enabled servers** in offshore rigs and remote substations.
- Used **Azure Automation** to apply patches and maintain configurations.
- Field data was ingested into **Azure Data Explorer** for real-time analytics.
- **Azure Purview** and **Azure Policy** ensured data classification and auditability.

**Results:**

- Automated reporting reduced manual effort by 90%.
- Compliance scores improved significantly with traceable configuration enforcement.
- Improved environmental impact visibility led to better regulatory positioning.

## Hybrid Deployment Patterns and Best Practices

Across these case studies, several common architectural patterns emerge:

1. **Hybrid Identity with Azure AD**: Use Azure AD Connect or Azure AD B2C for unified authentication and conditional access.
2. **Local compute + cloud orchestration**: Run workloads locally (Azure Stack HCI, Edge, Arc) with centralized governance in Azure.
3. **Hybrid Data Pipelines**: Use Data Factory, Event Grid, or IoT Hub to synchronize data.

4. **Centralized Logging and Monitoring**: Aggregate logs via Log Analytics, monitor health with Azure Monitor.
5. **Infrastructure as Code**: Use ARM/Bicep or Terraform across environments, including on-prem via Azure Arc.

## Code Example: Hybrid Deployment with ARM Template and Arc

```
{
"$schema": "https://schema.management.azure.com/schemas/2019-04-01/deploymentTemplate.json#",
"contentVersion": "1.0.0.0",
"resources": [
{
"type": "Microsoft.HybridCompute/machines",
"apiVersion": "2022-03-10",
"name": "arc-server-01",
"location": "eastus",
"identity": {
"type": "SystemAssigned"
},
"properties": {
"osName": "Windows",
"osVersion": "2019"
```

```
}
}
]
}
```

This template registers an Arc-enabled server into Azure Resource Manager, enabling policy enforcement, tagging, and monitoring.

## Metrics for Success in Enterprise Hybrid Deployments

To evaluate the effectiveness of hybrid strategies, enterprises often track the following KPIs:

- **Deployment velocity** (e.g., time to provision infrastructure)
- **MTTR (Mean Time to Repair)** for incidents
- **Compliance score** across all assets
- **Cost efficiency** per workload
- **End-user satisfaction** (app responsiveness, service availability)
- **Security posture** (threat detection coverage, incident resolution)

## Lessons Learned

1. **Start with governance and identity**: Ensure consistent access and security before scaling services.

2. **Don't rip and replace—extend first**: Use Arc, API wrappers, and containers to gradually modernize.
3. **Invest in observability early**: Unified logging and alerting is critical for hybrid health.
4. **Ensure operational consistency**: Standardize pipelines, tagging, and automation across environments.
5. **Use hybrid as a stepping stone**: Hybrid cloud is not an end state—it's a path toward full modernization where feasible.

## Conclusion

Enterprise hybrid cloud deployments offer a pathway to modernization that is pragmatic, controlled, and scalable. By leveraging Azure's hybrid capabilities, organizations can optimize their infrastructure investments, maintain regulatory compliance, and deliver modern experiences to users without compromising on performance or security. Real-world case studies demonstrate that success hinges not on perfection, but on strategy, iteration, and alignment between business and IT goals.

# Hybrid Scenarios in Regulated Industries

Regulated industries—such as healthcare, finance, government, and energy—face heightened scrutiny when adopting new technologies. Security, compliance, data sovereignty, and auditing requirements often delay or complicate cloud migrations. Hybrid cloud provides a strategic middle ground, allowing organizations in these sectors to modernize while remaining compliant with industry-specific regulations and regional laws.

This section explores real-world hybrid cloud scenarios in regulated industries, with a focus on the architectural strategies, security controls, compliance patterns, and governance models that enable successful implementations using Microsoft Azure's hybrid capabilities.

## Key Challenges in Regulated Industries

1. **Data Sovereignty**: Certain data (e.g., patient health records or financial transactions) must remain within specific geographic boundaries.
2. **Legacy Systems**: Critical applications may still run on mainframes or older platforms not easily migrated to the cloud.
3. **Security Requirements**: Enforced encryption, audit logging, and intrusion detection are mandatory.
4. **Regulatory Compliance**: Organizations must adhere to frameworks like HIPAA, GDPR, CJIS, PCI-DSS, FedRAMP, and ISO 27001.
5. **Auditability**: All activities—including admin operations and data access—must be fully traceable.
6. **Resiliency**: Systems must support high availability and disaster recovery while meeting strict SLAs.

Hybrid cloud solves many of these challenges by allowing sensitive workloads to remain on-premises or in edge locations while integrating with Azure's cloud-native capabilities for scalability, analytics, automation, and security.

## Use Case: Healthcare Provider with HIPAA Compliance

### Scenario

A large hospital network needed to modernize its Electronic Health Record (EHR) system, improve patient analytics, and introduce telehealth features—all while maintaining HIPAA compliance.

**Hybrid Design**

- **Azure Stack HCI** deployed in each data center for local EHR application hosting.
- **Azure Arc-enabled SQL Servers** allowed centralized monitoring and policy enforcement across on-prem and cloud.
- **Azure Blob Storage** used to store scanned patient documents with server-side encryption and private endpoints.
- **Azure API Management** exposed controlled APIs for telehealth integrations.
- **Azure Key Vault** and **Microsoft Defender for Cloud** enforced encryption and real-time threat detection.

**Compliance Measures**

- All ePHI (electronic Protected Health Information) data remained on-premises.
- Telehealth traffic tunneled through **Azure VPN Gateway** with strict ACLs.
- Role-based access policies enforced using **Azure AD Conditional Access** and MFA.
- Activity logs retained in **Log Analytics** with a 7-year retention period.

```
# Enabling diagnostic settings on an Arc-enabled SQL Server
```

```
Set-AzDiagnosticSetting -ResourceId
"/subscriptions/{subId}/resourceGroups/{rg}/providers/
Microsoft.HybridCompute/machines/sql01" `

-WorkspaceId
"/subscriptions/{subId}/resourceGroups/{rg}/providers/
Microsoft.OperationalInsights/workspaces/loganalytics01" `

-Enabled $true
```

## Use Case: Government Agency with CJIS Compliance

### Scenario

A U.S. law enforcement agency was required to modernize its data sharing and analytics systems while maintaining Criminal Justice Information Services (CJIS) compliance.

### Hybrid Architecture

- **Azure Government Cloud** used for compliant services (Key Vault, SQL Database, App Services).
- Critical case files stored locally in CJIS-audited data centers.
- **Azure Arc** brought governance and monitoring capabilities to local servers.
- Secure VPN and **ExpressRoute** ensured encrypted, high-throughput connectivity.
- Azure Sentinel used for SIEM (Security Information and Event Management) across both environments.

**Operational Strategy**

- Every administrator action audited through **Azure Activity Logs** and **Windows Event Forwarding**.
- Deployed **Azure Policy** to ensure only compliant configurations (e.g., no public IPs, enforced encryption).
- **Azure Lighthouse** used to delegate access to third-party compliance auditors without exposing underlying infrastructure.

```
// Sample KQL query to identify non-compliant Arc servers

ConfigurationData

| where ConfigurationName == "AzureCIS" and ComplianceState != "Compliant"

| project Resource, Setting, ComplianceState
```

## Use Case: Financial Institution with PCI-DSS Obligations

**Scenario**

A payment processing company needed to isolate its cardholder data environment (CDE) while integrating fraud detection services hosted in Azure.

**Hybrid Cloud Solution**

- Core CDE systems retained in a locked-down on-prem environment.

- **Azure Stack Edge** deployed in data centers to run fraud detection inference models close to transaction origin.

- **Azure Functions**, **Event Grid**, and **Cosmos DB** supported real-time event streaming and scoring in the cloud.

- Integration and communication secured through **Private Link** and **Azure Firewall**.

### Security Controls

- **Azure Policy** enforced FIPS 140-2 validated encryption.

- Cardholder data tokenized locally before transit to Azure.

- All DevOps pipelines configured to restrict deployments to pre-approved templates and locations.

## Use Case: Energy Sector with NERC CIP Regulations

### Scenario

A utility provider managing power generation and smart grid operations needed to improve data analytics and patching automation while conforming to NERC CIP (Critical Infrastructure Protection) standards.

### Hybrid Architecture

- **Azure Arc-enabled servers** onboarded substations and field devices.

- **Azure Monitor** used to collect telemetry across environments.
- **Azure Automation** enabled scheduled patching and compliance scanning using **Hybrid Runbook Workers**.
- Data replication implemented via **Azure Data Factory** for analytics workloads in Azure Synapse.

```
# Schedule patch deployment on Arc-enabled servers

Start-AzAutomationRunbook -AutomationAccountName "ComplianceAutomation" `

-Name "PatchManagement" `

-Parameters @{"TargetGroup" = "SubstationServers"; "Window" = "02:00-04:00"}
```

**Results**

- Reduced patching time by 50%.
- Maintained air-gapped environments with secure update mechanisms.
- Enabled executive-level dashboards to demonstrate compliance posture.

## Governance and Risk Management

To support regulatory audits and internal compliance, enterprises implement comprehensive risk management frameworks across hybrid environments:

- **Azure Blueprints** for consistent landing zone deployments
- **Azure Defender** for threat detection in hybrid infrastructure
- **Key Vault** for centralized secret and certificate management
- **Azure Purview** for data classification and lineage tracking
- **Log Analytics** and **Sentinel** for audit logging and incident response

## Sample Blueprint Artifact: Enforcing Regulatory Tags

```
{
"policyDefinitionId": "/providers/Microsoft.Authorization/policyDefinitions/requireTag",
"parameters": {
"tagName": { "value": "ComplianceOwner" }
},
"dependsOn": []
}
```

Apply this blueprint across all subscriptions and Arc resources to ensure traceability and ownership.

## Recommendations for Regulated Environments

1. **Start with a compliance gap assessment** using tools like Azure Security Center and Compliance Manager.
2. **Define data boundaries** using Private Link, ExpressRoute, and local data residency options.
3. **Use Azure Arc to bring non-Azure resources under governance**.
4. **Encrypt everything**—at rest, in transit, and in use.
5. **Retain logs** according to industry-specific retention periods (e.g., 7 years for HIPAA).
6. **Implement RBAC and Conditional Access** with continuous evaluation policies.
7. **Audit DevOps practices** to prevent policy drift and unauthorized deployments.
8. **Conduct quarterly tabletop exercises** to validate incident response readiness.

## Conclusion

Regulated industries cannot compromise on security, privacy, or compliance—and they don't have to. Hybrid cloud with Microsoft Azure provides a robust and flexible architecture for these sectors to innovate without breaching trust or violating mandates. Whether it's healthcare, finance, energy, or public services, hybrid cloud enables organizations to modernize, automate, and scale securely—while maintaining absolute control over sensitive assets and workloads. With the right planning, tooling, and governance, hybrid cloud becomes not a risk—but a powerful enabler of digital transformation in even the most highly regulated environments.

# Disaster Recovery and Business Continuity Plans

Disaster Recovery (DR) and Business Continuity Planning (BCP) are foundational pillars of enterprise IT strategy—especially in hybrid cloud environments. The goal is to ensure that critical services remain operational, or are restored swiftly, in the event of failures such as cyberattacks, hardware faults, power outages, natural disasters, or human error. For organizations operating across both on-premises and cloud infrastructures, crafting a unified DR/BCP framework is essential.

This section explores DR and BCP best practices, design patterns, Azure-native tools, real-world hybrid DR scenarios, and how to validate readiness through testing and automation. It also outlines how hybrid resiliency is achieved without compromising compliance, performance, or cost-effectiveness.

## Core Concepts of Disaster Recovery and BCP

- **Disaster Recovery (DR)** focuses on restoring IT systems and data after a disruption.

- **Business Continuity (BCP)** encompasses broader organizational preparedness, including personnel, processes, and physical locations.

- **Recovery Time Objective (RTO)**: The targeted duration to restore a service.

- **Recovery Point Objective (RPO)**: The acceptable amount of data loss measured in time.

- **High Availability (HA)**: Ensures service continuity during localized failures, not just after disasters.

A hybrid cloud DR plan must take into account:

- On-premises infrastructure and dependencies
- Cloud-native services and PaaS workloads
- Networking (connectivity between sites, VPN, ExpressRoute)
- Authentication and identity services
- Data replication and backup strategies
- Application interdependencies

## Azure Services for DR and BCP

Azure provides several tools and services to support hybrid DR and BCP strategies:

- **Azure Site Recovery (ASR)**: Replicates workloads from on-premises or other clouds to Azure.
- **Azure Backup**: Provides long-term, secure data backups for VMs, files, SQL databases, and more.
- **Azure Files with Geo-Redundant Storage (GRS)**: Ensures file share resiliency.
- **Azure Availability Zones**: Enables intra-region redundancy.

- **Azure Traffic Manager / Front Door**: Automates global failover for applications.
- **Azure Arc**: Enables DR governance for non-Azure resources.

## DR Strategy: Tiered Application Recovery

A common best practice is to classify applications into tiers based on business criticality:

- **Tier 0**: Identity and Access (e.g., Active Directory, Azure AD Connect)
- **Tier 1**: Mission-critical services (e.g., ERP, payment gateways)
- **Tier 2**: Important but less time-sensitive services (e.g., HR systems)
- **Tier 3**: Archival, batch processing, dev/test environments

RTO and RPO targets vary by tier. For example, Tier 0 services may require <15 minutes RTO, while Tier 3 services might tolerate 24–48 hours.

## Scenario 1: On-Premises to Azure DR with Site Recovery

### Context

A logistics company hosts critical applications on a private data center and wants a cloud-based DR strategy without building a secondary site.

**Solution**

- **Azure Site Recovery** replicates VMs to a paired Azure region.
- Failover is triggered manually or automatically based on thresholds.
- **Azure Automation** and **Runbooks** reconfigure DNS and load balancers post-failover.
- **Azure Monitor** tracks replication health and provides alerting.

```
# Enable replication of a VM to Azure

Set-AzRecoveryServicesAsrReplicationProtectedItem -
ProtectionContainer "onPremContainer" `

-ReplicationProtectedItem "vm-erp01" `

-RecoveryAzureStorageAccountId
"/subscriptions/{id}/resourceGroups/{rg}/providers/
Microsoft.Storage/storageAccounts/recoverystorage"
```

**Result**

- Reduced DR infrastructure costs by 60%
- Monthly failover tests conducted with no service interruption
- Achieved an RTO of under 30 minutes for mission-critical VMs

## Scenario 2: DR for Azure Stack HCI Workloads

### Context

A regional healthcare provider runs patient-facing applications on **Azure Stack HCI** to ensure low-latency access and data residency.

### Hybrid DR Approach

- **Azure Backup** used for VM-level backups stored in Azure GRS vaults.
- ASR used to replicate only Tier 1 VMs to Azure.
- **ExpressRoute** ensures encrypted connectivity between the HCI cluster and Azure.
- **Azure Arc** enables management and policy enforcement across both environments.

### Operational Plan

- Daily incremental backups + weekly full backup
- Monthly full DR simulation in staging subscription
- Alert-based triggers configured in Azure Monitor to initiate escalation workflows

### Key Takeaways

- Hybrid DR maintains compliance with regional health data regulations
- Staff can access systems within 20 minutes of localized failure

- DR documentation automated and stored in **Azure DevOps Wiki**

## Scenario 3: DR for Multi-Tier Applications

### Context

An e-commerce company hosts its web app frontend on Azure App Services and backend on a mix of Azure SQL, on-prem databases, and internal APIs.

### Strategy

- Use **Azure Front Door** to direct traffic between primary and backup frontends.
- Replicate on-prem data to **Azure SQL Managed Instance** using transactional replication.
- APIs containerized and deployed redundantly in **Azure Kubernetes Service** and on-prem.
- DR playbooks stored in **Azure Automation Account** and executed via runbooks.

### Failover Workflow

1. Detection of outage via Azure Monitor alert
2. DNS updated to point traffic to Azure-hosted backup site
3. Scripts re-point APIs to Azure SQL
4. Load test validation run to confirm readiness

### Benefits

- RTO of 10 minutes for the entire stack

- Seamless failover tested quarterly with zero user complaints
- Improved DevOps alignment with BCP through CI/CD triggers

## DR Testing and Validation

A DR plan is only as good as its testing schedule. Azure enables automated and manual testing options:

- **ASR Test Failover**: Non-disruptive validation using isolated virtual networks.
- **Azure DevTest Labs**: Simulate real-world outages.
- **Chaos Engineering**: Introduce controlled faults to validate resilience (e.g., using Azure Chaos Studio).
- **Audit Reports**: Use **Azure Monitor Logs** and **Workbooks** to generate evidence for compliance audits.

```
// Query for DR test execution logs
AzureDiagnostics
| where Category == "SiteRecovery" and OperationName == "TestFailover"
| project Resource, ActivityId, Status, TimeGenerated
```

## Compliance and Documentation

Most industry regulations require formalized, auditable BCP plans. Azure helps fulfill these requirements:

- Store all runbooks, diagrams, and recovery steps in **Azure DevOps**, **SharePoint**, or **Confluence**.

- Use **Azure Blueprints** to define compliant infrastructure templates.

- Automate evidence collection via **Log Analytics** and **Sentinel**.

- Include DR planning as part of regular internal and external compliance assessments.

## Automation for DR Execution

Automation accelerates response time and reduces human error during high-pressure scenarios:

- **Azure Automation** Runbooks for post-failover tasks (e.g., IP reassignments, DNS updates)

- **Logic Apps** for alert-based triggers and ITSM notifications

- **PowerShell** / **Azure CLI** scripts stored in GitHub with versioning and audit trails

```
# Runbook example: update DNS record

$dnsZone = Get-AzDnsZone -Name "company.com"

Set-AzDnsRecordSet -ResourceGroupName "RG" -ZoneName $dnsZone.Name -Name "app" -RecordType A -IPv4Address "10.10.10.50"
```

## Cost Optimization

DR infrastructure must be cost-effective. Azure enables:

- **Pay-as-you-go** storage and compute for replica VMs
- **Auto-shutdown policies** for test environments
- **Azure Reserved Instances** for always-on DR resources
- **Storage tiering** to archive infrequently accessed backups

Balance between cost and recovery speed by choosing hot, warm, or cold standby models:

- **Hot**: Always-on duplicates (fastest, most expensive)
- **Warm**: Pre-configured systems (moderate cost, RTO ~minutes)
- **Cold**: Backup only, restored on demand (cheapest, longest RTO)

## Best Practices

1. **Map dependencies** using Azure Resource Graph and service maps
2. **Document and version control all DR plans**
3. **Conduct quarterly DR drills** with full cross-team involvement
4. **Review RTO and RPO targets** annually against business requirements
5. **Secure backups and DR data** using encryption and Key Vault

6. **Monitor replication health and alert on drift**
7. **Include identity services** (AD, DNS) in DR planning
8. **Build dashboards** to track DR readiness in Azure Workbooks

## Conclusion

Disaster recovery and business continuity are non-negotiable elements of modern hybrid cloud architecture. Azure equips organizations with the tools and services necessary to build, test, and execute robust DR strategies across cloud and on-prem environments. By aligning DR/BCP with automation, observability, and governance, enterprises can ensure resilience against disruption, compliance with regulations, and continuity of critical operations—no matter the challenge.

# Lessons Learned from Hybrid Cloud Implementations

Organizations across every industry are embracing hybrid cloud strategies to modernize infrastructure, improve agility, and drive innovation—without losing control over critical assets. While hybrid deployments bring tremendous benefits, they also introduce operational, architectural, and cultural complexities that can only be fully understood through real-world experience.

This section captures the lessons learned from numerous hybrid cloud implementations using Microsoft Azure. These insights are drawn from failures, successes, and everything in between—focusing on practical advice that can help future adopters avoid common pitfalls, maximize ROI, and build resilient hybrid environments that scale.

## 1. Begin with Governance and Identity

One of the most common mistakes in hybrid projects is treating identity, access control, and governance as an afterthought. In hybrid environments, managing multiple identity providers or fragmented RBAC (role-based access control) leads to increased attack surfaces, shadow IT, and compliance risks.

**What Worked:**

- **Deploy Azure AD Connect early** to synchronize identities between on-prem AD and Azure AD.
- **Adopt Conditional Access Policies** with MFA to protect access to both environments.
- Use **Privileged Identity Management (PIM)** for just-in-time access to sensitive resources.
- **Standardize role definitions and scopes** across on-prem and Azure resources.

**What Didn't:**

- Delaying identity synchronization until after migration introduced authentication mismatches.
- Hardcoding credentials in scripts or configs led to audit failures.

```
# Example: Assigning a role to a user for Arc-enabled resource

New-AzRoleAssignment -ObjectId $userId -RoleDefinitionName "Contributor" -Scope "/subscriptions/$subscriptionId/
```

resourceGroups/$rgName/providers/Microsoft.HybridCompute/machines/arc-server01"

## 2. Start Small, Scale Strategically

Many enterprises attempted massive hybrid rollouts without first validating architecture patterns or assessing organizational readiness. This often led to extended timelines and budget overruns.

**What Worked:**

- **Pilot programs** involving 1–2 business units helped refine automation, monitoring, and support models.
- Choosing non-critical systems for initial hybrid migration allowed safe experimentation.
- **MVP-style deployments** enabled rapid feedback loops and executive buy-in.

**What Didn't:**

- "Big bang" migrations overwhelmed operations teams.
- Neglecting change management led to internal resistance.

## 3. Network and Connectivity Planning is Critical

Hybrid cloud success hinges on a resilient, secure, and well-architected network. Many issues in early hybrid deployments stemmed from assumptions about bandwidth, latency, DNS routing, and overlapping IP address spaces.

**What Worked:**

- Using **ExpressRoute** or **VPN Gateway** for encrypted, low-latency connections.
- Implementing **Azure Private Link** to access services without traversing the public internet.
- Establishing **DNS zones and resolvers** with clear routing rules between environments.

**What Didn't:**

- Poorly designed IP schemes caused subnet conflicts and hindered connectivity.
- Relying solely on public endpoints introduced security gaps.

## 4. Monitor Everything, Not Just the Cloud

Observability should span both cloud and on-prem infrastructure. Many organizations initially focused their monitoring efforts on Azure services, neglecting legacy systems, resulting in blind spots during outages or performance issues.

**What Worked:**

- Deploying **Azure Monitor agents** and integrating with on-prem tools like SCOM and Prometheus.
- Centralizing logs via **Log Analytics Workspaces** and normalizing telemetry formats.

- Building shared **Azure Workbooks** to visualize hybrid metrics and KPIs.

**What Didn't:**

- Lack of unified dashboards caused duplicate effort and delayed troubleshooting.
- Not collecting diagnostic logs from on-prem resources led to audit and compliance gaps.

```
// Example: Monitor CPU usage across hybrid servers

Perf

| where ObjectName == "Processor" and CounterName == "% Processor Time"

| summarize avg(CounterValue) by Computer, bin(TimeGenerated, 5m)
```

## 5. Automate for Resilience, Not Just Efficiency

Automation is often framed as a way to reduce manual effort—but in hybrid environments, it's just as much about enforcing consistency and enabling rapid recovery.

**What Worked:**

- Automating common remediation tasks (e.g., restarting services, freeing disk space).
- Using **Azure Automation**, **Logic Apps**, and **GitHub Actions** to handle hybrid orchestration.

- Standardizing Infrastructure as Code (IaC) with **Bicep** or **Terraform**, even for Arc-enabled resources.

**What Didn't:**

- Ad-hoc scripting without version control created maintenance nightmares.
- Failing to build idempotent workflows led to errors during re-runs.

```
# GitHub Actions workflow deploying hybrid app to Arc-enabled server

jobs:

deploy:

runs-on: self-hosted

steps:

- name: Checkout

uses: actions/checkout@v3

- name: Deploy App

run: |

Copy-Item -Path ".\build\app.zip" -Destination "\\arc-server01\apps"

Invoke-Command -ComputerName "arc-server01" -ScriptBlock { Expand-Archive -Path "C:\apps\app.zip" -DestinationPath "C:\apps\app" }
```

## 6. Legacy Doesn’t Mean Untouchable

A common misconception is that legacy systems can’t participate in hybrid architectures. Many organizations succeeded by wrapping, refactoring, or containerizing legacy workloads rather than rewriting them.

**What Worked:**

- Using **API gateways** (e.g., Azure API Management) to expose legacy services securely.
- Deploying **Azure Arc-enabled Kubernetes** for sidecar patterns and incremental modernization.
- Containerizing legacy .NET apps and hosting them on **Azure Stack HCI**.

**What Didn't:**

- Avoiding legacy modernization altogether led to ballooning technical debt.
- Failing to isolate legacy apps increased lateral movement risks during security incidents.

## 7. Build for Failover from Day One

Disaster Recovery (DR) and Business Continuity Planning (BCP) are often bolted on after hybrid systems go live. This leaves teams scrambling when incidents occur.

**What Worked:**

- Architecting DR into every deployment using **Azure Site Recovery**, **Azure Backup**, and **Traffic Manager**.
- Automating DR drills using **Azure Automation** and tracking via **Workbooks**.
- Establishing clearly documented **runbooks** and escalation workflows.

**What Didn't:**

- Relying solely on manual recovery processes during outages.
- Lack of DR validation led to extended downtime in early production failures.

## 8. Tagging and Metadata are Game-Changers

Tags and naming conventions are often underestimated until cost, governance, or access issues arise.

**What Worked:**

- Enforcing **mandatory tags** via **Azure Policy** (e.g., Environment, Owner, CostCenter).
- Aligning tags with **billing reports** and **access scopes**.
- Using metadata in queries and dashboards for more meaningful insights.

```
{
"if": {
"field": "tags['Environment']",
"equals": "[parameters('expectedEnvironment')]"
},
"then": {
"effect": "auditIfNotExists"
}
}
```

**What Didn't:**

- Free-form or inconsistent tags caused data sprawl.
- No enforcement led to orphaned or miscategorized resources.

## 9. Cloud Skills ≠ Hybrid Skills

Even seasoned cloud teams found hybrid environments challenging due to the need to integrate legacy systems, physical infrastructure, and specialized tooling.

**What Worked:**

- Cross-training teams on both Azure and traditional systems.

- Embedding site reliability engineering (SRE) practices across teams.
- Creating **shared playbooks** and **shadowing sessions** between cloud and infra teams.

**What Didn't:**

- Assuming cloud-native experience translates directly to hybrid.
- No investment in upskilling led to slow adoption and low confidence.

## 10. Hybrid is a Strategy, Not a Shortcut

Some organizations treated hybrid cloud as a temporary stepping stone to full cloud adoption. Others embraced it as a long-term strategy. Both approaches work—what matters is intentionality.

**What Worked:**

- Aligning hybrid architecture with **business outcomes**, not just technical feasibility.
- Defining **hybrid maturity models** with KPIs for governance, operations, and modernization.
- Continually reassessing hybrid footprint based on **cost**, **compliance**, and **user experience**.

**What Didn't:**

- Treating hybrid as a stop-gap led to inconsistent investment and tool fragmentation.
- No roadmap = no direction.

## Conclusion

Hybrid cloud isn't just about bridging environments—it's about bridging eras, people, and processes. The lessons learned across real-world deployments highlight that hybrid success is less about tools and more about culture, planning, and execution. By applying the principles of governance, automation, observability, and gradual modernization, enterprises can harness the best of both worlds: the innovation of cloud and the control of on-premises infrastructure. Hybrid cloud is not a compromise—it's a competitive advantage, when done right.

# Chapter 10: Future-Proofing Your Hybrid Strategy

## Emerging Technologies and Trends

As hybrid cloud adoption matures, enterprises must continually adapt their architectures, processes, and skillsets to remain competitive and resilient. The pace of technological advancement shows no signs of slowing—driven by artificial intelligence, edge computing, quantum innovation, advanced networking, and zero trust security. These trends are not only shaping how hybrid clouds are built and managed, but also redefining what is possible across industries.

This section examines the most impactful emerging technologies and trends that are shaping the future of hybrid cloud. It provides strategic insights into how organizations can harness these advancements to build flexible, intelligent, and future-ready hybrid environments using Microsoft Azure's ecosystem and capabilities.

### 1. AI and Machine Learning at the Edge

Edge AI is quickly transforming the hybrid landscape. Rather than sending all data to the cloud for analysis, workloads such as real-time video analytics, predictive maintenance, and anomaly detection are increasingly processed locally on edge devices—often powered by embedded AI chips or GPU-enabled infrastructure.

**Key Trends:**

- **AI inference at the edge** using services like **Azure Stack Edge**.

- **Model training in the cloud**, then deployment to edge for execution.
- **Integration with Azure Machine Learning** for lifecycle management of models.

**Benefits:**

- Reduced latency and bandwidth usage.
- Improved data privacy and compliance.
- Faster response times for mission-critical systems.

**Example:**

A manufacturing plant uses Azure Stack Edge to run trained models that detect anomalies in production line images. These models are deployed and updated using Azure Machine Learning pipelines and Azure IoT Edge runtime.

```
# IoT Edge deployment manifest for an AI module

modules:

aiModule:

version: "1.0"

type: "docker"

status: "running"

restartPolicy: "always"

settings:
```

image: contoso.azurecr.io/image-detection-ai:latest

createOptions: {}

## 2. Confidential Computing

Confidential computing is revolutionizing data security by allowing sensitive data to be processed in a secure, hardware-backed Trusted Execution Environment (TEE). Even cloud providers cannot access data inside TEEs, making this ideal for regulated industries.

**Azure Technologies:**

- **Azure Confidential VMs** using AMD SEV-SNP.
- **Azure Confidential Containers** running on Kubernetes with enclave support.
- **Azure SQL Always Encrypted with secure enclaves** for data-in-use protection.

**Scenarios:**

- Protecting IP in financial algorithms.
- Running analytics on encrypted healthcare datasets.
- Collaborating across companies without exposing proprietary data.

**Strategic Consideration:**

Organizations planning hybrid architectures should future-proof by identifying sensitive workloads that may benefit from confidential computing, and align data governance strategies accordingly.

## 3. Serverless and Event-Driven Hybrid Architectures

Serverless computing, already a staple in the cloud, is making its way into hybrid setups. Organizations can now build reactive, event-driven systems that run across cloud and edge, leveraging **Azure Functions**, **Logic Apps**, and **Event Grid**.

**Patterns:**

- Use **Azure Functions** to extend legacy apps with new cloud-based capabilities.
- Route on-prem event streams (e.g., IoT sensor data) into cloud workflows using **Event Grid** and **Service Bus**.
- Implement **event-sourced systems** that support analytics, alerts, and actions in real-time.

**Example:**

A retailer captures in-store transactions and routes them via Azure Arc-enabled Kubernetes into Event Grid, triggering real-time inventory updates and customer behavior insights.

```
# Create an Event Grid subscription to trigger a Logic App

New-AzEventGridSubscription -ResourceGroupName "RetailRG"
`
```

-TopicName "transaction-events" `

-EndpointType "WebHook" `

-Endpoint "https://logicapp-contoso.azurewebsites.net/api/transactions"

## 4. 5G and Advanced Networking

The rollout of 5G is enabling ultra-low-latency, high-bandwidth connectivity, unlocking new use cases in autonomous vehicles, telemedicine, and immersive experiences. Azure's hybrid cloud strategy incorporates these advances via:

- **Azure Private 5G Core** for deploying private cellular networks.
- **Azure Network Function Manager** to orchestrate virtual network functions (VNFs).
- **Integration with edge appliances and SD-WAN** for optimized traffic management.

**Impact:**

- Enhanced capabilities at remote/branch locations.
- Real-time media processing and AR/VR in field services.
- Secure, isolated networks for industrial use cases.

## 5. Multi-Cloud and Poly-Cloud Adoption

Though Azure may be the primary cloud, many enterprises adopt multi-cloud strategies for risk mitigation, cost efficiency, or regulatory compliance. Hybrid cloud architectures must now accommodate:

- Unified visibility and governance across cloud providers.
- Interoperable APIs and data exchange.
- Standardized identity and policy enforcement.

**Azure Capabilities:**

- **Azure Arc** extends governance to AWS and GCP.
- **Azure Purview** scans and catalogs data across environments.
- **Azure Lighthouse** allows service providers to manage multiple customer tenants.

**Best Practice:**

Design hybrid architectures to be **cloud-agnostic**, favoring containerized workloads, IaC, and open standards like OIDC and OAuth2.

## 6. Sustainability and Green IT

Sustainability is becoming a board-level priority. Hybrid environments must factor in energy usage, carbon footprint, and resource optimization.

**Azure Innovations:**

- **Microsoft Sustainability Manager** provides dashboards and impact assessments.
- **Carbon-aware computing** lets you shift workloads to greener regions or timeframes.
- **Right-sizing tools** help optimize resource usage across on-prem and Azure.

**Actionable Tips:**

- Use Azure Advisor to identify idle resources.
- Archive cold data using **Azure Blob Storage Archive Tier.**
- Replace aging on-prem infrastructure with energy-efficient Azure Stack HCI clusters.

## 7. Quantum Computing and Hybrid Simulation

While still emerging, quantum computing will eventually transform optimization, cryptography, and materials science. Azure's hybrid readiness includes:

- **Azure Quantum** for developing and testing quantum algorithms.
- Hybrid workloads combining quantum and classical compute (e.g., AI + Q#).
- Secure APIs for integrating quantum workloads with existing business processes.

Though not immediately actionable for most organizations, building awareness and future skills in this domain is a valuable long-term investment.

## 8. Autonomous Operations with AI and AIOps

Modern hybrid environments are too complex to manage manually. The rise of **AIOps** (Artificial Intelligence for IT Operations) automates detection, diagnosis, and resolution of issues using machine learning.

**Tools:**

- **Azure Monitor Insights** and **Smart Detection.**
- **Log Analytics Machine Learning-based queries.**
- **Microsoft Copilot for Security and Azure** (emerging capability).

**Example:**

An Arc-enabled server with performance degradation automatically triggers an Azure Function to collect logs, analyzes patterns via Log Analytics ML, and proposes a resolution within Microsoft Sentinel.

```
Perf
| where ObjectName == "Processor" and CounterName == "% Processor Time"
| summarize avg(CounterValue) by bin(TimeGenerated, 1h)
| extend AlertSeverity = iif(avg_CounterValue > 90, "Critical", "Normal")
```

## 9. Decentralized Identity and Zero Trust

As hybrid grows, perimeter-based security models fail. Organizations must adopt **Zero Trust** principles and **Decentralized Identity** frameworks.

**Key Technologies:**

- **Azure AD Conditional Access with risk-based policies.**
- **Verifiable Credentials** and **Decentralized Identity (DID)**.
- **Azure Key Vault + Managed Identities** for secure app authentication.

**Strategy:**

Design hybrid applications to assume breach. Enforce continuous verification of users, devices, and workloads—no matter where they reside.

## 10. Intelligent DevOps and Platform Engineering

DevOps is evolving into **Platform Engineering**—where internal teams provide reusable platforms and tools for hybrid developers.

**Trends:**

- **Backstage** and **Developer Portals** for hybrid service catalogs.
- **GitOps + Azure Arc** for secure, auditable deployment pipelines.
- **Cross-platform observability** as a service using OpenTelemetry.

**Practice:**

Build hybrid platform teams that enable, not control. Provide abstraction layers (e.g., templates, policies, GitOps pipelines) that support secure and scalable hybrid development.

## Conclusion

Future-proofing your hybrid strategy means more than reacting to today's needs—it's about architecting for what's coming. Whether it's edge AI, confidential computing, quantum simulation, or zero trust, the path ahead demands adaptability, foresight, and innovation. Microsoft Azure's hybrid ecosystem is uniquely positioned to support these transformations. By embracing emerging technologies early and aligning them with business goals, organizations can ensure their hybrid cloud strategy is not just reactive—but visionary, resilient, and truly future-ready.

# Evolving Hybrid Strategies with AI and Edge Computing

As enterprise technology rapidly evolves, two of the most transformative forces reshaping hybrid cloud strategies are **Artificial Intelligence** (**AI**) and **Edge Computing**. Together, they unlock a new era of intelligent, real-time applications distributed across on-premises environments, public cloud infrastructure, and edge locations. This convergence empowers organizations to process data closer to where it's generated, make decisions in milliseconds, and continuously learn and adapt using cloud-scale intelligence.

In this section, we explore how AI and edge computing are redefining hybrid cloud architectures. We cover architectural principles, use cases, deployment patterns, integration with Microsoft Azure's hybrid toolchain, and real-world strategies for scaling AI and edge in regulated, distributed, or latency-sensitive environments.

## The AI + Edge Paradigm in Hybrid Cloud

Traditionally, enterprises have centralized data in cloud-based systems for processing and insight generation. However, with the rise of edge locations—such as factories, hospitals, vehicles, and remote offices—this approach is increasingly insufficient.

Key drivers of edge AI in hybrid environments:

- **Latency**: Real-time decisions cannot wait for cloud round-trips.
- **Bandwidth**: High-volume data (e.g., video, telemetry) is expensive to transmit.

- **Data Sovereignty**: Regulations often require local processing.

- **Resiliency**: Critical systems must function even if disconnected from the cloud.

AI at the edge ensures these constraints are met while still benefiting from the cloud's scale for training, orchestration, and long-term storage.

## Core Components of Azure AI + Edge Hybrid Architecture

To build AI-powered hybrid systems, Microsoft Azure offers a suite of services and integrations:

- **Azure Stack Edge**: An appliance that runs containers and VMs locally with GPU support.

- **Azure IoT Edge**: Enables the deployment of AI models and microservices to edge devices.

- **Azure Machine Learning (AML)**: Supports model training, versioning, and deployment across cloud and edge.

- **Azure Arc**: Brings cloud-native operations, governance, and GitOps to on-prem and edge compute.

- **Azure Cognitive Services**: Pretrained models for vision, speech, and language, with offline containerized options.

## Architecture Pattern: Train in the Cloud, Infer at the Edge

This is the dominant architecture pattern for hybrid AI workloads.

1. **Model Training**: Performed in Azure using powerful compute (e.g., Azure Machine Learning with GPU clusters).
2. **Model Packaging**: Once validated, models are converted into containerized formats.
3. **Edge Deployment**: Models are pushed to edge devices using Azure IoT Edge or Arc-enabled Kubernetes.
4. **Real-Time Inference**: Local devices use the model to infer outcomes from sensor data, video, etc.
5. **Telemetry + Feedback Loop**: Results are optionally sent back to the cloud for retraining or analytics.

```
# Example: Register and deploy a model with Azure ML to an IoT Edge device

from azureml.core import Workspace, Model

from azureml.core.webservice import AciWebservice, Webservice

ws = Workspace.from_config()

model = Model.register(model_path="model.pkl", model_name="predictor", workspace=ws)

inference_config = InferenceConfig(entry_script="score.py", environment=env)

deployment_config = AciWebservice.deploy_configuration(cpu_cores=1, memory_gb=1)
```

```
service = Model.deploy(workspace=ws, name="predictor-service", models=[model],

inference_config=inference_config, deployment_config=deployment_config)

service.wait_for_deployment(show_output=True)
```

## Real-World Use Cases of AI + Edge in Hybrid Cloud

### 1. Manufacturing and Predictive Maintenance

- **Challenge**: Unplanned equipment downtime leads to millions in losses.
- **Solution**: Deploy ML models trained on vibration, temperature, and acoustic data to Azure Stack Edge in the plant. Models detect anomalies in real time and alert technicians.
- **Benefit**: Increased uptime, reduced maintenance costs, and local compliance.

### 2. Healthcare and Medical Imaging

- **Challenge**: MRI and CT image processing is bandwidth-intensive and latency-sensitive.
- **Solution**: AI models for image classification and segmentation run on edge hardware in hospitals. Inferences are made in seconds, and only results are sent to cloud-based systems.

- **Benefit**: Faster diagnoses, improved patient outcomes, compliance with data residency rules.

**3. Retail and Customer Analytics**

- **Challenge**: Understanding customer behavior in stores requires real-time video analytics.

- **Solution**: Cameras stream video to local Azure Stack Edge devices. Models detect foot traffic, dwell times, and sentiment. Insights are aggregated in Azure Synapse for trend analysis.

- **Benefit**: Enhanced merchandising decisions and customer engagement.

**4. Energy and Smart Grid Optimization**

- **Challenge**: Grid systems must react to energy demand and faults instantly.

- **Solution**: AI models run on edge nodes in substations to detect voltage anomalies and forecast consumption patterns.

- **Benefit**: Improved energy efficiency, grid stability, and outage prevention.

## Operationalizing AI at the Edge

Deploying models is only one part of the puzzle. True AI operationalization (MLOps) at the edge involves:

- **Version control** for models and inference logic

- **Monitoring inference performance and drift**
- **Automated retraining pipelines** triggered by cloud telemetry
- **Secure deployment pipelines** using GitOps with Azure Arc

Azure Machine Learning supports **end-to-end MLOps pipelines**, including data labeling, experimentation, CI/CD integration, and deployment management across environments.

```
# Example GitHub Actions workflow for edge model deployment

jobs:

deploy_model:

runs-on: ubuntu-latest

steps:

- uses: actions/checkout@v3

- name: Package model

run: |

docker build -t edge-ai-model .

- name: Push to Azure Container Registry

run: |

az acr login—name myacr

docker tag edge-ai-model myacr.azurecr.io/edge-ai-model:latest
```

docker push myacr.azurecr.io/edge-ai-model:latest

- name: Deploy to IoT Edge

run: |

az iot edge deployment create—config-id modeldeploy—hub-name MyIoTHub \

—content ./deployment.json—target-condition "tags.location='store01'"

## Governance and Security Considerations

Hybrid AI and edge workloads operate outside traditional data centers and must address specific security concerns:

- **Device identity and attestation**: Use Azure IoT Hub Device Provisioning Service.
- **Secure edge runtime**: Isolate workloads using container boundaries.
- **Model integrity**: Ensure signed, tamper-evident model packages.
- **Compliance enforcement**: Apply Azure Policy for Arc-enabled edge nodes.

Azure Arc and Defender for IoT/Edge help enforce consistent governance across these distributed environments, ensuring visibility, control, and compliance even in offline or partially connected scenarios.

## Designing for Offline Scenarios

Edge deployments must handle intermittent connectivity. Best practices include:

- **Local caching of models and data schemas**
- **Store-and-forward telemetry** using Azure IoT Hub offline buffers
- **Graceful degradation** of functionality based on available compute or power
- **Deferred sync** strategies for delayed model updates or logs

## Cost Optimization Strategies

While edge computing reduces data egress and latency, costs must still be managed:

- Use **Azure Percept** or low-power edge devices where GPU is not required.
- Offload non-critical inference tasks to cloud-based APIs.
- Monitor and optimize container sizes and model complexity.
- Use **Azure Reservations** and **Edge Zones** for predictable infrastructure pricing.

## Future Trends and Evolving Models

The AI + Edge space continues to evolve with trends such as:

- **Federated Learning**: Train models across edge devices without centralizing data.

- **TinyML**: Run models on microcontrollers (e.g., for wearables, IoT sensors).

- **Neural Architecture Search (NAS)**: Automatically create optimal models for edge hardware.

- **LLM at the Edge**: Running compressed transformer models on-premises for natural language interactions (e.g., copilots for field technicians).

Microsoft's investments in **OpenAI models, ONNX Runtime**, and **Azure Cognitive Services containers** ensure that hybrid cloud users can adopt these advancements as they mature.

## Best Practices for AI + Edge in Hybrid Strategy

1. **Use a centralized ML platform (AML)** for lifecycle management across environments.
2. **Validate models** in sandboxed edge environments before production rollout.
3. **Align model updates with CI/CD** to ensure consistent behavior.
4. **Design for failure**: Edge devices must operate autonomously if disconnected.
5. **Apply zero trust principles**: Authenticate all devices, users, and services.
6. **Leverage standard protocols** (MQTT, HTTPS) for interoperability.
7. **Enable observability**: Log model usage, performance, and drift metrics.

## Conclusion

The integration of AI and edge computing into hybrid cloud architectures represents a leap forward in what enterprises can achieve. It transforms static infrastructure into intelligent systems capable of autonomous decision-making, local optimization, and adaptive performance. Microsoft Azure provides the tools to not only experiment with these capabilities, but to operationalize them at scale.

To evolve your hybrid strategy, you must think beyond just connecting clouds and data centers—toward building an intelligent, decentralized fabric that runs wherever your business operates. Edge AI is not the future. It's here. And those who adopt it today will define the standards of tomorrow.

# Skills and Team Structures for Hybrid Success

The shift to hybrid cloud architecture is not just a technological evolution—it is a people and process transformation. As organizations extend their workloads across on-premises, public cloud, and edge environments, the required skills and team structures must also evolve. Traditional IT roles are merging with cloud-centric disciplines, and cross-functional collaboration has become essential to maintain agility, compliance, and operational excellence.

This section explores the competencies needed to thrive in hybrid environments, the team structures that support effective execution, and strategies for upskilling and talent development. Drawing from real-world implementations, it outlines how to build high-performing teams that are aligned with the principles of modern hybrid cloud architectures powered by Microsoft Azure.

## The Changing Role of IT in the Hybrid Era

Legacy IT teams were often organized around infrastructure domains—network, storage, servers, and applications. Cloud adoption introduced roles such as cloud architects, DevOps engineers, and platform engineers. In hybrid environments, these roles blend, and new responsibilities emerge that span both physical and virtual infrastructure.

**Key Shifts:**

- From **infrastructure management** to **platform enablement**
- From **reactive operations** to **proactive optimization and automation**
- From **siloed roles** to **cross-functional collaboration**
- From **manual provisioning** to **Infrastructure as Code and GitOps**

## Core Skills for Hybrid Cloud Professionals

To succeed in hybrid cloud operations, teams need a broad and adaptable skillset. Below are the core competencies grouped by functional areas:

**1. Infrastructure and Platform Engineering**

- Deep understanding of **Azure Arc**, **Azure Stack HCI**, and **ExpressRoute**

- Familiarity with **virtualization (VMware, Hyper-V)** and **container orchestration (AKS, Arc Kubernetes)**
- Network routing, DNS, and hybrid connectivity troubleshooting

**2. Cloud Architecture and Governance**

- Azure Resource Manager (ARM), Bicep, and Terraform for hybrid deployments
- Azure Policy, Blueprints, and RBAC for compliance enforcement
- Cost control and resource optimization strategies

**3. DevOps and Automation**

- CI/CD pipelines using **Azure DevOps**, **GitHub Actions**, or **Jenkins**
- Azure CLI, PowerShell, and REST API scripting
- Automated runbooks, Logic Apps, and workflow orchestration

```
# Azure DevOps pipeline snippet for hybrid deployment
jobs:
- job: DeployToArc
pool:
name: OnPremAgentPool
```

steps:

- task: PowerShell@2

inputs:

targetType: 'inline'

script: |

az login—identity

az deployment group create—resource-group HybridRG—template-file main.bicep

**4. Security and Compliance**

- Zero Trust principles and secure identity management with Azure AD
- Familiarity with regulatory frameworks (HIPAA, PCI-DSS, GDPR)
- Incident response planning and SIEM/SOAR integration (Azure Sentinel)

**5. Data and AI**

- Data ingestion and hybrid pipelines with Azure Data Factory
- Model deployment via Azure Machine Learning to Arc-enabled endpoints

- Understanding of edge analytics and data retention policies

### 6. Monitoring and Observability

- Kusto Query Language (KQL) for diagnostics and insights
- Integration with legacy tools (SCOM, Nagios, Splunk)
- Azure Monitor, Log Analytics, and Workbooks for unified visibility

## Team Structures for Hybrid Cloud Success

A hybrid-ready organization needs to reorganize around **collaboration, agility, and shared responsibility**. Here are several proven models:

### 1. Platform Engineering Teams

Platform engineers build and maintain reusable components—templates, automation, pipelines, monitoring tools—that other teams can consume. They act as internal service providers.

**Responsibilities:**

- Develop and maintain hybrid landing zones
- Enforce tagging, naming, and security standards
- Automate provisioning of infrastructure and services

### 2. Cloud Center of Excellence (CCoE)

A CCoE is a cross-functional team that provides governance, evangelism, training, and standards for hybrid and cloud operations.

**Key Functions:**

- Define hybrid architectural patterns and best practices
- Review solutions and guide adoption of new services
- Act as a liaison between business units and IT

### 3. Site Reliability Engineering (SRE)

SREs focus on operational excellence, automation, and service health. They apply engineering principles to operations and incident management.

**Key Responsibilities:**

- Establish SLAs, SLOs, and error budgets
- Create runbooks and response playbooks for hybrid systems
- Continuously improve deployment and monitoring pipelines

### 4. Embedded DevOps Teams

Rather than centralized DevOps roles, each product or service team includes DevOps engineers responsible for automating delivery, managing infrastructure, and ensuring compliance.

**Benefits:**

- Faster iteration and shorter feedback loops
- Contextual understanding of application and infrastructure needs
- Better alignment between developers and operations

## Skill Development and Talent Strategies

As hybrid complexity increases, a proactive approach to skill development is essential.

**Upskilling Approaches:**

- **Role-based learning paths** via Microsoft Learn (e.g., Azure Administrator, DevOps Engineer)
- **Certifications**: AZ-104, AZ-305, AZ-500, AZ-700, AZ-400, DP-203
- **Hands-on labs and sandboxes** using Azure DevTest Labs or free tier subscriptions
- **Hackathons and game days** to practice DR, incident response, and performance optimization

**Building a Talent Pipeline:**

- Partner with universities or coding bootcamps for hybrid cloud skill development

- Sponsor internal reskilling programs for traditional IT staff
- Recognize and reward learning milestones across teams

```
# Example: Assign Azure role to a learner sandbox environment
New-AzRoleAssignment -ObjectId $learnerId -RoleDefinitionName "Contributor" `
-Scope "/subscriptions/$subId/resourceGroups/LabRG"
```

## Cultural Shifts and Soft Skills

Technology alone doesn't guarantee hybrid success. The organizational culture must also evolve.

**Critical Attributes:**

- **Empathy and collaboration**: Especially across teams with different tech backgrounds
- **Adaptability**: Hybrid environments evolve quickly; so must people
- **Ownership**: Teams must own not just code but reliability, security, and compliance
- **Communication**: Clear documentation, runbooks, and status updates are vital in hybrid teams

## Collaboration Models and Tools

Hybrid cloud teams are often distributed geographically, making collaboration tools essential:

- **Azure DevOps and GitHub Enterprise** for code, backlog, and pipelines
- **Microsoft Teams** with shared channels and Planner for task management
- **Visual Studio Code + Live Share** for real-time code reviews and pairing
- **Wikis and docs**: Document every playbook, architecture, and decision rationale

## Aligning Roles with the Hybrid Lifecycle

Each stage of the hybrid lifecycle—plan, build, operate, optimize—requires involvement from different stakeholders.

| Lifecycle Stage | Roles Involved | Key Deliverables |
|---|---|---|
| Plan | Architects, Security, Finance | Landing zone design, Budget, Governance policies |
| Build | DevOps, Platform Engineering | IaC, Pipelines, Access configuration |
| Operate | SREs, IT Admins, SOC | Monitoring dashboards, Alerts, Incident runbooks |
| Optimize | FinOps, Data Engineers, Cloud Analysts | Cost reports, Performance metrics, Usage insights |

This alignment ensures accountability and effective lifecycle management.

## Common Pitfalls and Lessons Learned

1. **Underestimating identity complexity**: Hybrid environments require seamless identity integration.

2. **Over-reliance on cloud-native skills**: On-prem knowledge remains essential.
3. **Ignoring process documentation**: Lack of repeatable playbooks causes chaos during incidents.
4. **Siloed teams**: Prevents shared learning and leads to duplication of effort.
5. **Lack of automation**: Manual changes introduce risk and technical debt.

### Conclusion

The evolution of hybrid cloud strategies demands a parallel evolution in the people and teams that implement them. Organizations that invest in broadening their talent, breaking down silos, and fostering a culture of learning and collaboration will be best positioned to take advantage of Azure's hybrid capabilities. The path to hybrid cloud success is not just paved with infrastructure—but with empowered, skilled, and connected teams working together toward shared outcomes.

## Continuous Optimization and Innovation

In the fast-paced world of hybrid cloud, standing still means falling behind. Continuous optimization and innovation are not optional—they are essential for maintaining performance, controlling costs, ensuring security, and delivering value to end users. Hybrid environments, by their nature, require a dynamic approach that continuously evolves to reflect changing workloads, business priorities, user expectations, and technology capabilities.

This section explores a practical, strategic framework for continuous improvement across hybrid cloud deployments. It includes optimization tactics across cost, performance, security, and governance domains, as well as guidance on creating a culture of innovation through experimentation, feedback loops, and agile practices—all within the context of Microsoft Azure's hybrid toolset.

## The Need for Continuous Optimization

Hybrid cloud environments are complex and distributed. Without proactive optimization, organizations risk:

- Overprovisioned and underutilized infrastructure
- Mounting cloud and on-premises costs
- Security vulnerabilities and compliance gaps
- Reduced application performance and user satisfaction

Optimization must be embedded as an ongoing practice—not a one-time project. It should be measurable, automated where possible, and aligned to business outcomes.

## Optimization Domains in Hybrid Environments

### 1. Cost Optimization

Managing costs across both cloud and on-prem infrastructure is a top priority. Hybrid strategies often incur hidden expenses due to:

- Overlapping toolsets
- Redundant compute/storage resources
- Inefficient networking
- Lack of visibility into usage

**Strategies:**

- **Tag resources** consistently for chargeback and cost tracking.
- Use **Azure Cost Management and Billing** to analyze spend across subscriptions and resource groups.
- Optimize storage using **tiered options** (e.g., Hot, Cool, Archive for Azure Blob).
- Implement **Auto-Shutdown** and **Scaling Policies** for VMs and Kubernetes clusters.
- Use **Azure Reservations** for predictable workloads and **Spot Instances** for interruptible jobs.
- Decommission or consolidate legacy infrastructure where hybrid usage declines.

```
# Example: Set auto-shutdown for a VM to reduce idle cost

$vm = Get-AzVM -Name "HybridTestVM" -ResourceGroupName "HybridRG"

$vm | Set-AzVMAutoShutdown -Time 2200 -TimeZone "UTC"
```

**2. Performance Optimization**

Performance tuning in a hybrid setup involves both cloud-native services and legacy systems.

**Best Practices:**

- Use **Azure Monitor** and **Log Analytics** to identify latency hotspots and underperforming components.

- Optimize database performance using **Query Performance Insight** for SQL and **Index Advisor**.

- Cache frequently accessed data at the edge with **Azure Front Door**, **Azure CDN**, or **Azure Cache for Redis**.

- Review **network throughput** and use **ExpressRoute** for consistent latency-sensitive traffic.

**3. Security Optimization**

Security is a continuously moving target. Hybrid environments increase the surface area for threats and require centralized, automated protection mechanisms.

**Recommendations:**

- Regularly scan for vulnerabilities using **Microsoft Defender for Cloud** and **Azure Security Center**.

- Enforce **Just-In-Time (JIT) VM access**, **MFA**, and **Conditional Access Policies**.

- Rotate secrets and certificates using **Azure Key Vault** with **Azure Automation**.

- Monitor anomalies and threats with **Microsoft Sentinel**, integrating signals from on-prem and cloud.

```
// Detect JIT access requests across hybrid VMs

SecurityAlert
```

```
| where ExtendedProperties has "Just-In-Time"

| summarize count() by Computer, TimeGenerated
```

**4. Governance and Compliance Optimization**

Effective governance ensures that your hybrid estate remains compliant, controlled, and aligned with organizational policies.

**Tactics:**

- Enforce **naming conventions** and **mandatory tags** using **Azure Policy**.
- Audit infrastructure with **Azure Resource Graph** to identify shadow IT.
- Set up **Management Groups** and **Blueprints** to organize resources across teams or departments.
- Automate remediation of policy violations using **Azure Automation Runbooks**.

```
{

"if": {

"field": "tags['Environment']",

"equals": "Production"

},

"then": {

"effect": "audit"
```

}

}

## Building a Culture of Continuous Innovation

Optimization supports performance and efficiency. Innovation enables transformation. Together, they future-proof your hybrid strategy.

**Core Pillars of Innovation:**

1. **Agility**: Teams can experiment and iterate quickly.
2. **Empowerment**: Developers and engineers are encouraged to challenge the status quo.
3. **Automation**: Manual processes are eliminated to free up time for innovation.
4. **Measurement**: Data-driven decisions guide product and platform evolution.

**Ways to Foster Innovation:**

- **Create innovation sandboxes** using isolated subscriptions or resource groups for experimentation.

- **Host internal hackathons** to generate ideas and test new architectures.

- **Use feature flags and canary releases** to test changes in hybrid applications without full rollouts.

- **Integrate feedback loops** from users into CI/CD pipelines to drive rapid iterations.

## Operationalizing Continuous Improvement

Implementing continuous optimization and innovation requires a framework that aligns people, process, and technology.

**The Improvement Loop:**

1. **Observe** – Collect metrics, logs, traces, and feedback.
2. **Analyze** – Use Azure Monitor, KQL, and dashboards to identify trends and outliers.
3. **Improve** – Apply changes via IaC, update pipelines, adjust policies.
4. **Validate** – Measure the impact of optimizations against baseline KPIs.
5. **Automate** – Codify improvements into reusable automation workflows or templates.

**Sample Metrics to Track:**

| Area | Metric | Tool/Service |
|---|---|---|
| Cost | Cost per app/user/unit | Azure Cost Management |
| Performance | Response time, CPU utilization | Azure Monitor, App Insights |
| Security | Failed logins, threat alerts | Microsoft Sentinel, Defender |
| Governance | Policy compliance rate | Azure Policy, Compliance Manager |
| Developer Velocity | Build/deploy frequency | Azure DevOps, GitHub Actions |
| Incident Response | MTTR, alert resolution time | Log Analytics, Azure Automation |

## Leveraging Innovation from the Azure Ecosystem

Microsoft continually releases new hybrid capabilities that can be used to optimize and evolve your environment:

- **Azure Arc**: Extending policy, automation, and GitOps to Kubernetes, SQL, and VMs—anywhere.
- **Azure Automanage**: Automated operations for Windows Server VMs, both in Azure and hybrid.
- **Azure Chaos Studio**: Resilience testing using real-world fault injection.
- **Azure Percept and Stack Edge**: Prebuilt platforms for deploying AI at the edge.
- **Azure Well-Architected Framework (WAF)**: Assessment and guidance for improving reliability, cost, security, and performance.

## Team Alignment for Optimization

Optimization is not just the job of IT—it's a shared responsibility. Successful organizations embed optimization goals into team KPIs and review cycles.

| Role | Optimization Responsibility |
|---|---|
| Cloud Architects | Standardize patterns, evaluate new tech |
| DevOps Engineers | Automate deployments, enforce IaC and policies |
| SREs | Reduce toil, improve availability and latency |
| SecOps | Ensure threat detection and policy compliance |
| FinOps | Analyze and reduce wasteful spending |
| App Teams | Track usage, performance, and user feedback |

## Avoiding Common Pitfalls

1. **Ignoring on-prem optimization**: Hybrid means both sides of the house must be continuously improved.
2. **Overengineering**: Simplicity wins—optimize for outcomes, not technical perfection.
3. **Lack of ownership**: Every team must own the operational health of what they build or manage.
4. **Failure to iterate**: Optimization is ongoing, not quarterly.
5. **No visibility**: You can't improve what you don't measure—invest in observability.

## Conclusion

Continuous optimization and innovation are what transform a hybrid deployment from a functional architecture into a strategic asset. By combining performance tuning, cost control, governance enforcement, and a culture of experimentation, enterprises can ensure their hybrid environments remain efficient, secure, and ready to adapt. Microsoft Azure's hybrid capabilities—backed by automation, observability, and AI—enable organizations not just to keep up with change, but to lead it. Make optimization a habit, not a project. Make innovation a culture, not an initiative. That is how hybrid cloud becomes a driver of long-term success.

# Chapter 11: Appendices

## Glossary of Terms

Understanding the terminology used throughout hybrid cloud discussions is critical for clarity, communication, and success in implementation. This glossary serves as a reference point for both technical and non-technical readers, offering clear, concise definitions of key terms, acronyms, and concepts relevant to Microsoft Azure and hybrid cloud architectures.

### A

**Active Directory (AD)**

A directory service developed by Microsoft for Windows domain networks. AD is essential in hybrid identity setups where on-premises authentication is extended to cloud services.

**Azure Active Directory (Azure AD)**

Microsoft's cloud-based identity and access management service. Used to authenticate users, enforce policies, and secure hybrid environments via integration with Azure AD Connect.

**Azure Arc**

A set of technologies that extend Azure management and governance to non-Azure environments, including on-premises servers, Kubernetes clusters, and third-party clouds.

**Azure Automation**

A service that allows for the automation of tasks and orchestration of workflows across hybrid environments using runbooks, DSC (Desired State Configuration), and hybrid workers.

**Azure App Service**

A platform-as-a-service (PaaS) offering for hosting web applications, RESTful APIs, and mobile back ends, often used in hybrid applications for modern frontend hosting.

**Azure Availability Zones**

Physically separate locations within an Azure region, designed to ensure high availability. Used in hybrid DR designs to enhance fault tolerance for Azure-hosted services.

## B

**Backup Vault**

A storage container in Azure used to hold backup data. Supports VMs, SQL Server, Azure Files, and more, and is crucial for implementing hybrid backup strategies.

**Bicep**

A domain-specific language (DSL) for deploying Azure resources declaratively. Used to define infrastructure as code in a human-readable syntax.

**Blueprints**

Azure Blueprints help you define and enforce a repeatable set of Azure resources, policies, and role assignments. Useful for standardized hybrid landing zones.

## C

### CI/CD (Continuous Integration/Continuous Deployment)

A set of practices that automate the build, test, and deployment of code. CI/CD pipelines in hybrid environments manage both cloud and on-prem deployments.

### Cloud Shell

A browser-accessible shell in Azure for managing resources using PowerShell or Bash, often used for scripting hybrid configurations.

### Conditional Access

A feature of Azure AD that enforces access control decisions based on user, location, device, and application. Essential for securing hybrid access.

### Cost Management + Billing

Azure's built-in service for monitoring, allocating, and optimizing cloud costs. Supports tracking hybrid spend through tags and management groups.

## D

### Disaster Recovery (DR)

Processes and tools used to restore IT systems after a failure. In hybrid environments, DR typically includes Azure Site Recovery and offline backup strategies.

### Data Box

A family of physical and virtual appliances used for transferring large volumes of data into or out of Azure in hybrid data migration scenarios.

### Defender for Cloud

Microsoft's extended detection and response (XDR) solution offering integrated threat protection for hybrid workloads across VMs, containers, databases, and more.

### DNS (Domain Name System)

A naming system that translates domain names to IP addresses. Hybrid architectures often require split-brain DNS or custom DNS forwarding rules.

## E

### Edge Computing

A paradigm in which computation is performed closer to data sources or end users. Azure Stack Edge enables edge deployments for AI and analytics in hybrid setups.

### ExpressRoute

A dedicated, private connection from an on-premises network to Azure, offering increased reliability and performance compared to public internet connections.

## F

### Failover

The process of switching to a redundant or standby system upon failure. In hybrid DR plans, failover typically redirects workloads to Azure-hosted services.

**Firewall (Azure Firewall)**

A managed, cloud-based network security service that protects Azure Virtual Network resources, often integrated with hybrid networks for perimeter defense.

## G

**GitOps**

A model for managing infrastructure and application deployments using Git repositories as the single source of truth. Azure Arc enables GitOps for hybrid Kubernetes.

**Governance**

The organizational policies, processes, and tools used to control and manage hybrid cloud environments, including Azure Policy, tagging standards, and cost controls.

## H

**Hybrid Cloud**

A computing environment that combines public cloud and on-premises resources, allowing data and applications to be shared between them.

**Hybrid Identity**

An identity model where user identities span both on-premises directories (e.g., AD) and cloud-based identity providers (e.g., Azure AD).

## I

### Infrastructure as Code (IaC)

The practice of managing and provisioning infrastructure through machine-readable definition files. Common tools include Bicep, Terraform, and ARM templates.

### IoT Edge

A component of Azure IoT that enables running cloud workloads on edge devices, useful for hybrid scenarios requiring local processing of sensor data.

## J

### Just-In-Time (JIT) Access

A security feature that reduces attack surfaces by allowing temporary access to Azure VMs. Often used in hybrid security strategies to limit exposure.

## K

### Kusto Query Language (KQL)

A powerful query language used in Azure Log Analytics and Azure Data Explorer for extracting insights from telemetry data.

## L

### Log Analytics

A feature within Azure Monitor that collects and analyzes telemetry from across cloud and hybrid resources using KQL.

### Lighthouse

Azure Lighthouse enables cross-tenant management, allowing service providers or large organizations to manage multiple hybrid environments securely.

## M

### Managed Identity

An automatically managed identity in Azure Active Directory for applications to use when connecting to resources securely, often replacing credentials in hybrid apps.

### Microsoft Sentinel

A scalable, cloud-native SIEM (Security Information and Event Management) and SOAR (Security Orchestration, Automation, and Response) solution.

## N

### Network Security Group (NSG)

Controls inbound and outbound traffic at the subnet or NIC level within Azure. Used to enforce network rules in hybrid environments.

### NSG Flow Logs

Logs capturing IP flow information through NSGs. Can be sent to Log Analytics or Event Hubs for analysis in hybrid network monitoring.

## O

### Operational Insights

Azure Monitor insights modules that provide tailored dashboards for VMs, containers, networks, and other workloads.

### OMS Agent

The legacy agent used to send data to Log Analytics. Now replaced by the Azure Monitor Agent (AMA) in modern hybrid monitoring setups.

## P

### Policy (Azure Policy)

A governance tool that enforces rules on resources, ensuring compliance and consistency across environments.

### Private Link

Azure service enabling private access to Azure PaaS services from on-prem or VNet resources without exposing them to the internet.

## Q

### Quota

Resource limits imposed per subscription or region. Understanding quotas is critical when planning capacity in hybrid deployments.

## R

### RBAC (Role-Based Access Control)

A method of regulating access to Azure resources based on user roles. Essential for secure delegation in hybrid environments.

### Recovery Services Vault

Stores backup and site recovery metadata. Central to any Azure-based DR strategy in a hybrid model.

## S

### Service Principal

An identity created for use with applications, hosted services, and automated tools to access Azure resources.

### Site-to-Site VPN

A connection between an on-premises network and Azure via VPN Gateway, often used in hybrid network designs.

### Storage Account

An Azure resource that provides access to scalable cloud storage (Blobs, Queues, Tables, Files) and is commonly extended to on-premises via File Sync.

## T

### Terraform

An open-source IaC tool that enables safe and predictable resource creation and management, commonly used in hybrid cloud deployments.

### Tags

Key-value pairs attached to resources for categorization and cost allocation. Critical for governance and reporting in hybrid operations.

## U

### Update Management

Azure Automation feature that manages OS updates for Windows and Linux across Azure and on-premises VMs.

## V

### Virtual Network (VNet)

A logically isolated network in Azure. VNets connect to on-prem networks via VPN or ExpressRoute in hybrid configurations.

### VM Extensions

Scripts or applications that are deployed to VMs for configuration, management, or monitoring, often used in automation.

## W

### Workbooks

Azure Monitor tool for building interactive reports and dashboards to visualize hybrid resource performance and health.

### Windows Admin Center

A locally deployed management console that integrates with Azure services for managing Windows Server instances on-premises and in the cloud.

## Z

### Zero Trust

A security framework that assumes no implicit trust and verifies every access attempt. Applies to users, devices, and applications in hybrid environments.

---

This glossary should serve as a living document to support deeper understanding throughout your hybrid cloud journey. As new services and concepts emerge, especially within the ever-evolving Azure ecosystem, revisiting and expanding this glossary ensures teams remain aligned, informed, and empowered to manage complexity with confidence.

# Resources for Further Learning

Hybrid cloud computing is a constantly evolving field, influenced by rapid advancements in cloud platforms, edge computing, artificial intelligence, security frameworks, and DevOps practices. Staying current requires ongoing education through curated content, hands-on experimentation, and engagement with the global tech community. This section offers a comprehensive collection of resources—spanning documentation, learning platforms, certification paths, books, labs, open-source projects, and community hubs—that can guide professionals and teams along their hybrid cloud journey.

## Official Microsoft Learning Paths

Microsoft provides structured learning paths tailored to various roles, technologies, and certification levels. These are ideal for both beginners and seasoned professionals looking to expand or refresh their skills.

**Azure Learning Paths on Microsoft Learn**

Microsoft Learn offers self-paced modules and interactive labs for Azure hybrid services, including:

- **Azure Arc:**https://learn.microsoft.com/en-us/training/paths/azure-arc/
- **Azure Stack HCI:**https://learn.microsoft.com/en-us/training/paths/azure-stack-hci/
- **Hybrid Identity with Azure AD:**https://learn.microsoft.com/en-us/training/modules/hybrid-identity-introduction/
- **Azure Monitor and Log Analytics:**https://learn.microsoft.com/en-us/training/paths/monitor-azure-infrastructure/

Each path includes guided labs, quizzes, and sandbox environments for hands-on practice without requiring your own subscription.

## Certification Programs

Certifications validate your skills and increase career mobility. For hybrid and cloud professionals, the following certifications are especially relevant:

**Foundational**

- **AZ-900: Microsoft Azure Fundamentals**

For individuals beginning their cloud journey. Covers core concepts, pricing, SLA, and compliance.

**Administrator/Operations**

- **AZ-104: Microsoft Azure Administrator**

Focuses on managing Azure subscriptions, identities, compute, networking, and storage.

- **AZ-500: Microsoft Azure Security Technologies**

Ideal for professionals securing hybrid and cloud environments using built-in Azure tools.

**Architect/Advanced**

- **AZ-305: Azure Solutions Architect Expert**

Covers solution design including identity, governance, compute, and DR across hybrid and cloud.

- **AZ-700: Designing and Implementing Azure Networking Solutions**

Emphasizes hybrid connectivity, routing, and network security.

**DevOps**

- **AZ-400: Designing and Implementing Microsoft DevOps Solutions**

Integrates CI/CD pipelines, GitOps, IaC, and monitoring for both cloud and hybrid applications.

**Data and AI**

- **DP-203: Data Engineering on Microsoft Azure**

  Includes hybrid data integration, governance, and analytics.

All certification prep materials are available via Microsoft Learn and can be supplemented with practice exams from platforms like Whizlabs, MeasureUp, or Udemy.

## Books and Guides

For in-depth understanding and architectural guidance, these books are recommended:

- **"Exam Ref AZ-305 Designing Microsoft Azure Infrastructure Solutions" – Microsoft Press**

  Offers exam prep and architectural insights for hybrid cloud workloads.

- **"Hybrid Cloud for Architects" – Packt Publishing**

  Explores cloud migration, integration, and best practices for hybrid systems.

- **"Azure for Architects" – Ritesh Modi**

  Updated editions cover emerging patterns like AI at the edge, IoT, and hybrid security.

- **"Cloud Strategy: A Decision-based Approach to Successful Cloud Migration" – Gregor Hohpe**

A vendor-neutral, decision-driven guide to cloud and hybrid transitions.

## Hands-On Labs and Sandboxes

Experimentation accelerates learning. These platforms provide real-world exercises in safe environments:

- **Microsoft Hands-on Labs:**https://learn.microsoft.com/en-us/training/azure/
- **Microsoft Azure Sandbox (free tier):** Included in Microsoft Learn paths; provides temporary access to Azure services for learning.
- **GitHub Labs and Repositories:** Search for "Azure Arc Jumpstart" or "Azure Quickstart Templates" for lab-ready code.
    - https://github.com/microsoft/azure_arc
    - https://github.com/Azure/azure-quickstart-templates

Example: Deploy a VM with monitoring using a quickstart template

az group create—name HybridLabRG—location eastus

az deployment group create \

—resource-group HybridLabRG \

—template-uri https://raw.githubusercontent.com/Azure/azure-quickstart-templates/master/101-vm-simple-linux/azuredeploy.json

## Architecture Center and Reference Architectures

The **Microsoft Azure Architecture Center** provides vetted guidance, blueprints, and design principles:

- https://learn.microsoft.com/en-us/azure/architecture/

Highlighted hybrid architectures:

- **Hybrid network with VPN and ExpressRoute**
- **Hybrid identity with Azure AD and AD DS**
- **Hybrid data analytics with Azure Synapse and on-prem SQL**

These come with downloadable diagrams, ARM/Bicep templates, and decision trees to guide implementation.

## Open Source Projects and Community Templates

Many hybrid and edge solutions are built using open source and community-driven tools:

- **Azure Arc Jumpstart:**https://github.com/microsoft/azure_arc

  Includes end-to-end scenarios with automation for Arc-enabled servers, Kubernetes, and data services.

- **Enterprise Scale Landing Zones:**https://github.com/Azure/Enterprise-Scale

  Templates and policies for scalable, secure Azure environments, extendable to hybrid models.

- **Terraform Modules for Azure Hybrid:** https://registry.terraform.io/providers/hashicorp/azurerm

Open-source infrastructure code for hybrid services and policy-as-code.

## Community and Ecosystem

Being active in the global Azure community offers invaluable opportunities to learn from peers and experts.

### Microsoft Tech Community

- https://techcommunity.microsoft.com/
- Dedicated forums for hybrid, identity, security, and more.

### Azure Friday

- https://azure.microsoft.com/en-us/resources/videos/azure-friday/
- Weekly videos from Scott Hanselman and product teams featuring real-world Azure implementations.

### Microsoft Reactor Events

- https://developer.microsoft.com/en-us/reactor/
- Free virtual and in-person events hosted by Microsoft, featuring hands-on workshops and expert talks.

**User Groups and Meetups**

- https://www.meetup.com/topics/azure/
- Connect with Azure professionals in your area.

**Conferences**

- **Microsoft Ignite:** Premier conference with deep dives into hybrid architectures and roadmap announcements.
- **Microsoft Build:** Developer-focused sessions often covering DevOps, automation, and hybrid app development.

## Blogs and Podcasts

Keep up with trends, tutorials, and product updates through trusted blogs and shows:

- **Azure Blog:**https://azure.microsoft.com/en-us/blog/
- **CloudSkills.fm (Podcast)**
- **The Azure Podcast:** Hosted by Microsoft cloud advocates and engineers.
- **Thomas Maurer (Microsoft PM for Azure Hybrid):**https://www.thomasmaurer.ch/
- **John Savill's Technical Training:** YouTube series covering everything from Arc to advanced governance.

## Sample Learning Path for Hybrid Cloud Professionals

| Week | Focus Area | Resources |
|---|---|---|
| 1 | Hybrid Fundamentals | AZ-900, Microsoft Learn Intro to Hybrid Cloud |
| 2 | Azure Arc and Stack HCI | Learn modules, GitHub Jumpstart |
| 3 | Identity and Security | AZ-500 path, Conditional Access labs |
| 4 | Monitoring and Automation | KQL tutorials, Azure Monitor Workbooks |
| 5 | Infrastructure as Code (IaC) | Bicep, Terraform labs, GitHub Actions |
| 6 | Governance and Landing Zones | Enterprise Scale Blueprint, Policy deep dive |
| 7 | DR and BCP | Azure Site Recovery Labs, Sentinel integration |
| 8 | Capstone Project | Build a hybrid deployment, submit via GitHub |

## Conclusion

The hybrid cloud learning journey is continuous, and success requires more than just understanding technology—it demands curiosity, community, and experimentation. With the right resources, anyone can become proficient in hybrid cloud strategy, design, and operations. Whether you're an administrator, architect, engineer, or executive, the tools and content listed in this section will empower you to stay current, solve problems creatively, and lead confidently in the hybrid era.

# Sample Projects and Code Snippets

To solidify the principles and practices of hybrid cloud computing, hands-on experience is essential. This section provides sample projects and curated code snippets that span a wide range of real-world scenarios. These examples are designed to give practical exposure to Azure's hybrid capabilities, covering infrastructure provisioning, workload migration, hybrid networking, monitoring, automation, and application deployment across on-premises and cloud environments.

Each project includes a high-level objective, suggested tools and services, relevant code or scripts, and key takeaways. These templates can be extended and adapted to your specific enterprise needs or used as foundational labs in training sessions.

## Project 1: Deploy and Manage an Arc-Enabled Server

**Objective:** Connect an on-premises Windows or Linux VM to Azure using Azure Arc, apply policy, enable monitoring, and secure with Defender for Cloud.

**Technologies Used:** Azure Arc, Azure Policy, Log Analytics, Defender for Servers

**Steps:**

1. Install the Azure Connected Machine agent on the VM.
2. Register the server to a resource group in Azure using a script.
3. Enable diagnostics and Defender for Servers via Azure Security Center.
4. Assign a policy initiative (e.g., apply a required tag or install an extension).

```
# Windows registration script
$resourceGroup = "ArcServers"
$location = "eastus"
$subscriptionId = "<your-subscription-id>"
az connectedmachine connect—resource-group $resourceGroup `
—location $location—subscription $subscriptionId `
—name "onprem-sql01"
```

**Key Takeaways:**

- Azure Arc enables cloud-native governance over on-prem servers.
- Policies can enforce consistency without manual effort.
- Telemetry flows into Log Analytics for centralized monitoring.

---

## Project 2: Create a Hybrid Network Using VPN Gateway

**Objective:** Establish secure communication between an on-premises network and Azure Virtual Network using a Site-to-Site VPN.

**Technologies Used:** Azure Virtual Network, VPN Gateway, Local Network Gateway, On-Prem VPN Device

**Steps:**

1. Configure a virtual network and subnet in Azure.

2. Create a VPN Gateway and public IP address.
3. Define a Local Network Gateway with your on-prem public IP and address space.
4. Create a Site-to-Site connection and configure your physical router or firewall.

az network vnet create \

—name HybridVNet—resource-group HybridRG \

—address-prefix 10.1.0.0/16—subnet-name GatewaySubnet—subnet-prefix 10.1.0.0/24

az network vpn-gateway create \

—name HybridVPN—resource-group HybridRG \

—vnet HybridVNet—public-ip-address HybridVPNPublicIP \

—gateway-type Vpn—vpn-type RouteBased

**Key Takeaways:**

- Hybrid networks provide secure, reliable paths between cloud and on-prem.

- Azure supports IPsec/IKE protocols compatible with most network devices.

- Once established, services like File Sync or SQL replication become feasible.

## Project 3: Deploy a Hybrid Kubernetes Cluster

**Objective:** Use Azure Arc to onboard an existing Kubernetes cluster and manage it through Azure, enabling GitOps-based deployment and policy enforcement.

**Technologies Used:** Azure Arc-enabled Kubernetes, GitHub Actions, Kustomize

**Steps:**

1. Deploy a Kubernetes cluster on-premises using AKS-HCI, Rancher, or another provider.
2. Install the Azure Arc agent to connect it to Azure.
3. Configure GitOps with a GitHub repository as the source of truth.
4. Deploy apps using YAML templates stored in Git.

az connectedk8s connect—name arc-k8s-cluster—resource-group HybridRG

az k8s-configuration create—name app-deployment \

—cluster-name arc-k8s-cluster—resource-group HybridRG \

—operator-instance-name flux—operator-namespace flux \

—repository-url https://github.com/contoso/hybrid-apps \

—scope cluster

**Key Takeaways:**

- Azure Arc enables consistent policy, monitoring, and deployment for non-Azure clusters.

- GitOps offers secure, auditable deployments based on pull requests.

- Supports multi-cloud and edge scenarios.

---

## Project 4: Hybrid Backup and Restore with Azure Backup

**Objective:** Configure backup for on-prem Windows Servers using the Microsoft Azure Recovery Services (MARS) agent.

**Technologies Used:** Azure Backup, Recovery Services Vault, MARS Agent

**Steps:**

1. Create a Recovery Services Vault in Azure.
2. Download the MARS agent from the vault interface.
3. Install and configure it on the on-prem server.
4. Define the backup schedule and retention policies.
5. Perform test restores and audit backup success rates.

**Key Takeaways:**

- Azure Backup protects on-prem systems without extra infrastructure.

- MARS agent provides granular file/folder level restore options.

- Vault supports long-term retention and compliance tracking.

---

## Project 5: Automate Hybrid Resource Reporting

**Objective:** Generate a daily report of all Arc-enabled servers and VMs in a subscription, along with their compliance state and tags.

**Technologies Used:** Azure Resource Graph, Kusto Query Language (KQL), Azure Logic Apps

**Sample KQL:**

```
Resources

| where type == "microsoft.hybridcompute/machines"

| extend tags = tostring(tags)

| project name, location, resourceGroup, subscriptionId, tags
```

**Logic App Workflow:**

- Trigger: Recurrence (Daily)
- Action 1: Run Resource Graph query
- Action 2: Format output as CSV
- Action 3: Send via email or upload to SharePoint

**Key Takeaways:**

- Automating inventory saves time and reduces human error.
- KQL enables rich querying across resource types and attributes.

- Useful for audit preparation and governance enforcement.

---

## Project 6: Build a Hybrid Monitoring Dashboard

**Objective:** Visualize telemetry from Azure VMs and on-prem Arc-enabled servers using Azure Monitor Workbooks.

**Technologies Used:** Azure Monitor, Log Analytics, Azure Arc

**Steps:**

1. Ensure diagnostics and agent extensions are enabled for all VMs.
2. Use KQL queries to gather performance, availability, and event log data.
3. Create visualizations (line charts, bar charts, pie charts) in Workbooks.
4. Share dashboards with teams via RBAC.

Perf

| where ObjectName == "LogicalDisk" and CounterName == "% Free Space"

| summarize avg(CounterValue) by bin(TimeGenerated, 1h), Computer

| render timechart

**Key Takeaways:**

- Workbooks provide deep visibility into hybrid workloads.

- Customizable for infrastructure, security, or app-focused views.
- KQL is the glue for meaningful hybrid insights.

---

## Project 7: Deploy a Hybrid App with API Management and On-Prem Backend

**Objective:** Expose an on-prem web API securely via Azure API Management (APIM) using an internal VNet and hybrid connection.

**Technologies Used:** Azure API Management, Azure Virtual Network, VPN Gateway

**Steps:**

1. Deploy APIM in an internal VNet.
2. Connect to on-prem network via Site-to-Site VPN.
3. Define API endpoints that forward to your internal backend.
4. Apply policies for rate limiting, header injection, and OAuth validation.

**Sample Policy:**

```
<policies>

<inbound>

<base />

<set-header name="x-api-client" exists-action="override">

<value>HybridAppClient</value>
```

```
</set-header>

</inbound>

</policies>
```

**Key Takeaways:**

- APIM acts as a secure, centralized entry point for legacy services.
- Hybrid connectivity allows gradual modernization without replatforming.
- Combines the benefits of modern API lifecycle with legacy systems.

---

## Summary

These sample projects cover a wide range of hybrid scenarios, from infrastructure provisioning and connectivity to monitoring, automation, and application delivery. Each project can be used independently or combined into a comprehensive enterprise lab or pilot program. By working through these examples, teams can gain not only technical proficiency but also architectural awareness, operational maturity, and governance alignment—paving the way for successful hybrid cloud adoption.

Remember, real transformation comes not from tools alone but from how they're used—continuously, collaboratively, and purposefully. Let these projects be the foundation for your own hybrid innovation.

# API Reference Guide

As hybrid environments continue to mature, programmatic access to infrastructure and services becomes essential for automation, consistency, scalability, and integration. Microsoft Azure provides a rich and comprehensive API surface across REST, CLI, SDKs, and PowerShell that enables developers, DevOps engineers, and platform teams to manage hybrid resources in a secure, repeatable, and auditable way.

This API reference guide outlines the key Azure API endpoints, SDK libraries, CLI commands, PowerShell modules, and authentication strategies needed to interact with Azure services from hybrid environments. It also highlights common hybrid use cases such as managing Azure Arc resources, automating site recovery, orchestrating backups, and integrating with on-prem systems.

## API Access Fundamentals

Azure supports several ways to interact with its services programmatically:

- **REST APIs** – Direct HTTP interface to all Azure services.
- **Azure CLI** – Cross-platform command-line interface.
- **Azure PowerShell** – Module-based scripting support for automation.
- **SDKs** – Available in C#, Java, Python, JavaScript/TypeScript, Go, and others.
- **ARM/Bicep Templates** – Declarative resource provisioning through infrastructure-as-code.

**Authentication and Authorization**

Before calling any API, you must authenticate using Azure Active Directory (Azure AD). The most common methods include:

- **Service Principal (Client ID + Secret/Certificate)**
- **Managed Identity (system-assigned or user-assigned)**
- **Interactive login (for development or manual tasks)**

**Example: Acquiring a token with CLI**

az account get-access-token—resource https://management.azure.com/

**Example: Using a Service Principal with curl**

curl -X POST -H "Content-Type: application/x-www-form-urlencoded" \

-d "grant_type=client_credentials&client_id=<client-id>&client_secret=<cli
\

https://login.microsoftonline.com/<tenant-id>/oauth2/token

## Azure Resource Manager (ARM) REST API

ARM is the control plane for all Azure resources. You can use it to manage virtual machines, storage, networking, hybrid resources, policies, and more.

**Base URL Format:**

https://management.azure.com/{resourceId}?api-version={api-version}

**Example: List all Arc-enabled servers in a subscription**

GET https://management.azure.com/subscriptions/{subscriptionId}/providers/Microsoft.HybridCompute/machines?api-version=2022-03-10

Authorization: Bearer {access_token}

**Response Example:**

{

"value": [

{

"id": "/subscriptions/abc/resourceGroups/HybridRG/providers/Microsoft.HybridCompute/machines/onprem-server01",

"name": "onprem-server01",

"type": "Microsoft.HybridCompute/machines",

"location": "eastus",

"properties": {

"osName": "Windows",

"osVersion": "2019"

}

}

]

}

## Common Hybrid APIs

### Azure Arc – Servers and Kubernetes

**Register Arc-enabled server:**

az connectedmachine connect—resource-group HybridRG—location eastus—name onprem-sql01

**List Arc resources via REST:**

GET /subscriptions/{subId}/resourceGroups/{rg}/providers/Microsoft.HybridCompute/machines?api-version=2022-03-10

**Assign policy to Arc-enabled resource:**

az policy assignment create \

—name "enforce-tag-environment" \

—policy "/providers/Microsoft.Authorization/policyDefinitions/require-tag-environment" \

—scope "/subscriptions/<subId>/resourceGroups/HybridRG/providers/Microsoft.HybridCompute/machines/onprem-sql01"

### Azure Site Recovery (ASR)

**Enable replication:**

az backup protection enable-for-vm \

—resource-group HybridRG \

—vault-name BackupVault01 \

—vm onpremVM \

—policy-name DefaultPolicy

**Trigger failover:**

az backup recoverypoint list \

—vault-name BackupVault01—resource-group HybridRG \

—container-name IaasVMContainer;iaasvmcontainerv2;HybridRG;onpremVM \

—item-name onpremVM

**Azure Monitor and Log Analytics**

**Query logs via REST API:**

POST https://api.loganalytics.io/v1/workspaces/{workspaceId}/query

Authorization: Bearer {access_token}

Content-Type: application/json

{

"query": "Heartbeat | summarize count() by Computer"

}

**PowerShell Example:**

Search-AzGraph -Query "resources | where type == 'microsoft.hybridcompute/machines'"

## SDK Highlights

Azure provides SDKs for most modern languages. Each SDK follows consistent patterns and includes authentication helpers.

**Python SDK Example: List Arc-enabled servers**

```
from azure.identity import DefaultAzureCredential

from azure.mgmt.hybridcompute import HybridComputeManagementClient

credential = DefaultAzureCredential()

client = HybridComputeManagementClient(credential, subscription_id)

machines = client.machines.list_by_subscription()

for machine in machines:

print(machine.name, machine.location)
```

**.NET SDK Example: Create Resource Group**

```
var credential = new DefaultAzureCredential();

var armClient = new ArmClient(credential);

SubscriptionResource subscription = armClient.GetDefaultSubscription();

ResourceGroupData rgData = new ResourceGroupData(AzureLocation.WestUS);
```

```
ResourceGroupResource rg = await subscription.GetResourceGroups().CreateOrUpdateAsync("HybridRG", rgData);
```

## ARM Template / Bicep Snippets

Declarative deployments using Bicep or ARM templates offer reusable, scalable provisioning across hybrid resources.

**Bicep: Arc-enabled Server**

```
resource arcServer 'Microsoft.HybridCompute/machines@2022-03-10' = {
name: 'onprem-sql01'
location: 'eastus'
identity: {
type: 'SystemAssigned'
}
properties: {
osName: 'Windows'
osVersion: '2019'
}
}
```

**Assign Azure Policy to all Arc servers**

```
{
```

```
"type": "Microsoft.Authorization/policyAssignments",

"name": "enforceTagEnvironment",

"properties": {

"scope": "/subscriptions/0000-0000-0000/resourceGroups/HybridRG",

"policyDefinitionId": "/providers/Microsoft.Authorization/policyDefinitions/require-tag-environment",

"parameters": {

"tagName": {

"value": "Environment"

}

}

}

}
```

## PowerShell Modules

Azure PowerShell allows scripting across hybrid and cloud resources:

- **Az.HybridCompute**
- **Az.ConnectedMachine**
- **Az.ResourceGraph**
- **Az.PolicyInsights**

**Get all connected machines:**

```
Get-AzConnectedMachine | Format-Table Name, Location, Status
```

**Apply Update Management schedule:**

```
Register-AzAutomationScheduledRunbook `
-AutomationAccountName "HybridAutomation" `
-RunbookName "UpdateWindowsVMs" `
-ScheduleName "WeeklyPatch" `
-Parameters @{ "ComputerGroup" = "ProductionServers" }
```

## Integration Scenarios

Hybrid cloud APIs are often used in orchestration with other platforms:

### CI/CD Pipelines

- Use GitHub Actions, Azure DevOps, or Jenkins to deploy to Arc-connected environments.
- Incorporate API calls for provisioning, tagging, monitoring, and rollback.

### ServiceNow and ITSM

- Trigger automated ticket creation via Logic Apps or REST hooks on policy violations.
- Enrich incident data with API calls to Log Analytics and Azure Resource Graph.

#### On-Prem Automation Tools

- Integrate System Center Orchestrator, Ansible, or Puppet with Azure REST APIs.
- Schedule syncs, backups, or compliance checks from internal cron jobs or runbooks.

---

## Tips for Using APIs Securely

- Always use **least privilege** principles for service principals and identities.
- Enable **API throttling awareness** with exponential backoff in scripts.
- Audit API usage through **Azure AD Sign-in Logs** and **Activity Logs**.
- Secure secrets with **Key Vault** instead of storing credentials in code.
- Use **API Management** to abstract and control access to custom APIs in hybrid apps.

---

## Conclusion

APIs are the glue that connects hybrid environments into a seamless, automated, and governed system. Whether you're orchestrating deployments, enforcing compliance, collecting telemetry, or managing DR, programmatic access enables you to move faster, with precision and consistency. This guide is not exhaustive, but it provides the foundation for exploring Azure's rich hybrid automation ecosystem. As Azure continues to evolve, so too will its APIs—unlocking even more possibilities for managing infrastructure at scale, from the data center to the cloud and beyond.

# Frequently Asked Questions

This section compiles the most frequently asked questions (FAQs) about hybrid cloud architectures, tools, and operational practices with Microsoft Azure. These questions span foundational topics, technical design considerations, implementation details, and strategic alignment. Whether you're a decision-maker, architect, developer, or operations engineer, these questions and their answers will help reinforce core concepts, clear up common misunderstandings, and guide successful hybrid deployments.

## General Hybrid Cloud Questions

### What is a hybrid cloud environment?

A hybrid cloud environment combines on-premises infrastructure (or private cloud) with public cloud services, allowing data and applications to move between the two environments. This architecture offers flexibility, scalability, control, and compliance advantages.

### Why choose a hybrid cloud strategy?

Organizations choose hybrid cloud for several reasons:

- Compliance with data sovereignty laws
- Gradual cloud adoption/migration
- Continued use of legacy infrastructure

- Reduced latency for edge computing
- Improved business continuity and disaster recovery

**What's the difference between multi-cloud and hybrid cloud?**

- **Hybrid cloud** integrates private/on-prem systems with a single public cloud provider (e.g., Azure).
- **Multi-cloud** uses services from multiple public cloud providers (e.g., Azure + AWS).

**What are the disadvantages of hybrid cloud?**

- Increased complexity in networking and identity management
- Challenges in monitoring and observability
- Higher upfront costs for establishing hybrid connectivity
- Governance risks if not properly enforced across environments

---

## Azure-Specific Questions

**What Azure services support hybrid cloud?**

Azure provides a robust suite of hybrid cloud services:

- **Azure Arc**: Extend Azure management to on-prem, edge, and multi-cloud

- **Azure Stack HCI/Edge/Hub**: Run Azure services locally
- **Azure Site Recovery**: Disaster recovery for hybrid workloads
- **Azure Backup**: Backup on-prem and cloud resources
- **Azure Monitor**: Unified monitoring across environments
- **Azure Active Directory**: Hybrid identity and access management
- **Azure ExpressRoute / VPN Gateway**: Secure hybrid connectivity
- **Azure Policy and Blueprints**: Governance for hybrid infrastructure

**Can I deploy Azure services in my own data center?**

Yes, using Azure Stack products (e.g., Azure Stack HCI, Azure Stack Hub), you can run Azure services like virtual machines, App Services, AKS, and databases within your own data center with consistent APIs and tools.

**What is Azure Arc and why is it important?**

Azure Arc is a bridge that extends Azure management and governance to resources outside of Azure—such as on-premises servers, Kubernetes clusters, SQL instances, and more. Arc enables unified inventory, policy enforcement, monitoring, and automation using Azure-native tools.

**How does Azure handle hybrid identity?**

Azure uses **Azure AD Connect** to sync identities from on-prem Active Directory to Azure Active Directory. Hybrid identity solutions can include password hash sync, pass-through authentication, or federated identity with AD FS. Conditional Access and MFA policies can be applied to both cloud and on-prem users.

---

## Networking and Connectivity

**How do I connect my on-prem network to Azure securely?**

There are two primary options:

- **Azure VPN Gateway**: Encrypted IPsec connection over the public internet.

- **Azure ExpressRoute**: Private, dedicated connectivity with higher performance and SLA.

**Can I route all internet traffic through Azure from on-prem?**

Yes, but it's not recommended unless there's a strong use case. Routing all internet-bound traffic from on-premises through Azure introduces performance, cost, and complexity considerations. Instead, route only specific traffic or use a Secure Web Gateway alongside Azure Firewall.

**What are best practices for hybrid network design?**

- Use **Hub-and-Spoke** or **Virtual WAN** architectures in Azure.

- Plan IP address ranges carefully to avoid overlaps.

- Implement **DNS forwarding** to allow name resolution across environments.

- Use **Azure Firewall** or **NVA appliances** for traffic inspection and segmentation.

- Monitor network health with **Network Watcher** and **Connection Monitor**.

---

## Security and Compliance

**How is security enforced in hybrid environments?**

Security in hybrid environments relies on a combination of:

- **Identity management** via Azure AD

- **Conditional Access and MFA**

- **Role-Based Access Control (RBAC)**

- **Defender for Cloud** for threat detection

- **Policy and Compliance Scanning**

- **Encryption** at rest and in transit

- **Log Analytics and Microsoft Sentinel** for SIEM/SOAR capabilities

**How do I handle regulatory compliance in hybrid cloud?**

Azure helps address compliance through:

- **Compliance Manager** with control mapping and evidence tracking
- **Azure Policy** to enforce configurations
- **Customer Lockbox** for controlled access
- **Geo-redundant storage** with location-based access controls
- **Blueprints** that align to standards like ISO 27001, NIST, and HIPAA

**Is Azure HIPAA/GDPR/PCI compliant?**

Azure offers services and configurations that support compliance with HIPAA, GDPR, PCI DSS, and other standards. Responsibility is shared between Microsoft and the customer—Microsoft secures the platform, and the customer secures their applications and data.

## Monitoring, Automation, and Management

**How can I monitor on-prem systems with Azure Monitor?**

Install the **Azure Monitor Agent (AMA)** or the **Log Analytics Agent** on your on-prem VMs. Use **Azure Arc** to register non-Azure machines and ingest telemetry into Azure Monitor and Log Analytics.

**Can I use Azure Automation for on-prem servers?**

Yes. Deploy **Hybrid Runbook Workers** to on-premises machines, allowing them to execute automation runbooks defined in Azure Automation.

```
Register-AzAutomationHybridWorkerGroup `
```

-AutomationAccountName "HybridAuto" `

-ResourceGroupName "HybridRG" `

-GroupName "ProdRunbookGroup"

**What's the best way to keep hybrid resources compliant?**

- Apply **initiative definitions** using Azure Policy.
- Run **compliance scans** across all Arc-connected resources.
- Use **Defender for Cloud recommendations** to close gaps.
- Automatically remediate violations using **automation scripts** or **Logic Apps**.

---

## Disaster Recovery and Business Continuity

**How does DR work in hybrid environments?**

Azure supports multiple disaster recovery patterns:

- **Azure Site Recovery** for VM-level replication and failover.
- **Backup Vaults** for long-term retention and restore capabilities.
- **Cross-region replication** for Azure services like SQL, Blob Storage.
- **Custom runbooks** to orchestrate failover and failback.

**Can I replicate on-prem VMs to Azure for DR?**

Yes. Azure Site Recovery supports replication of Hyper-V, VMware, and physical machines to Azure for hot or warm standby.

**How often should I test my DR plans?**

At least **once per quarter**, or more frequently in regulated industries. Use **ASR test failovers** and **chaos engineering** tools like **Azure Chaos Studio** to validate resilience.

## DevOps and CI/CD

**Can I deploy to on-prem infrastructure from Azure DevOps?**

Yes. Use **self-hosted agents** in your on-prem environment, and target Arc-enabled Kubernetes clusters or servers.

```
jobs:

- job: deploy

pool:

name: OnPremAgentPool

steps:

- script: |

./deploy-service.ps1
```

**Can I use GitOps with Arc-enabled clusters?**

Yes. Azure Arc supports GitOps with Flux or other operators. Changes pushed to your Git repository are automatically synchronized to your hybrid clusters.

## Architecture and Best Practices

**What are common architectural patterns in hybrid cloud?**

- **Cloud Bursting**: Scale out to Azure when on-prem resources reach capacity.
- **Edge Processing**: Perform inference or analytics at the edge using Azure Stack Edge.
- **Lift-and-Shift**: Move existing workloads to Azure with minimal changes.
- **Refactor with Hybrid Services**: Use Azure Functions, Logic Apps, and APIM to enhance legacy apps without replacing them.

**How do I modernize legacy systems in hybrid setups?**

- Wrap legacy services with APIs (via API Management).
- Refactor into microservices and deploy to Azure Kubernetes Service (AKS).
- Use **containers** to isolate and modernize older applications.
- Migrate data to Azure SQL Managed Instance or Azure Cosmos DB.

---

## Troubleshooting and Support

**How do I troubleshoot hybrid connectivity issues?**

- Use **Azure Network Watcher** to run IP flow verification and connection troubleshooting.
- Check **VPN Gateway or ExpressRoute logs** for latency, packet loss, or dropped tunnels.
- Use **Log Analytics queries** to detect downtime or configuration drift.

**Where can I get help with Azure hybrid features?**

- **Microsoft Support**: Submit support tickets via the Azure Portal.
- **Docs and Learn**: Refer to documentation and guided learning paths.
- **Tech Community**: Ask questions and share solutions with peers.
- **GitHub**: Raise issues or contribute to hybrid-related repos like Azure Arc Jumpstart.

---

## Conclusion

As hybrid cloud adoption continues to grow, so do the questions surrounding its architecture, operations, and strategy. These FAQs reflect real-world challenges and solutions, offering a valuable knowledge base for individuals and organizations at any stage of their hybrid journey. Whether you're planning a pilot, managing production environments, or exploring future innovations, understanding the nuances of hybrid deployments is key to building resilient, secure, and future-ready systems. Use this FAQ as a living reference to guide decisions, validate assumptions, and strengthen your hybrid cloud foundation.

www.ingramcontent.com/pod-product-compliance
Lightning Source LLC
LaVergne TN
LVHW101612210926
848480LV00008B/47

*9798230461098*